D1121894

THE
WIT
AND
WISDOM
OF
YOGI BERRA

THE
WIT
AND
WISDOM
OF
YOGI BERRA

Phil Pepe

TRIUMPH
BOOKS
CHICAGO

Library of Congress Cataloging-in-Publication Data

Pepe, Phil.
    The wit and wisdom of Yogi Berra.
    "An Associated Features Book."
    1. Berra, Yogi, 1925–   .   2. Baseball players—
United States—Biography.   I. Title.
GV865.B4P46   1988   796.357'092'4 [B]   88-13574
ISBN 1-57243-472-4

This book is available in quantity at special discounts for your group or organization. For further information, contact:
Triumph Books
601 South LaSalle Street
Suite 500
Chicago, Illinois, 60605
(312) 939-3330
Fax (312) 663-3557

Printed in the United States of America
ISBN 1-57243-472-4

Contents

Acknowledgments

So many people helped in the writing of this book that it would be impossible to list them all and foolish to try.

The public relations staffs of the Yankees, Mets, and Astros were extremely generous with their time and their files.

Others whose help contributed greatly are mentioned in the pages that follow. I hope they will accept that mention as my profound thanks for their help and cooperation.

But I would be remiss if I did not make special mention of two people—Zander Hollander, whose idea this book was, and Yogi Berra, for being the kind of good guy who makes people want to talk about him.

Foreword

It had been 14 years since Yogi Berra was fired by George Steinbrenner as manager of the New York Yankees; 14 years since he had set foot in Yankee Stadium.

Many had tried over the years to get him to return to Yankee Stadium, to heal old wounds, put aside past differences. None had succeeded.

He was invited to appear at Old-Timers Day, but he always declined.

There was a ceremony on August 21, 1988. The Yankees were to permanently retire uniform No. 8, which had been worn by two Hall of Fame catchers: Berra and his predecessor and mentor, Bill Dickey. Plaques were to be erected in their honor in Monument Park, out in center field. Berra failed to attend. He remained adamant in his promise never to set foot in Yankee Stadium "as long as *he* owns the team."

Now, outside forces were at work to bring about a reconciliation. Mickey Mantle, Roger Maris, and Elston Howard had passed on. Joe DiMaggio was gravely ill. Three Hall of Fame Yankees remained—elder statesmen, the last links to the grand old dynasty.

There was Phil Rizzuto, still broadcasting Yankees games, but nearing retirement; Whitey Ford, who made occasional visits to the big ballpark; and Yogi Berra, who continued his boycott.

Berra's sons, Larry, Tim, and Dale, appealed to their father to let bygones be bygones.

"Dad," they implored, "you belong in Yankee Stadium. You're a Yankee. You have grandchildren who have never seen you there."

Yogi weakened. He made it known that if someone could arrange to bring him together with George Steinbrenner, he would be amenable to a reconciliation. But it had to be done right, and it had to be the right time and the right place.

The right time was the winter of 1999. The right place was the new Yogi Berra Museum on the campus of Montclair State University. Steinbrenner agreed to come to Yogi, the mountain going to Mohammed.

They met. They embraced. The hatchet was buried. Steinbrenner beamed and said he felt good about having Yogi back in the Yankee family.

There would be a day at Yankee Stadium for Berra the following season. He would be showered with gifts, including replicas of all his lost World Series rings. And his grandchildren would see their grandfather on the field at Yankee Stadium, back where he belonged, receiving a thunderous ovation from the crowd. He would be a regular visitor to the stadium that made him famous, and which he had helped to make famous. He would throw out the first ball on Opening Day and at the World Series. Yogi Berra was home, at last.

Why had Berra decided to put aside past differences and return to Yankee Stadium? His answer was typically simple, typically to the point, typically Berra.

"It was time," he said.

Introduction

The sportswriter was nonplussed. He was visibly disturbed when he encountered Yogi Berra in a hotel lobby one morning.

"It's ridiculous," the sportswriter said. "This place is a rip-off."

"What'sa matter?" Berra inquired.

"I just had breakfast in the coffee shop," the sportswriter complained. "Orange juice, coffee, and an English muffin. Eight dollars and seventy-five cents. It's a rip-off, I tell you."

"Well," Berra replied. "That's because they have to import those English muffins."

Outside the rain fell steadily in torrents, pelting the small window and cascading down in a steady stream. Inside, in a small cubicle of a room, Mets manager Yogi Berra talked with reporters. The room was hot and steamy from the September humidity and too small for the five reporters trying to squeeze their way in, hoping to get close enough to catch every word.

His hat was off and his shoeless feet were propped up on an antique desk, and Yogi Berra was in a rare reflective, talkative mood.

"I'm proud of this club," he said. "I'll be proud of these guys even if we don't win. Don't forget, boy, they were thirteen games under .500; now we're two over."

"Even if we don't win . . . hell, I've had a good life. I've had times you wish you were not managing . . . lots of times, even before this year. . . . I'd lay in bed and say, 'What the hell do I have to do this for?' and then we'd win a few and I'd say, 'It's a great life.' Carm's good. She says, 'Don't let it bother you.' I'll tell you who else is good. Scheffing. He calls me up and says, 'Hang in there, do the best you can.' He understands."

This was Chicago, the last Saturday of the 1973 season, and the rain would continue, hard enough so they'd have to cancel the game. The Mets were close now, close to their second miracle, and Yogi Berra had brought them there—just two days and two victories from winning a division title in an unbelievable year.

He was in the second year of a two-year contract, and it was no secret that he was fighting for his job, his life. If the Mets didn't win, if they didn't turn things around, he probably would not be back. His future was at stake. His life. The only life he had known for almost 30 years.

In July he was in last place. In August the fans booed him, yelled for his head. In September he was in first place. Funny game, baseball. Hero yesterday, bum today, hero again tomorrow.

Through it all Yogi Berra remained calm. Through it all he remained patient. Through it all he remained confident. Through it all Yogi Berra remained Yogi Berra.

During the long, frustrating summer, reporters would come to him and ask what he thought of his team's chances. He would never give up. He *couldn't* give up. It wasn't in his nature. Things looked bleak, they appeared futile, but Yogi would find some reason for optimism, some reason for hope.

It was at one of these sessions that he uttered perhaps the most famous of all "Berraisms," a single sentence that would be repeated for years to come, that would be quoted as a sign of perseverance and the never-say-die spirit by football coaches, baseball managers, and even presidential candidates. Someone had had the temerity to suggest to Berra that the Mets were dead, that their chances appeared hopeless. Berra would hear none of it. "It ain't over 'til it's over," he said in that simplistic way he had of stating the obvious.

He would win the thing. Naturally. He usually did. He was lucky. He was Yogi Berra and he had something, some indefinable thing called "Berra luck"—whatever that was.

It would represent his greatest accomplishment, his finest hour as a manager, a leader of men, and a homespun philosopher. But nothing is forever in the managing business and his greatest hour would be followed by setbacks, disappointments, and failure. And in this business, all that is normally followed by unemployment.

The Mets were never able to duplicate their 1973 success, which should have been interpreted as a testimony to the leadership of their manager. Instead, it was the manager who suffered the consequences and paid the price for the Mets' fifth-place finish in 1974. When things did not improve as rapidly in 1975 as fans, press, and management thought they should, Berra was fired as manager on August 5 and replaced. The Mets were in third place, having posted a record of 56–63.

For the remainder of the season the Mets would lose one game more than they won and after a winning record in 1976, they would suffer through seven consecutive losing seasons before winning more games than they lost.

As usual, Berra did not remain out of baseball for long. Fired in August, he spent the remainder of the season as a man of leisure, but that winter his old buddy, Billy Martin, called and invited him to return to the Yankees as a coach. It was a glorious homecoming for Berra, a return to the scene of his greatest triumphs: Yankee Stadium.

He coached for eight years through a steady stream of Yankee managers, from Billy Martin to Bob Lemon to Martin again to Dick Howser to Gene Michael to Lemon, again to Michael, to Clyde King, and to Martin again—surviving each change, each time being passed over for the job and not regretting the slight.

Inevitably, Berra's number came up. When Billy Martin was fired after his third term for punching a marshmallow salesman in a Minneapolis hotel, Berra was asked to replace him as manager of the Yankees. You don't say "no" to George Steinbrenner. And the idea of being manager had never left Yogi's mind. He accepted the job with full knowledge of the consequences.

The Yankees finished third under Berra's leadership in 1984, compiling a record of 87–75. Yogi did a good job of managing under the conditions, considering the material he had. Everybody thought so—or almost everybody. George Steinbrenner disagreed.

He criticized Berra privately and publicly, second-guessed him, threatened him. Finally, only 16 games into the 1985 season, with his team still in the starting blocks, Berra was fired as manager of the Yankees. This time it hurt more than the previous two incidents had. Berra was bitter. He refused to be seen in public, stayed away from ballparks all season, and absented himself from the game he loved so much, the game he graced for years.

Eventually his friend and neighbor, Dr. John McMullen, owner of the Houston Astros, offered him a job as a coach. He would be the perfect assistant to help break in the Astros' new manager, Hal Lanier. It was not New York. It was not the Yankees. But it was baseball. Yogi accepted.

In their 25 years of existence, the Houston Astros had won only one division championship. They had not won in six years. In his first year as coach, Berra watched the Astros win the National League West. Naturally, they said it again: Berra luck.

Berra's boyhood friend, Joe Garagiola, says, "He's one of those Christmas Eve guys. There are people like that. There are people who are December 17 guys or October 19 guys. Me, I'm an April 10 guy. And there are people who are Christmas Eve guys. Every day in their lives is Christmas Eve. Stan Musial was always a Christmas Eve guy. So is Yogi."

When people would mention Berra luck to him, Yogi would flash that silly grin of his and say, "I'd rather be lucky than good." Yet he was both—lucky *and* good.

He won three Most Valuable Player Awards and was voted into the Hall of Fame, baseball's supreme honor. He won two pennants in his first three years as a manager, the first manager in almost 40 years to win pennants in both the American and National Leagues. He always bounced right. While others— more famous, more intelligent, better educated, higher paid— piled up business failure after business failure, everything he touched became 14-carat gold.

He invested in a bowling alley with Phil Rizzuto and sold out at a handsome profit during the bowling boom. A year later he bought the place back for half as much as he received when he sold it.

He put some money in and contributed his name to a small soft drink company, Yoo-Hoo, and was named a vice president.

He became one of America's most lovable characters. His face, beautifully ugly, guaranteed him instant recognition. It was a natural for television commercials—"Yogi Berra is one of those sissies who uses his wife's hair spray," said the voice, and there was Yogi Berra shooting a spray onto his black hair. It didn't help his looks, although it sure helped his bank account.

When he uttered something funny it was usually accidental, but people never believed that. He became the master of the malapropism, the father of the faux pas. He spoke and people laughed and he didn't even know what they were laughing at. So he laughed, too.

Funny guy, that Yog. That face, that build, that voice, that name, those remarks. What a scream!

He never went beyond the eighth grade in school, yet he has a native intelligence, an innate wisdom, and a wonderfully simple way of cutting through all the folderol and getting to the heart of a matter. When he says something that seems funny, it really isn't funny at all; it is wise. He expresses himself simply and naturally.

The first time he said something funny, accidentally of course, people laughed. They laughed not with him but at him. Soon everybody was telling Yogi Berra stories. Real ones. And when there were no more real ones to tell, they made up stories and attributed them to Berra. And everybody laughed, even Yogi. He was the foil for their jokes, just as there have been foils for years. He was Lou Costello and Harpo Marx and Stan Laurel and Jerry Lewis, playing the buffoon to someone else's straight man.

The stories they made up about him didn't hurt Yogi. In fact, they helped him. They helped him become more lovable, more recognized, more in demand for commercials. They laughed at him, and Yogi laughed all the way to the bank.

One Yogi Berra story even hit me personally. I can vouch for its veracity. I was a young reporter for the New York *World Telegram and Sun*. I had covered the Yankees for a year, and many people called me by my last name. They had since I was a kid. It was short, catchy, easy to remember. Yogi Berra had his life story ghostwritten, and there was this big autograph party at one of New York's large department stores. My editor thought it might be a good idea for me to go over and do a piece on the autograph party. My reward for showing up was a copy of the book. Naturally, I had to have it autographed.

"Would you mind signing it, Yog?" I asked.

"Sure," he said, taking my pen and opening the book. He began writing "To Pepe," then he paused. "Hey, what's your last name?"

I laughed. Yogi laughed. Then he wrote, "Best Wishes, Yogi Berra."

Well, it seemed funny then. I've told the story many times. It always got a laugh. Not a real big laugh, more of a bemused smile, usually followed by the comment, "That's Yogi for you."

He can't go anywhere without being recognized. There was a cartoon character on television named Yogi Bear. An obvious steal. The bear is a big, hulking animal with a gruff voice, a kind of innocent, bumbling creature. I suppose if Yogi Berra were an animal, he would be a bear—big, bumbling, and lovable.

There was a kid on a Little League team in Saddle River, New Jersey. He was a catcher, and the other kids called him Yogi. It's an endearing nickname, a tribute to his ability as a catcher. I suppose there must be thousands of kid catchers on Little League diamonds and sandlots all over the country called Yogi.

My daughter once had a soft, furry, lovable cat. The cat's name was Yogi. It was not meant to be insulting; a child does not give a pet cat an insulting name.

There are lots of stories in this book that are attributed to Yogi Berra. Some of them are true. Many of them aren't. I must admit I don't know for certain which are true and which are apocryphal. The years have made it difficult to separate truth from fiction.

I consider Yogi Berra a friend of mine. I hope he feels the same about me. I know this: he hasn't a malicious bone in his body. I never heard him say a bad word about anyone. And I never heard anyone say a bad word about him. I want Yogi Berra to know that the stories repeated here are not meant to demean or ridicule him. I have never known him to intentionally hurt anyone; I would never intentionally hurt him.

THE
WIT
AND
WISDOM
OF
YOGI BERRA

1

Pal Joey

"I remember the first time I went to Yogi's house in Montclair," Joe Garagiola recalled with a smile. "I didn't know the first thing about New Jersey and I knew even less about Montclair. Naturally, I got lost.

"I made it to the town, all right, but I must have taken the wrong turn, because I couldn't find the street I was looking for. So I stopped to call Yogi for directions. I was near some big building, the Museum of Science, the sign said, but for some reason the people of Montclair call it The Library. When I told somebody my problem and asked where I was, he replied, 'Just say you're at The Library. Your friend will know where you are. Everybody in Montclair knows The Library.'

"So I called. 'Hey, Yog,' I said, 'I'm lost.'

" 'Where are ya?' he said.

" 'Some guy says to tell you I'm at The Library.'

" 'Oh,' he said, 'you ain't too far, just a couple of blocks. Only don't go that way, come this way.' "

They were like bookends . . . like reflections in a looking glass. Joe Garagiola and Yogi Berra were so much alike as kids, it was almost as if they were the same person.

They grew up in St. Louis, in a section known as The Hill. It was also called Dago Hill—a little patch of land not far from the heart of town. It sat there atop a hill like an island of privacy in the sea of activity that was the metropolis of St. Louis. The Hill was like a city within a city, inhabited in the main by Italian immigrants and their families living in neat, one-family brick houses.

It was not necessary to leave The Hill to subsist. Right there were the essentials of life—homes, churches, Italian groceries, bakeries, shoemakers, barbers, fruit and vegetable markets, and taverns. In that respect it was not unlike any first or second generation Italian neighborhood in any large metropolitan city in the United States of its time.

The time was soon after the Depression. In another time it might have been called a ghetto, and the people who lived there might have been considered poor enough to qualify for welfare. But the people of The Hill were too proud to accept charity, and the young ones never thought of themselves as poor. As long as there was food on the table and a pair of shoes to wear to church on Sunday and games to play like stoop ball and softball, how could they be poor?

"How long have I known Yogi?" Joe Garagiola asked. "I can't remember not knowing him."

The Garagiolas lived at 5446 Elizabeth Avenue on The Hill, in a small, one-family brick house. Directly across the street, at 5447 Elizabeth Avenue in an identical house, lived the Berras— Pietro and Paulina. They had come to St. Louis from the little town of Malvaglio in the north of Italy, near Milan. The Berras had four sons and one daughter. They named the youngest son Lawrence Peter. They called him Lawdie.

Lawdie Berra was eight months older than Joey Garagiola. As kids they were practically inseparable. Their families were practically inseparable. Papa Berra and Papa Garagiola worked together, baking clay at the kilns of the Laclede-Christy Clay Products Company. Their two oldest boys worked together at Ruggieri's Restaurant, still a landmark on The Hill.

Yogi was Joey's best man when he married Audrie; Joe was

Yogi's best man when he married Carmen. The Garagiolas had a boy, the Berras had a boy; the Garagiolas had another boy, the Berras had another boy; the Berras had a third boy, the Garagiolas had a girl.

"Our lives," says Joe, "are parallel."

What are the odds that two kids, born to Italian immigrant parents, living across the street from one another in a small St. Louis neighborhood, would, at one time, make up one-eighth of the starting catchers in the major leagues? How coincidental is it that both of them not only would play the same position but would throw right-handed and bat left-handed and that they would wind up living and raising families in the New York area—Berra in Montclair, New Jersey, Garagiola in Scarsdale, New York—and that both would be eminently successful in their careers, Joe Garagiola in television, Yogi Berra as manager of the New York Mets?

And yet, the boys who grew up with them on the Hill would not have been surprised that Joey and Lawdie would earn their livings in sports. It was sports that consumed them during their entire young lives, occupying their every waking moments, keeping them off the streets—or on the streets—playing their little games tirelessly and endlessly.

They played softball without mitts and football with rolled-up newspapers or bundles of rags tied in a knot. They played when and where they could, improvising their make-shift games, but on The Hill summer was the best of times. School was out, and the whole day was available for playing their games. The boys would get up early and have their breakfasts of bread and coffee, laced with sugar and lightened with evaporated milk, and then the truck from Laclede-Christy would come. Their fathers would pile on and go off to work, and the moment the truck was out of sight, the boys on The Hill would begin their summer games.

They played all day, usually without stopping for lunch. Then at 4:30 the whistle blew at the Blackmer Post Pipe Company. That was the signal for the game to end, no matter if the score was tied and there were two outs and the bases loaded in the last of the ninth inning.

At 5 P.M. sharp, the truck from Laclede-Christy pulled up at Elizabeth Avenue and unloaded a group of hungry fathers. The 4:30 whistle gave a boy just enough time to get home, pick up a metal beer bucket, dash down to Fassi's Tavern, have the bucket filled with cold, draught beer, and get it home and on the table before pop walked in the door. And heaven help you if the beer was not on the table when pop walked in the door.

There were times, when he got older, that Lawdie missed dinner completely. He was too busy playing baseball, which was then as it is now his great love.

One historic summer afternoon Lawdie Berra became "Yogi" for all time. It happens in any era, in any city, to a great many kids. A group goes to a movie, enjoys it, singles out a particularly interesting character with a strange name, pins one of their group with the name, and sometimes it sticks. Yogi stuck.

Lawdie Berra's movie was a travelogue about India featuring a Hindu fakir called a yogi who sat there with his arms folded and his knees crossed and a look of solemnity and sadness on his face. It occurred to one of their gang, Jack Maguire, that the Indian fakir, the yogi, looked like Lawdie Berra in one of his contemplative moods. From that day to this, Lawdie Berra has been Yogi to millions of Americans, to his friends, even to his wife.

The name was not meant to be insulting. If anything, it was endearing, something kids did then as they do now—their own private thing. It is out of such things that people are dubbed Moose or Rocky or Butch or Doc. Lawrence Peter Berra, called Lawdie by his family, became Yogi.

"As a kid, Yogi wasn't the town dummy—nothing like that," points out Garagiola, adding that his friend did have one idiosyncrasy. "He ate the strangest things. One of his favorites for lunch was to take a loaf of Italian bread, split it in half, put bananas on the bread, then smear mustard on the bananas. Johnny Columbo would watch Yogi eating his bananas and mustard sandwich and it would make him so sick to his stomach that he couldn't eat his own lunch and Yogi would wind up with Johnny's cheese sandwich in addition to his own banana sandwich."

Thinking back over the years, Garagiola's remembrances of his pal Yogi are that he was "a likeable guy. I guess we had our share of fights like all kids do, but nothing major, nothing that I can remember now. I just remember that Yogi was a likable guy and the best athlete in the neighborhood."

It wasn't an award or a prize he won, but as Garagiola points out, "Kids always determine who the best player is by themselves." They have the judgment of a super scout, and a foolproof way of showing who they think is best. He is always the first one picked when sides are chosen for their games. Yogi Berra was always the first one picked in any sport, always the one you wanted with you, not against you. He was the best at baseball, the best at football, even the best at pitching horseshoes.

When the kids of The Hill played football—touch football—Yogi would always switch sides when it was fourth down so that he could be on the side of the team with the ball. He was the best kicker in the neighborhood, a skill he developed playing soccer. He could kick the ball farther and straighter than anybody else, so he became the punting specialist on fourth down for both sides. In the huddle, he would always call the plays for his side.

Garagiola remembers one incident that occurred in Tower Grove Park, where the kids of The Hill often went to play.

"It was," says Joe, "just like a scene from a class B movie. On this day we were playing on one end of the field, and the South West High School football team was working out at the other end. Well, a football got loose and came to our end and Yogi picked it up and kicked it back—a tremendous kick. He was wearing sneakers, and he must have kicked that football 50 yards. So the coach came over and wanted to know who kicked the ball. We told him it was Yogi. Right there, the coach asked him to come to South West High to play football.

"Yogi said he couldn't because he had to go to work. But the coach was persistent. 'Just come to school three days a week,' he said."

But high school was a luxury the Berras couldn't afford. Yogi had to go to work as soon as possible, which was after he left Wade School, a vocational school, after the eighth grade. He worked at a variety of jobs. He loaded and unloaded cases of soda on a Pepsi-Cola truck, and later his brother, Mike, helped get him a job as a tack-puller with the Johansen Shoe Company. In the process of putting soles on women's shoes, the sole was cemented to the frame and tacks were put in to keep the soles adhering to the frames while the cement was drying. When the cement was dry, the tacks would have to be pulled out of the soles. That was Yogi's job, and his pay depended on how many pairs of shoes he completed. He was good for about $35 a week.

As a means of supplementing his income, and just because he enjoyed it, Yogi played sandlot baseball for $5 or $10 a game. And when the local Irish-American club staged weekly boxing shows, Yogi Berra became one of its more prominent attractions. He estimates he fought 14 times at the club at $5 per fight and was never defeated.

But it was baseball at which he excelled, and it was baseball that coursed through his veins. He was determined to be a baseball player, just like his hero, Ducky Medwick.

"We followed baseball on the radio," says Joe Garagiola, "when we were lucky enough to find somebody with a radio. Or we followed it with bubble gum cards. Like all kids, we had our individual heroes. Yogi's was Joe Medwick. Occasionally we would get to see the Cardinals play through the Knot Hole Gang program. They put us in left field, right near Medwick, and that's how he came to be Yogi's favorite player. That's why I can't figure out why Yogi and I began batting left-handed. We're both right-handed in everything else we do. Usually, kids will imitate their heroes, hit like they hit. If Yogi imitated anybody, it would have been Medwick, and he hit right-handed."

When Garagiola talks of his friend, it almost borders on hero worship. Here is the big television star, the sophisticated, urbane raconteur who is as glib as they come, who can make small talk with presidents, kings, and pontiffs, yet Joe Garagiola sometimes gives the impression that Yogi Berra was all he ever wanted to be.

It is understandable. What Yogi Berra did, he did naturally, his gift of natural ability emanating from a far greater power. Yogi Berra is what many men would like to be—a famous and gifted athlete.

When Joe Garagiola talks of Yogi Berra's ability as a baseball player, it is with reverence and awe and with the understanding of one who has been there but has fallen short; yet he speaks without envy. Never that, for no man can be more pleased with another's success than Joe Garagiola is with the success of Yogi Berra.

"Because he's such a pleasant guy," Garagiola explains, "not spoiled, not vain, just such a basic, simple, humble man. There's a lot going on inside him. I just wish he could say it better, because he has so much to say. He could also say some other things about people who have hurt him, but he won't do it. He's such a decent guy. And let me tell you something else; Yogi is no dope. If he tells you something, he may not be able to explain it as well as somebody else, but you can go to the bank on it."

Among so many other things he is, Yogi Berra is the world's greatest sports fan. He can tell you what's going on in any sport at any time. He can identify the best interior linemen in college football, and he can name the six best defensemen in the National Hockey League.

"Once while I was still working in St. Louis," Garagiola remembers, "I had to come to New York for something, so I called Yogi and asked him if we could get together for dinner. We met in the city, had dinner, then he said, 'Hey, come with me, I'm goin' to the Garden. There's a college kid playing there I wanna see.' I went with him, and that night we saw Oscar Robertson set a Madison Square Garden scoring record. Oscar was only a sophomore, but Yogi knew all about him. His interest in sports is boundless, and so is his knowledge.

"One Saturday we're doing the Yankees on the 'Game of the Week.' Yogi is playing left field and I notice him waving Mickey Mantle over from right center into straightaway center. I can't even remember who the hitter was, but after the game I asked Yogi why he moved Mantle.

" 'Mickey doesn't know it,' he said, 'but that guy never pulls the ball with two strikes on him.'

"The guy is anything but dumb. Paul Richards once said he was the toughest hitter in baseball in the eighth and ninth innings when the game was on the bases. He has the greatest concentration of any man I've ever known. He's a super card player, great at gin rummy. He has the ability to shut out everything else and concentrate on what he's doing, which is what made him such a great hitter, especially in clutch situations. If he says he's going to play cards, bombs could be going off in that room, he'll be concentrating on that card game.

"He was the same way as a hitter. If I were to make a composite of the perfect ballplayer, the one thing I would want from Yogi would be his thinking in the batter's box. You know the story about how his manager told him he had to think along with the pitcher when he was at bat and Yogi began grumbling. 'How can you think and hit at the same time?' he asked.

"He has a way of getting right to the core of the matter. He never thought himself into a slump. If you listen to him, he never was in a slump. There were times when he wasn't hitting, but he never believed he was in a slump. He could make that distinction between not hitting and being in a slump.

"Another thing about him that made him so remarkable as a player," Garagiola continued, "was his durability playing a position where it's almost impossible to avoid cuts or bruises or broken bones. Every catcher has to play hurt, but he played a lot of years for the Yankees during which he caught almost every game.

"One year he wasn't hitting well, and people kept making excuses for him. The papers talked about an allergy on his hands. Allergy, hell. That was a case of nerves. And there wasn't anything wrong with him that year except that his mother was dying and he couldn't concentrate on playing baseball. That's the kind of guy he is. He'd do anything for you. He'd give you half of whatever he had. If he hit a double, he'd gladly give you a single. He's a man who's good to his family, a sensitive man, not a guy who's going to do lines for you. He's not a funny guy and he shouldn't be depicted as a funny guy."

Garagiola could remember only twice when Yogi got angry as a kid. Once was at the Roosevelt High School field when some boys were ridiculing him, telling him he wasn't such a good hitter.

"He bet them a dollar he could hit a ball on the hill behind the field. He hit one nine miles and won his dollar. The other time was when some kids came down and wrecked the baseball field we had made on Sublette Avenue. That was his pride and joy, and he was so mad that if he had caught those kids in the act, he would have torn them apart."

The field was on an old clay mine right near where there is now a street called Berra's Court. With two old wrecked cars for dugouts, the Stags A.C., Berra's team, had the neatest baseball diamond in town. The Stags were Berra's first team. He was 11 years old.

As Yogi got older and grew bigger, his reputation as a hitter

The following year the Works Progress Administration, an agency formed under President Franklin D. Roosevelt's New Deal to provide work for needy persons, put on a month-long baseball clinic at Sherman Park in St. Louis with major leaguers as instructors and scouts, ever on the lookout for talent, in attendance at every session. Players were divided into various teams, tournaments were held, and the scouts got a chance to look at the boys under game conditions. When the month was concluded, the Cardinals offered a professional contract to Garagiola.

"I asked for a $500 bonus and they agreed," Joe recalls. "The reason I said $500 was that was the amount remaining on the mortgage of our house. In later years, I told my father if he had grew with him. He switched from the Stags to the Edmonds because they had uniforms, and then to the Stockham Post, an American Legion team that made the national semifinals two straight years.

Berra and Garagiola took turns pitching and catching, and although the Stockham Post lost once in the semis to a team from Illinois and another time to the Sunsets of California with Nippy Jones and Gene Mauch, the two kids from Elizabeth Avenue were earning a reputation in baseball in the St. Louis area.

The local newspapers reported their progress through the American Legion tournament, and Jack Maguire's father was a St. Louis Cardinal scout, so the names Berra and Garagiola were not unknown to the Cardinals or the St. Louis Browns.

Joey Garagiola had used his father's homemade wine to bribe the Cardinal clubhouse man into letting him into Cardinal tryout camps, and eventually Joe began hustling bats for two dollars a session while getting in a workout. The Cardinals invited him to go to Springfield, Missouri, to one of their minor league affiliates, to work as a part-time groundskeeper and part-time batting practice catcher.

had a $10,000 mortgage, I would have been the first bonus baby in baseball history."

Joey Garagiola was a happy young man. His boyhood dream had come true. He would go off to play professional baseball in Springfield in the 1942 season. But what about his pal, Yogi Berra?

While a scout named Dee Walsh had talked to Cardinal General Manager Branch Rickey about Garagiola, Yogi Berra had Jack Maguire talking for him. The Cardinals were willing to give Yogi a contract as well, but there would be no bonus.

"The boy is too clumsy and too slow," Rickey said. "He'll never make anything more than a triple A ballplayer at best, and I'm looking for boys who can go all the way to the big leagues."

Maguire pleaded and Rickey relented. "All right," he said, "I'm willing to give him a $250 bonus, but that's all he's worth."

Jack Maguire reported Rickey's offer to Berra and beseeched him to take the $250.

"Nothin' doin'," said Yogi, his pride hurt. "I want the same as Joey got."

It was no deal as far as the Cardinals were concerned, and Yogi Berra went back to work in the shoe factory and his pal Joey went off to win fame and fortune with the Cardinals.

"He was hurt and I didn't blame him," Garagiola said many years later. "Yogi is supersensitive as it is. But he was eight months older, and it hurt him that I got a contract and he didn't, especially since whenever we went to work out with the Cardinals, he kept popping the ball onto that screen in right field. He didn't look like the Spalding Guide's model ballplayer, that's true, but he felt he deserved to get as much as I did. In his mind and heart he knew he was the better ballplayer. And I knew it, too."

Nobody has ever satisfactorily explained why the Cardinals let Yogi Berra get away. Some say it was simply poor judgment, an honest mistake on the part of Branch Rickey, who rarely made mistakes when it came to judging talent. Others say Rickey knew he was leaving the Cardinals that year to take a similar post with the Brooklyn Dodgers and he wanted Berra for his new club. His staunchest followers and disciples insist Mr. Rickey was too honorable a man to do a thing like that.

"That may be," says Joe Garagiola, "but why do you think I was in Springfield the year before? The Cardinals stashed me there so that nobody would see me and get interested in me. They wanted to sign me as soon as I came of age. I don't know for sure, but I'd have to say, based on everything I know, based on all the evidence and on how well Yogi did in those tryouts, that Mr. Rickey was trying to stash him for the Dodgers."

Garagiola's theory seems to have a basis in fact. The following year, after Rickey moved to Brooklyn, the Dodgers wired Berra and invited him to leave immediately for their training camp at Bear Mountain, New York, and sign a bonus contract.

No amount of money was specified, and Berra never found out if the Dodgers were going to pay him more than his pal Joey. It didn't matter. Brooklyn was too late. Yogi Berra had already made other plans.

2

Hero on the Hill

It probably was accidental, based solely on alphabetical order, and if it was an accident, it was a marvelous one; but if it was planned, it was a stroke of genius and the perpetrator is to be commended.

However it happened, when the 1946 Newark Bears of the International League went on the road, a rookie catcher from St. Louis named Lawrence Peter Berra was assigned to room with a rookie infielder from Seattle, Washington, named Robert Williams Brown. It would have been impossible to scrutinize the entire Yankee farm system, indeed, even the whole of professional baseball, and find two individuals with such completely diverse interests.

Both had nicknames. Berra was Yogi for reasons already explained. Brown was Doc for reasons that will soon become obvious. But that was where the similarity of the two roommates ended.

The contrast between the two rookies was striking, Berra with his eighth-grade education; Brown, a college graduate, spending the off-season studying medicine at Tulane University. He would enter the medical profession after a brief and moderately successful major league career. He would become a prominent cardiologist in Texas and would return to baseball in 1985 as president of the American League.

Conversations between Berra and Brown must have been classic; their evenings together must have been unique. One such evening, after an exhausting day at the ball park and a leisurely dinner, they returned to their room to relax. Hotels did not have television in those days. Reading was the baseball player's only diversion, his only escape from the boredom of long, tedious road trips. And so Brown reached for one of his medical texts, while Berra dipped into his seemingly inexhaustible supply of the classics—Superman comics, perhaps, or Batman and Robin, or Mutt and Jeff.

Time passed, each reading in silence. Finally, as the hour became late and sleep drew near, Bobby Brown closed his huge, thick text with a satisfied slam and an accompanying sigh.

Moments later, Berra turned the last page of his book.

"Boy," he said, "that was a good one. How did yours come out?"

Yogi Berra's disappointment at not being signed by the Cardinals was short-lived, and his hurt pride was quickly mended. He had been working at the shoe factory just a few months when his big break came. A man named Johnny Schulte paid a call to the Berra home on Elizabeth Avenue.

Schulte was the bullpen coach for the New York Yankees, who had just wiped out the Cardinals in the World Series. He lived in the St. Louis area and had been asked by the Yankee general manager, George Weiss, to look up this Berra kid and "see what he's got. If you like what you see, sign him to a contract."

Weiss, it seems, had gotten a tip on Berra in the form of a letter from Leo Browne, commander of the Stockham Post, Yogi's American Legion team. Browne had been an umpire in the Eastern League when Weiss ran the New Haven club there.

"All the kid wants," Browne wrote, "is a $500 bonus. He'll take whatever salary you offer."

Schulte had never seen Berra play, but he had heard enough about him and liked the way the kid handled himself in their short, casual workout. He offered Yogi a contract with the Yankees' Norfolk club.

"You'll get a $500 bonus and $90 a month," Schulte said. Likely, Berra never heard a thing beyond the "$500 bonus."

That was the magic number. He agreed to sign. Now he was a Yankee and on a par with his pal Joey.

It didn't take long for Yogi to realize life as a professional ballplayer was not all it was cracked up to be—at least not at that minor league level. His $500 bonus was payable if he remained with Norfolk for the entire year. And his salary, after taxes, came to $35 every two weeks. He could make twice as much at the shoe factory.

He spent only seven dollars a week for a room in a boardinghouse, but invariably he had eaten himself broke by the middle of the second week. Once, he went on a hunger strike, refusing to play until the Norfolk manager, Shaky Kain, went into his pocket and came up with enough money for Yogi to buy a couple of hamburgers and Cokes.

Instead of sending money home, a letter from Norfolk to 5447 Elizabeth Avenue, St. Louis, was usually a plea for cash. Mama Berra, the softhearted one, sent the money so her boy could eat. She also sent along a warning: "Don't tell your papa or he'll make you come home."

Mama Berra knew nothing about baseball, but she knew a lot about her boys. Instinctively, she realized this was her youngest son's heart, this was what he had to do. Yogi's three older brothers also knew, and they were eager for their kid brother to get the chance they never had.

"They could have been better than me," Yogi has said. "But they had to go to work."

His empty stomach couldn't stop Berra from attracting attention at Norfolk. Only 18 years old, he appeared in 111 games, batted a respectable .253, slugged seven homers, and drove in 56 runs, including an unbelievable 23 RBI in an incredible two-game spree.

Years later, when he was asked to explain how he was able to drive in 23 runs in just two games, Berra responded with the simplest and most logical of explanations.

"Every time I came to bat, there were men on base," he said.

But his success, like his disappointment, was short-lived—halted abruptly by something called World War II and a request from his government to help do something about ending that skirmish.

Berra collected his $500 bonus, put it in the bank, then joined the navy to see the world—at least some of it, but not under the most pleasant of circumstances. One of the more charming places he visited was Omaha Beach—as a rocket man on a 36-foot landing craft that took part in the D-Day invasion of Normandy.

Returning from overseas, Berra finished his tour of duty in New London, Connecticut, doing the one thing he liked best—playing baseball for the post team. In addition to playing games against other bases, the New London team occasionally competed against major league clubs. On one such occasion Berra slammed three hits off Ace Adams of the New York Giants as the New York manager, Mel Ott, looked on with great interest.

As soon as he could, Ott told his boss, Horace Stoneham, about the slugging sailor he had seen at New London. "He isn't much to look at," the Giant manager warned, "and he looks like he's doing everything wrong, but he can hit. He got a couple of hits off us on wild pitches."

With his owner's approval, Ott paid a call on Larry MacPhail, president of the Yankees, and made a proposition. "You had a kid catcher at Norfolk last year," Ott said. "Name is Berra. We're looking for a young catcher. We'll pay you $50,000 for his contract."

"Berra!" repeated MacPhail, his own interest peaked by such a generous offer. "He's not for sale. Not at any price."

Ott tried to change MacPhail's mind but failed. Disappointed, he left the Yankee office, and as soon as he was out of the room, MacPhail called his chief scout, Paul Krichell.

"Paul," MacPhail said, "do we have a kid catcher named Berra?"

"Yes," said Krichell. "He played at Norfolk last year. Pretty good hitter. He's in the navy now."

"Write him a letter and tell him I'd like to see him whenever he gets the chance."

The next time he got a weekend pass Berra made the trip from New London to Yankee Stadium to see Larry MacPhail. Johnny Schulte was waiting for Yogi, and he took the young sailor into the Yankee clubhouse to meet some of the players.

The late Pete Sheehy, the droll clubhouse custodian who worked for the Yankees from Babe Ruth's day until his death in 1985, took one look at the squat, round-shouldered, burly, gnomelike kid in the sailor suit that seemed two sizes too large and exclaimed: "Who the hell is that?"

Later, Schulte took Berra upstairs to the club's offices to meet Larry MacPhail. They had a pleasant chat that proved to be rewarding and encouraging for the young catcher.

"I like what I've heard about you," MacPhail said. "And you had a good year at Norfolk. As soon as you're discharged, I'm going to send you to play for the Newark Bears."

Berra was walking on air. Not only was Newark the top farm team in the Yankee organization, but the city of Newark was only about 35 miles away from Yankee Stadium. A good year there and a fellow was almost certain to be noticed and brought up to the big team.

By the time he was discharged and had caught up with the Newark team in Rochester, New York, the 1946 International League season was almost a month old. The Bears had a set team, and a good one. The Yankees were riding high. Their scouts had gathered the best baseball talent in the land, and with the war over, players were coming back and there were more good players on the Newark team than there were on some major league rosters. It was going to be very difficult for a young catcher, only 21 and with just one year of professional baseball behind him, to crack the Newark lineup.

Berra bided his time, waiting for his chance, which came, finally, in the first game of a Sunday doubleheader. Manager George Selkirk sent him up as a pinch-hitter and Yogi delivered an important base hit. Selkirk rewarded him with a start in the second game and Berra responded with two hits in three times at bat.

From that day on Berra was the Bears' regular catcher. There was still time to make an impression on the big brass, and Berra did just that. He appeared in 77 games, batted .314, hit 15 homers, drove in 59 runs, and was called up to the Yankees for the last week of the 1946 season.

He managed to get in seven games with the Yankees. In his first major league game, he hit his first major league home run, off Jesse Flores of the Philadelphia Athletics. In his seven games he hit two homers, drove in four runs, and batted .364, then returned to The Hill content with his season and convinced that his time was near.

Back on The Hill, Berra was still second fiddle to his buddy, Joe Garagiola, who had starred for the Cardinals in the 1946 World Series, batting .316 in five games as the Cardinals beat the Boston Red Sox for the championship of baseball.

Yogi was happy for his friend and confident that he, too, was on his way toward becoming a big league star.

There would be a few bumpy roads along the way, however. He was a rookie in the Yankee spring training camp in 1947, and as a rookie, Berra would have to serve his apprenticeship not only on the field but in the dugout and the clubhouse. Because of his name and his unusual physique and looks, Berra soon became the brunt of jokes, not only from opponents but from his teammates, as well.

His manager, Bucky Harris, referred to him as The Ape. Mike Ryba, a Red Sox pitcher and no beauty contest winner himself, named Berra captain of his "All Ugly Team." Washington pitcher Ray Scarborough would mock Berra by first attracting his attention from across the field, then hanging with one hand from the top of the dugout and, with his other hand, scratching his stomach like a gorilla.

Charlie Keller, Yogi's Yankee teammate, said he was having a picture taken of Berra and himself side by side. "Then I'm going to take it home and tell my wife anytime she thinks I'm not so good-looking, she should take a look at you."

His Yankee teammates remembered the time the team was scheduled to play the Dodgers a preseason exhibition game at Brooklyn's Ebbets Field, which was not the easiest place to find, especially for a rookie from out of town. Much to their surprise Berra was waiting in the visitors' clubhouse when they arrived.

"I knew I was going to get lost," he explained, "so I left an hour early."

Berra took all the jokes in good-natured fashion. Besides, he was more concerned with making the team and somewhat frustrated that he was playing only about one game out of every two. The Yankees had more than their share of able catchers, and it was only injuries to Joe DiMaggio, Tommy Henrich, and Charlie Keller that depleted their outfield and opened up a spot for the rookie. Of the 83 games in which he appeared that year, Yogi played right field in 24 of them, was used as a pinch-hitter in eight, and caught only 51. He played mainly against right-handed pitchers but still showed a potent bat, hitting for a .280 average, cracking 11 homers, and driving in 54 runs, which was pretty good for a part-time player.

Having surpassed his buddy Joe Garagiola in all offensive categories, Berra became the new idol of The Hill—so much so that on the Yankees' last visit of the year to St. Louis, Yogi's friends and neighbors got together and gave him a "night" at Sportsman's Park. They collected a glittering assortment of gifts to present to their hero, including a new Nash sedan.

On occasions such as this it is customary for the recipient to say a few words of thanks to the people who put together such a night. Yogi Berra would have preferred hitting against fireballer Bob Feller without a batting helmet and with a pencil for a bat.

"Don't worry," said his pal Bobby Brown, "there's nothing to it. I'll help you with your speech. I'll make it nice and short."

True to his word, Brown wrote a nice little speech, only 22 words long, and Berra began the arduous task of trying to commit it to memory. He worked on it for weeks until he was sure he had it right. Nevertheless, he was frightened at the prospect of approaching that microphone in front of that large crowd.

When the fateful time arrived, Berra approached the microphone with trepidation and with a voice hoarse and stammering with nervousness, delivered his memorable address.

"I'm a lucky guy and I'm happy to be with the Yankees. I want to thank everyone for making this night necessary."

At first there was a silence from the crowd. Did they hear correctly? Then came a smattering of chuckles before it was drowned out by applause. They had heard right. Berra had inadvertently changed Bobby Brown's speech, substituting the word "necessary" for Brown's word "possible." It was the first Berraism that ever came to the attention of the public, and Yogi would never live it down.

Berra was more embarrassed, however, by what happened in his first World Series. Yogi was a rookie catcher, and the Dodgers were a running team, a daring team, with Jackie Robinson, PeeWee Reese, Pete Reiser, and Al Gionfriddo. Each of them could run. Each of them could steal a base. And they weren't afraid to gamble. In fact, they promised they would. In the newspaper stories leading up to the Series the Dodgers openly said they planned to run on the rookie catcher. It seemed the only way they could match the home run power of the Yankees. And they kept their promise.

Robinson and Reese, in particular, seemed to be able to steal a base whenever they wanted to. Eventually, Bucky Harris had to bench his rookie catcher. Berra's deficiency behind the plate enabled the Dodgers to use their strongest weapon to its greatest advantage and to extend the powerful Yankees to the seven-game limit before falling.

Worried about his throwing, Berra's hitting also suffered. He managed to get only three hits in 19 at-bats, a pitiful .158 average, although one of his hits was the first pinch-hit home run in World Series history, in game number three at Ebbets Field.

It was a humiliating experience for the young catcher, but Berra soothed his embarrassment with a World Series check for $5,830, more than he had earned for the entire season, and he went back to The Hill a hero, not a goat.

One night the newest celebrity on The Hill walked into a restaurant owned by Stan Musial and met "the prettiest girl I had ever seen in my life." She was Carmen Short, a blond waitress. "I fell in love with her the first time I saw her," Yogi said.

He eventually got up enough courage to ask Carmen Short for a date. Soon they were going together all the time, everywhere, all winter. Yogi took his girl to the movies, to basketball games, and on double dates with his best friend Joe Garagiola and his girl, Audrie Ross. Carmen and Yogi saw each other almost every night until Yogi had to leave for spring training. And it was that absence that hurt most and made him decide that the first chance he got, he would ask Carmen to be his wife.

They were engaged during the 1948 season, an announcement that was the social event of the year on The Hill. It even called for a radio interview by Harry Caray, who broadcast the Cardinal games.

"What does your mother think about your marrying a girl who isn't Italian?" Caray asked.

"She thinks it's all right. She likes Carm."

"What do the girls on The Hill think of it?"

"I don't know. Anyway, it don't matter. They had their chance."

Yogi's first team, the Stag A.C. Terrors of the Hill. Yogi is third from the left in the middle row; childhood friend Joe Garagiola is at the far left in the front row. *Photo courtesy of the N.Y. Yankees.*

A young Yogi scores for the Stockham Post team in an American Legion tournament game in 1942 in Hastings, Nebraska. The ump is Peaches Postlewait. *Photo courtesy of the N.Y. Yankees.*

Yogi with his parents in 1947, just before joining the majors. *Photo courtesy of UPI.*

Yogi and Carmen Short married on January 26, 1949. *Photo courtesy of UPI.*

Yogi pours for the groom and Stan Musial for the bride as they prepare to make a toast at the wedding breakfast of Joe Garagiola and Audrie Ross on November 5, 1949. *Photo courtesy of UPI.*

Larry Jr.
slides home
as Dad puts
the tag on.
*Photo courtesy
of UPI.*

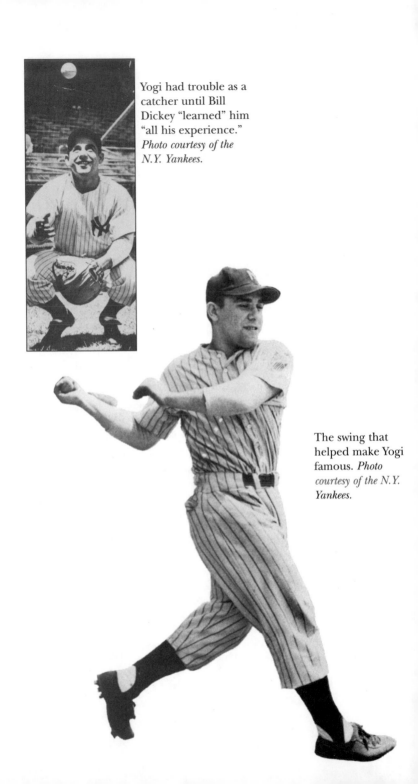

Yogi had trouble as a catcher until Bill Dickey "learned" him "all his experience." *Photo courtesy of the N.Y. Yankees.*

The swing that helped make Yogi famous. *Photo courtesy of the N.Y. Yankees.*

A reunion for Yogi and Joe Garagiola in St Petersburg, Florida, during spring training of 1947; they're a long way from good old Elizabeth Avenue. *Photo courtesy of the N.Y. Yankees.*

Yogi meets the mighty Babe Ruth on Babe Ruth Day in St Louis, 1948. *Photo courtesy of UPI.*

Charlie Keller (right) had this photo taken and told Yogi, "I'm going to take it home and tell my wife anytime she thinks I'm not so good-looking, she should take a look at you." *Photo courtesy of UPI.*

Yogi and Joe DiMaggio combined forces with a home run apiece in the final game of the 1950 World Series sweep of the Phillies. *Photo courtesy of UPI.*

Through hard work Yogi became the best American League catcher of the fifties. His catch here saved a wild pitch by Allie Reynolds in a game against the Washington Senators. *Photo courtesy of UPI.*

Happiness is when you've beaten the Brooklyn Dodgers in the sixth game to even the 1952 World Series. The winning pitcher, Vic Raschi, is front right; the one who saved Vic in relief, Allie Reynolds, is front left; Yogi and Mickey Mantle, each of whom homered, are behind them. *Photo courtesy of UPI.*

Barnstormers en route to Hawaii, already wreathed in leis (from left): Nelson Fox of the White Sox, Ed Lopat and Yogi Berra of the 1952 World Champion Yankees, Pee Wee Reese of the Dodgers, and Robin Roberts of the Phillies. *Photo courtesy of UPI.*

Yogi never hesitated to slide face first. *Photo courtesy of UPI.*

A meeting of the MVP minds: Phil Rizzuto, 1950 American League MVP; Yogi, 1951; and Bobby Schantz, 1952. *Photo courtesy of UPI.*

Yogi would add one more MVP plaque (for 1955) to the two shown here, from 1951 and 1954. *Photo courtesy of UPI.*

Yogi strolls on the "Ginza" while barnstorming in Japan during 1955. *Photo courtesy of UPI.*

Berra was as excited as Don Larsen after the big right-hander pitched a perfect game against the Brooklyn Dodgers in the 1956 World Series. *Photo courtesy of UPI.*

A one-time catcher who later became a heavyweight champion, Rocky Marciano once got some tips from Yogi at spring training in St. Petersburg, Florida. *Photo courtesy of the N.Y. Yankees.*

From left to right: Hank Bauer, Bob Turley, and Yogi celebrate after the Yankees won the sixth game of the 1957 World Series. But the Milwaukee Braves would later take the seventh game and the Series. *Photo courtesy of the N.Y. Yankees.*

Yogi with the famous (and sometimes infamous) Casey Stengel. *Photo courtesy of UPI.*

Called out on strikes under a new rule in 1957, Yogi squawked to no avail to umpire Ed Rommel. It happened on Opening Day against Washington in Yankee Stadium. *Photo courtesy of UPI.*

Photo courtesy of UPI.

3

"Is He Living Now?"

Baseball players live a lonely life on the road and will do anything to fight the boredom and find amusement during the long hours away from home. The time between games hangs heavy; the time on trains, in Yogi Berra's early days, and on planes, in more recent years, seems interminable.

On train rides or plane trips, restless athletes will choose their own device in an effort to pass the time. Some sleep. Some read. Many play cards. Others do crossword puzzles. And still others rely on word games.

Yogi Berra liked games, and among his favorites was Twenty Questions. The rules were simple. One player chose an object and his opponent would guess what that object was. The guesser got one clue—that the object was animal, vegetable, or mineral. Then the guesser could ask 20 questions, answered only by a yes or no, with which to guess the object.

During one game, Yogi Berra, the guesser, determined that the object, animal, was a person.

"Is he living?" Yogi asked.

"Yes," replied his opponent.

"Is he living now*?"*

Love had come to Yogi Berra at the age of 23 and after only one year in the big leagues, and with it he seemed to blossom as a man and flourish as a ballplayer. He established himself as a truly outstanding hitter in the 1948 season, but he also proved that he was no better as a catcher in 1948 than he had been in the 1947 World Series.

Emboldened by the success the Dodgers had enjoyed in running on Berra, American League teams followed the pattern that had been set. Yogi had trouble throwing and he had trouble catching and with all that to worry about, his hitting fell off.

On August 14 he was batting .271, a respectable average but not up to his potential. It was on that day that Yankee manager Bucky Harris decided to relieve the young man of mitt and mask and his duties as a catcher in an effort to save him as a hitter. Yogi had split his time between catcher and right field, and it was obvious to Harris that the young slugger was more effective as a hitter when he didn't have to worry about catching. So, on August 14 Harris moved Berra to right field, and he was there to stay.

It was uncanny. Relieved of the responsibility of catching, Berra was a hitting terror from that day on. He tore American League pitching apart, batting almost .400 for the final six weeks and finishing with a season's average of .305, 14 homers, and 98 runs batted in.

The Yankees came fast at the end but missed winning the American League pennant by three games, and Berra went home to The Hill to keep an important date. On January 26, 1949, Lawrence Peter Berra took the hand of Carmen Short in matrimony in a simple ceremony at St. Ambrose Church. For their honeymoon the Berras motored to New Orleans, then stopped off in Daytona Beach, Florida, on their way to St. Petersburg, where the Yankees had set up spring training camp for the 1949 season.

The new year brought surprises. The Yankees had dismissed Bucky Harris as manager and replaced him with Casey Stengel, part clown, part genius. Stengel was already 59 years old when he took over the reins of the Yankees. He had had two previous tries as a major league manager and had failed in both.

In nine seasons with the Brooklyn and Boston clubs in the National League, he could finish no higher than fifth in an eight-team league. But for five seasons he had managed with great success at Oakland in the Pacific Coast League, and he was the man the Yankees wanted to succeed Harris, despite great criticism from the New York press.

With him, Stengel brought two coaches. One was pitching coach Jim Turner. The other was to have an important role in the history of baseball, the Yankees, and Yogi Berra. He was Bill Dickey, considered by many to be the greatest catcher of all time. Officially, his job was that of hitting instructor. Unofficially, and perhaps more importantly, he was there to teach young Berra the rudiments, as well as the nuances, of catching.

Stengel had decided he was going to sink or swim with Berra, who would be his catcher no matter what. Casey not only recognized the potential of the squat slugger, he placed a high premium on a catcher who could hit and was durable enough to absorb the little hurts that were inevitable in that job. Berra qualified on both counts.

In later years, Stengel would articulate his theory about catchers when, as the septuagenarian manager of the brand-new New York Mets, he explained why a catcher, Hobie Landrith, was the infant team's first selection in the expansion draft.

"You have to have a catcher," Stengel said sagely, "because if you don't, you're likely to have a lot of passed balls."

Berra was eager to give catching a try on a full-time basis and excited to have such an illustrious former player as Dickey for his mentor. Yogi worked harder than anybody else in camp, and when a sportswriter asked him how he was coming along, he replied, "Great! Bill Dickey is learning me all his experience."

Berra attempted to conceal his disappointment when the season opened in Washington and he was not in the starting lineup. But he pinch-hit in the seventh, singled in the tying run, and was in the starting lineup the following day and most days thereafter.

It can hardly be considered a coincidence that for five straight years, beginning in 1949, the Yankees won five pennants and world championships and that for five straight years, beginning in 1949, Yogi Berra appeared at no other position for the Yankees but catcher. He caught 109 games in 1949, and then 148, 141, 140, 133, and he was perhaps the team's most valuable player over that span.

His reputation was growing by leaps and bounds and by blunders and malaprops. He came to the attention of the late Jimmy Cannon, fertile-minded syndicated sports columnist, who recognized Berra as a wonderful character to write about and jumped on the Berra bandwagon.

"One day recently," Cannon wrote, "Joe Page was talking to Berra about Enos Slaughter, whose passion, besides baseball, is hunting. 'He's tireless,' Page said. 'We were in the woods one time and Enos ducked in and out of the bushes so quick he got a cyst on his back.'

"'What the hell kind of a bird is a cyst?' Berra asked."

Berra wasn't quite so funny with a bat in his hands, particularly to opposing pitchers. And the improvement he was showing behind the bat was nothing short of incredible. The great Detroit left-hander, Hal Newhouser, indicated the esteem in which Berra was held when a sportswriter, discussing Berra, said: "You shouldn't have any trouble with him, he's strictly a bad ball hitter."

"Yeah," replied Newhouser, "but I defy anybody to throw him a good ball."

It was impossible for a pitcher to accumulate a dossier on the Yankee catcher. He hit the pitch over his head as well as he hit the pitch over the plate.

Casey Stengel loved Berra. For all his seeming bumbling and fumbling, Yogi was as astute a baseball man on the field as you could find. "My assistant manager," Stengel called him, only half in jest because Casey would frequently rely on Berra's judgment when it came time to make a manager's most difficult decision—whether to leave a pitcher in the game or take him out.

If Yogi said of a Yankee pitcher, "He ain't got nothin', Case," Stengel would usually bring in a new pitcher. If Yogi said, "He's still throwin' good, Case," the pitcher was usually allowed to continue.

"Mister Berra," Stengel would say during one of his frequent marathon monologues directed at reporters, usually with Berra within earshot, "may not be the prettiest man in this here game, but I would have to say that he is one of the three outstanding catchers in the American League because you've got Mickey Cochrane and Bill Dickey, and in the National League you got Roy Campanella and Gabby Hartnett, which was also great, and I would have to say that's pretty good company for a young feller."

Berra's baseball logic was simple yet sage and generally accurate. Before the 1949 All-Star Game, the American League team held a meeting in its clubhouse to review strategy for pitching to the National League hitters. When the name Stan Musial came up, everybody in the room had a theory on how to stop the great Cardinal outfielder.

After listening to the lively debate for some time, Berra had this to say: "You guys are trying to stop Musial in 15 minutes and the National League ain't figured a way to stop him in 15 years."

For all his simplistic good nature, Berra had a streak of anger that he would unfurl on special occasions, sort of as a weapon to pull out when all else failed. Several Yankee pitchers felt the full fury of the Berra wrath, none more than right-hander Vic Raschi.

"Raschi pitched better when I got him mad," Yogi pointed out. "When he got off the beam, I would go out there and say, 'You're supposed to be a pitcher. You been pitchin' for 15 years and you can't even get the ball over.' And he would get mad at me, he would go right down the other end while I went back to my end. Then we'd make up, though."

In 1949 Berra had a big year at bat with a .277 average, 20 homers, and 91 RBI. He had an even bigger year in 1950, and many people thought he deserved to be voted the American League's Most Valuable Player on the strength of his .322 average, 28 homers, and 124 RBI, which was third in the league. But Yogi was not disappointed when the MVP award went to his buddy Phil Rizzuto, who outhit Berra by only two points and scored 125 runs.

With less impressive statistics, .294, 27 homers, and 88 RBI, Berra was named Most Valuable Player by the Baseball Writers Association of America in 1951, a very big year for Yogi—in fact, almost an unforgettable one.

On July 12 Berra caught his first no-hit game, pitched by Allie Reynolds against the Cleveland Indians. On September 28 of the same year Reynolds held the Boston Red Sox hitless for eight innings, then retired the first two batters in the ninth inning, and faced the immortal Ted Williams for the final out of his second no-hitter. Reynolds overpowered Williams with a fastball and got him to loft a towering pop foul, between first base and home.

Yogi tore off his mask quickly and confidently and flung it a safe distance as he settled under the ball with Reynolds standing alongside, shouting encouragement. The ball popped in and out of the mitt and fell to the ground with a thud and with a groan from the crowd as a sinking feeling settled in the pit of Berra's stomach.

Yogi got a new ball and walked to the mound and placed it in Reynolds' glove, saying something to the pitcher as he did. Later, when he was asked what he said to Reynolds, Yogi replied: "I told him, 'Hey, you stepped on my foot.'"

Was it an omen? Was there a message in Yogi's goof of the easy pop? Would Williams line the next pitch for a single to right field to deprive Reynolds of his second no-hitter and make Berra a goat? It seemed inevitable, the only course for the fates to take.

But as Berra imagined Williams lining his single and contemplated what form of suicide he would take, Williams hit another, almost identical, pop fly between first and home. A sudden thought came to Berra's mind as he settled under the ball and prepared for the catch. "What if I drop this one, too?" But the mask was off and the glove was poised and the ball was coming down . . . right into the mitt. This time it didn't pop out, and Allie Reynolds had his second no-hitter of the season.

In the years that followed, Berra became one of the most feared hitters in baseball. He followed his 1951 success with a .273 average, 30 homers, and 98 RBI in 1952. In 1953 he batted .296, slugged 27 homers, and drove 108 runs across the plate as the Yankees won an unprecedented fifth straight world championship. During those five years the funny kid from The Hill had produced 132 homers and 509 RBI.

When the Yankees' string of successes was finally stopped in 1954, it was hardly Berra's fault. He had perhaps his greatest year, a .307 average, 22 homers, and 125 RBI, for which he received his second Most Valuable Player Award. The Yankees won a remarkable 103 games that year but still finished second, eight games behind the Cleveland Indians, who won the staggering total of 111 games, an American League record.

In 1955 the Yankees got back on the winning track, and Berra was named MVP for the third time on the strength of his .272 average, 27 homers, and 108 RBI.

For all his personal glory it was a game in which he played a supporting role that provided Berra with his greatest thrill in baseball. All he did was crouch behind the plate and catch 97 pitches, but it made him part of the most extraordinary and most celebrated one-man performance in baseball history.

The date was October 8, 1956, the fifth game of the World Series between the New York Yankees and the Brooklyn

Dodgers. Don Larsen, a much-traveled, less than spectacular major league pitcher, was on the mound that day, and he pitched the first perfect game in World Series history. When it was over, when Dale Mitchell, a pinch-hitter, was called out on strikes, it was Berra who was the most excited person in Yankee Stadium, more excited than Larsen himself. Yogi leaped into the air, then dashed to the mound and hurled himself into Larsen's arms, which made the pitcher utter a tender thought.

"Damn, you're heavy," he said.

Moments later the Yankee dressing room was bedlam. Players were yelling at the tops of their voices and sportswriters from all over the country were jamming into the room hoping to talk to the pitching hero. Television cameras whirred and flash bulbs popped as Larsen climbed on a bench in the middle of the room to tell it like it was.

Those who couldn't get close to Larsen settled for the manager's office, including one rookie reporter who asked Casey Stengel, "Is that the best game Larsen's ever pitched?"

Off in a secluded corner of the Yankee clubhouse Don Larsen's catcher, a lonely figure, sat in front of his locker stripped to the waist and smoking a cigarette. One solitary reporter approached, and as he drew near, Yogi Berra looked up, and before the reporter could ask a question, Berra asked one.

"What's new?"

The 1956 season ended with the Yankees winning another world championship. It had been another super year for Berra—30 homers, 105 runs batted in, and a .298 average. The kid from The Hill, a kid no more, was at the top of his game. The top of the world.

He had done it all—three Most Valuable Player Awards, nine straight years a member of the American League All-Star Team, eight pennants, and seven world championships in ten years. His salary was in the $70,000 range, and Carmen was expecting their third child. Everything was beautiful for Lawrence Peter Berra, who had recently moved his family to a new home in Montclair, New Jersey, a big, gracious Tudor-style mansion in an exclusive community that must have seemed like it was a thousand light-years away from The Hill.

"Wotta house," Berra told Jackie Farrell of the Yankees' public relations department. "Nothin' but rooms!"

4

Jackie and the Malaprops

Yogi and Carmen Berra took a trip to Rome one year, and somebody arranged for them to have an audience with Pope John XXIII. When they returned home, Jackie Farrell asked Yogi about it.

"I understand you had an audience with the Pope," Farrell said.

"No," Yogi replied, "but I saw him."

"Did you get to talk to him?"

"I sure did. We had a nice little chat."

"What did he say?"

"Ya know, he must read the papers a lot, because he said, 'Hello, Yogi.'"

"And what did you say?"

"I said, 'Hello, Pope.'"

There are some who will tell you that the Yogi Berra image that the public knows, the joke-cracking, humorous Yogi Berra, was really created by a little giant of a man, five feet and one inch, 108 pounds after a full meal, and with a mammoth wit. His name was Jackie Farrell and by way of introduction he would tell you that he used to be a boxing writer in Jersey City. One day in the late 1930s a fighter who went under the name of Marty O'Brien asked him for a favor.

"My kid is a singer, Jackie," Marty O'Brien said. "I'd like you to manage him."

"A singer!" Jackie shrieked. "What do I want with a singer? If your son was a boxer, I'd be interested. Crooners are a dime a dozen on Broadway."

"He was a skinny little kid from Hoboken," Jackie Farrell later recalled. "Maybe you've heard of him. His name is Frank Sinatra."

A promising sportswriting career came to a halt when Ed Barrow, general manager of the Yankees, asked Jackie Farrell if he would like to go to work for the ball club in its public relations department. Jackie jumped at the chance and later became director of the Speakers Bureau for the Yankees. It was there that Jackie and Yogi met.

Berra was one of the most popular Yankees in the decade of the fifties. He was in constant demand by groups who wanted him as a speaker at their functions. And since it was Jackie Farrell who arranged the speaking program for the Yankees, the two became fast friends.

It was Farrell who first recognized Berra as a character, one who had a knack for attracting people and making friends as well as a knack for saying the wrong thing at the right time.

Berra hated to make speeches, and he would rely on the clever and capable Farrell to write little speeches for him. And if Jackie slipped in a few malaprops, tossed off a couple of jokes, and came back and spread them around members of the press, well, just file it under the heading of public relations.

"Most of the things he really said," insisted Jackie Farrell, looking you straight in the eye and not even cracking a smile. "He just said funny things. He didn't mean them to be funny; they were unintentionally funny, but they came out funny.

"Like the one about the Pope. On the same trip, he went to the famed opera house at LaScala to see Tosca. I asked him how he liked it. 'Pretty good,' he said. 'Even the music was nice.'

"And the one about the house, 'Nothin' but rooms.' He really said that. He also said the house had beautiful landscraping outside.

"Once we were invited to an Italian-American dinner up in

Schenectady. I picked him up at his house, and we drove up the New York Thruway. We were driving and talking, and after awhile he says, 'Hey, where's this joint we're going?'

" 'Schenectady,' I say.

"We're driving along and there are signs saying, 'Albany 100 Miles, Albany 50 Miles.' Finally, he says, 'Hey, we're lost.'

" 'Whaddya mean we're lost?' I ask.

" 'Well,' he says, 'We been drivin' for a coupla hours lookin' for Schenectady and I ain't seen one sign that's got a town beginnin' with C.' "

Farrell never did deny that others came along and put words and stories in Berra's mouth. His, he vouched for. Even the one about the venetian blind.

According to Farrell, Carmen Berra went to do some shopping and forgot to tell Yogi that a man was coming to fix a broken venetian blind. Yogi went upstairs to take a nap. The doorbell rang and was answered by his oldest son, Larry.

"Hey, dad," shouted Larry. "The man is here for the venetian blind."

"Well, go in my pocket and give him a couple of bucks for a donation and get rid of him," Berra yelled back.

"You didn't have to make things up for Yogi," Farrell said. "He just said them. I love the guy, I really do. He's the most lovable guy in the world. He has the greatest nature you can imagine, but he says the damnedest things. Once I asked him what he does on the afternoon of a night game.

" 'I usually sleep for two hours,' he said, 'from one o'clock to four.' "

Farrell once swore he heard Berra say the Orioles would miss the injured Gus Triandos because, "He's the main clog in their machine," and that he didn't mind it when he had to wear glasses, "as long as I don't have to wear those contract lenses," and that it's not necessary to have expensive luggage because, "You only use it for traveling."

Eavesdropping helped Jackie Farrell add to his storehouse of

Berraisms. "I heard him gabbing with another player in the clubhouse, and they were talking about insurance," Farrell recalled. "Yogi had just taken out a big policy, and the other player said it was a waste of money. 'What the hell good will all that dough do you?' he asked.

" 'Well,' said Yogi, 'I'll get it when I die.' "

And then, said Farrell, there was the time several Yankees were standing around a hotel lobby talking about anything that popped into their minds. Somehow the subject turned to good luck, and somebody asked Berra what he would do if he found a million dollars in the street.

"I'd see if I could find the guy who lost it," Yogi replied, "and if he was poor, I'd give it back to him."

5

"Too Many Wrong Mistakes"

Baseball players are famous for their appetites, more gluttons than gourmets if the truth be known. But they are first to discover the best restaurants in town; at least the ones that offer the most food for the money.

Moving a team into a new city means establishing a beachhead on the best restaurant in town as quickly as possible. When the Washington Senators became the Minnesota Twins in 1961, the race was on to see who could find the best restaurant in the city of Minneapolis. It didn't take long for the players to settle on an elegant establishment, called simply, Charlie's. No trip to Minneapolis that first season would be complete without a trip to Charlie's, and even in the second season Yankee players looked forward to a visit to Minneapolis because it meant an evening at Charlie's.

On a Saturday night, after a matinee performance against the Twins, Yogi Berra returned to his room in the Radisson Hotel, showered and shaved and changed his clothes, then joined a group of his teammates assembling, as was their custom, in the hotel lobby.

"Where are you guys going?" Berra addressed pitcher Whitey Ford.

"Out to dinner," Ford said. "You coming?"

"Where are ya gonna eat?" Berra inquired.

"We thought we'd go to Charlie's," said Ford. "Where else?"

"Charlie's?" Berra screeched. "Nobody goes there anymore, it's too crowded."

It has been said that the professional athlete has two deaths. The first comes when he "dies" as an athlete, when he can no longer perform the skills he once performed so easily and gracefully and he must accept less of himself. Then, he must make plans to adjust to another life, a life after his athletic life.

Yogi Berra suffered a slow first death. He began to notice the signs in 1957. He was only 32, not old by any standard known to man except the standard of professional sports. He was still a productive athlete, still a feared hitter in the American League, but his credentials had slipped noticeably. He batted only .251, a drop of 47 points from the previous year. He hit 24 homers, six fewer than the previous year. And he drove home only 82 runs, off 23 from the year before.

In each of the next two years his batting average improved, but his run production declined, he was playing less, and he was taking longer to come back from minor injuries—a sure sign that an athlete is fading.

In the 1959 season, however, advancing age was less responsible for his failure to produce than the fact that Yogi was filled with concern for his mother, critically ill and sinking fast. Diabetes had dictated the removal of one leg, and now her eyesight was being taken away by the dread disease.

One day in May the Yankees were finishing up a series in Detroit. After a day off, they would move on to Kansas City for a series with the Athletics. Berra's mother was in a hospital, near death, and Yogi asked Casey Stengel for permission to use the day off to leave the team and fly to see his mother.

Stengel said it would be all right with him, and Berra made arrangements to take a noon flight. But he was awakened at 6 A.M. by the ringing of the telephone in his hotel room. The caller was a spokesman for St. John's hospital in St. Louis, advising him to be on the very next plane available or he might not see his mother alive. Yogi caught a 7:00 A.M. flight to St. Louis and was at the hospital by 11:00.

His father was there, and his sister and brothers all gathered around his mother's deathbed.

"Mom," he whispered, "it's me, Lawdie. It's me, mom, Lawdie. I've come to see you."

He thought he saw the old woman move and try to speak, but the words would not come. Then a priest came and gave her the last rights of the Roman Catholic Church, and within a few hours she was dead.

Doctors said it was a miracle she lasted so long. They expected her to be gone hours before, but she lingered near death as if she knew her baby boy was coming to see her and she didn't want to leave before he arrived.

When she died, Mrs. Berra was clutching a rosary in her hands, and Yogi took it from her and put it in his pocket. He still carries it with him.

She was only 64 years old, but she had suffered for two years and Yogi knew there was mercy in her passing. Still, he wished she had lived just a few more months, long enough to see him honored with a Day at Yankee Stadium. At the time, he was only the sixth Yankee so honored—Babe Ruth, Lou Gehrig, Joe Di-Maggio, Phil Rizzuto, Charlie Keller, and now, Yogi Berra.

There were 58 gifts presented to him and $9,800 in cash, which Yogi turned over to Columbia University for the purpose of establishing a Yogi Berra scholarship fund for deserving scholar-athletes.

By the 1960 season Berra was little more than a part-time player, and most of that time was spent playing left field. He was 35 years old, and he had succumbed to another sign of advancing age by wearing eyeglasses in the field and at bat. It was time to step aside for youth, and a young man named Elston Howard had taken the number one catching job away from Berra.

Even at age 35, Berra had some big hits left in his potent bat. He played in only 120 games but batted .276, hit 15 homers, and drove home 62 runs as the Yankees won another pennant.

But they lost the World Series in a wild and weird seven games to the Pittsburgh Pirates. The final game was the one in which Bill Virdon's ground ball to shortstop hit a pebble, bounced up, and hit Yankee shortstop Tony Kubek on the Adam's apple, preventing him from starting a game-ending double play. The Pirates tied the game and won it on Bill Mazeroski's sudden-death home run off Ralph Terry.

Later, when Berra was asked how the powerful Yankees could lose to a team such as the Pirates, Yogi had the answer: "We made too many wrong mistakes," he said.

It was the last game Casey Stengel ever managed for the Yankees. When the 1961 season began, Stengel was in enforced retirement and replaced by Ralph Houk, who had been one of Stengel's coaches and whose entire major league playing career had consisted of 158 games in eight seasons, less than 20 games a season. Houk was just another of the promising young Yankee catchers who languished on the bench because Yogi Berra was catching almost every game for more than 15 years.

The 1961 season was one of those unbelievable, once-in-a-lifetime years for the Yankees. Baseball underwent its first expansion in 60 years, with the American League going from eight teams to ten. With expansion, the schedule increased from 154 games to 162, which was to be the cause of a raging controversy.

With the aid of the extra eight games and, according to many, because of the dilution of talent caused by expansion, Roger Maris hit 61 home runs, breaking the most cherished of all baseball records, Babe Ruth's 60 home runs, set in 1927. There were many who said Maris did not deserve the record because he had many more batting opportunities as a result of the extended schedule. Others said a record is a record, a season is a season, and Maris hit more home runs in a season than Babe Ruth and the length of their respective seasons had no bearing on that fact.

Attempting to solve the problem and satisfy both arguments,

Baseball Commissioner Ford C. Frick said Maris's record would go into the books with an asterisk to denote a 162-game schedule and Babe Ruth's record would remain in the books as the norm for a 154-game schedule. Instead of settling the controversy, Frick's decision created greater argument.

In addition to Maris, the Yankees had five other players who hit 20 or more homers, including Mickey Mantle, who had slugged 54 and looked like he would be the one to surpass Ruth until an injury forced him to miss the last nine games of the season. Bill "Moose" Skowron hit 28 homers, Elston Howard and John Blanchard hit 21 each, and Yogi Berra, at the age of 36, slugged 22 out of the park. The Yankees won 109 games and finished eight games ahead of the Detroit Tigers, and Whitey Ford won 25 games pitching every fourth day for the first time in his career.

Berra also drove in 61 runs. He was now pretty much a full-time outfielder, settling in left field because Maris had proved himself to be among the best right fielders in baseball once he joined the Yankees in 1960. Prior to the arrival of Maris, Berra had played both left field and right field. One day, a reporter in search of a story asked him which field he liked best.

"Chicago," Yogi said.

Berra was a better than average left fielder. He had an accurate, if not strong, throwing arm, and he was amazingly sure-handed. He would catch anything he got his glove on, but the years had slowed him to the point where he often let balls drop in front of him. In one game the Yankees were beaten when Berra let a drive get past him in the ninth inning, allowing the tying and leading runs to score. It was a ball that had appeared catchable, and even Berra later admitted he should have tried to make the catch.

"I just nonchalanted it," he explained.

Berra was in left field in four of the five games in the 1961 World Series against the Cincinnati Reds. Late in one game in

Yankee Stadium, with the shadows falling on left field, Berra came in hard for a sinking line drive, lost the ball momentarily, and it slammed off his glove, ricocheted, and broke his glasses. While two Cincinnati players whirled around the bases, shortstop Tony Kubek went out to run the ball down before going to the aid of his teammate. There was blood pouring from a cut on his hand, and there were tears of embarrassment and frustration welling in his eyes.

Manager Houk came out and decided it was best to remove Berra from the game. He was not the first player to be victimized by the autumn shadows that fell in left field of Yankee Stadium during a World Series game played on an October afternoon.

Norm Siebern, a gifted hitter and adequate fielder, had been practically run out of New York because of the humiliation he suffered in game four of the 1958 World Series when he lost two fly balls in the sun. He went on to a successful career with four other American League teams, finishing with a lifetime batting average of .272. But he would always be remembered for his goofs in the 1958 World Series at Yankee Stadium.

Even a veteran player like Yogi Berra had his troubles with the sun, and as he walked off the field alongside Manager Houk, Tony Kubek heard him explain: "It gets late early out there."

The Yankees went on to win another world championship, but it would be the last one that Berra would really enjoy. He had contributed a home run, three RBI, and a .273 average against the Reds, but the 1962 season was one of pain—not physical pain but the emotional pain of knowing he had not produced as he had in the past. He would play in only 86 games, and his statistics would be the lowest in his 16 years with the Yankees, a .224 average, 10 homers, and 35 RBI.

But he remained the same old, lovable Yogi Berra, idolized and admired by fans and respected and loved by his teammates. Because of his popularity, the Yankees decided to use Berra in a newspaper advertisement in conjunction with the Schrafft Restaurant chain, which had signed that year to sponsor Yankee games on radio and television.

The first thing that hit you in the ad was the smiling, unmistakable face of Yogi Berra gazing out at you. Then, underneath, were the words—Yogi's words supposedly:

> ON BEHALF OF THE YANKEE ORGANIZATION, IT IS INCUMBENT UPON ME TO REMARK THAT THE DELICACIES SERVED IN SCHRAFFT'S RESTAURANT ARE A CULINARY TREAT THAT WILL SATIATE EVEN THE MOST DISCRIMINATING PALATE.

Naturally, his teammates twitted Berra about his polysyllabic vocabulary.

"You guys thought I couldn't speak a foreign language, huh?" he is said to have replied.

As a teammate and a friend, Berra was a joy. His generosity and camaraderie is attested to by Tony Kubek.

"Carmen would often take the three boys and go to visit her parents on their farm outside of St. Louis," said the former Yankee shortstop turned NBC broadcaster. "They usually went during the season because school was out, and that would leave Yogi all alone in that big house in Montclair. So, he would invite some of us who were living in hotels or motels to come and stay with him at the house while Carmen and the boys were away.

"We had a great time. There was Mantle and Maris, Bobby Richardson and Joe DiMaestri and myself. Yogi would drive us back and forth from the Stadium and we swam in his pool and he would go out and stock the refrigerator with food. All the food was on him. He would cook us big steaks on his outdoor barbecue. We didn't even mind when he asked us to do a little work.

"They had just put the pool in and there were all these rocks and boulders laying around and we all pitched in and cleared them out of the way for him. It saved him ten dollars a day, he said, but we didn't mind. It was the least we could do. He was such a great host and he was going out of his way to feed us and show us a good time. We thought it was very generous of him until a few years later, when he admitted he had an ulterior motive.

" 'The only reason I treated you,' he said, 'was because I was scared to stay in that big house all by myself.' "

The end was at hand for Berra in the 1963 season, and in recognition of that fact, as well as in an attempt to reward him for all the great years he had given them, the Yankees made Yogi a player-coach. He was more coach than player, however, appearing in only 64 games and coming to bat only 147 times. He hit only eight home runs and drove in 28 runs, but as if to make it one last hurrah, he batted a lusty .293, his highest average in seven seasons.

In the 1963 World Series, the Yankees played as if they were merely going through the motions. Later, hindsighters would say it was a sign that the Yankee dynasty was coming to an end, but that theory does an injustice to the Los Angeles Dodgers—particularly to the pitchers of the Los Angeles Dodgers. One look at the blazing fastball and the crackling curve of Sandy Koufax was enough to convince them they were overmatched.

"Is this trip necessary?" asked one Yankee when the team, down two games to none, journeyed all the way to southern California for the next two games.

"Are you sure there aren't any Jewish holidays coming up?" asked another, thinking about having to face Koufax one more time.

Don Drysdale and Johnny Podres were almost as formidable as Koufax and the Yankees dropped four straight to the Dodgers. For Yogi Berra, it was a World Series of nonparticipation. The extent of his participation was one pinch-hit appearance, in game number three, when he was sent up to hit for Jim Bouton with the Dodgers leading, 1–0, in the eighth inning. Berra hit the ball hard against Drysdale but lined it to the second baseman. It would not only be his only appearance in the 1963 World Series, it was to be his last appearance ever in a World Series.

All through the 1963 season Yogi Berra lived with a secret. In spring training that year Ralph Houk had asked to have a private chat with him.

"Mr. Topping and Mr. Webb," said Houk, referring to the Yankees' millionaire owners, "have asked me if I would be interested in moving up as general manager. Roy Hamey wants to retire, and they want me to take the job. I said I would. They asked me who I would want to replace me as manager, and I said I wanted you to manage the club next year. They said it was all right with them. How do you feel about it?"

Naturally, Berra was overjoyed. He realized his playing career was at an end, and he welcomed the opportunity to remain associated with the game he loved so much. He wanted to stay on in any capacity. To manage the Yankees, well, that was beyond his wildest dreams.

His first step was to accept the job as coach for the 1963 season. It was a way to break him into the idea of managing, for Yogi to familiarize himself with his future job by sitting close to Houk and studying his moves, asking him questions. It was also a way of establishing Berra's managerial credentials with the press and the public. Berra kept Houk's promise to himself through the season, during which the Yankees won a third straight American League championship under Houk and their 14th league title in Berra's 17 years with the club.

When the World Series ended, Berra knew he had played his last game. When he retired as a player, he took with him a pageful of records.

The man who had suffered the humiliation of being removed

from behind the plate as a rookie in the 1947 World Series had set a record for most home runs by a catcher (313—he also hit 45 as an outfielder); for the most consecutive errorless games as a catcher (148); and for accepting the most consecutive chances without an error (950).

He held World Series records for participation in the most series (14), the most series games (75), the most times on the winning side (10), the most at-bats (259), and the most hits (71).

It was the end of a truly remarkable career of a man who was deemed unworthy of a $500 bonus by one of the most astute minds in baseball history, yet went on to become one of the great catchers of all time. But while it was the end of one career, another career was just beginning.

6

The Harmonica

One of the responsibilities of managing a major league baseball team is to deal with the press. It was the part of the job Yogi Berra liked least. In a one-to-one relationship he was fine, very informative and interesting, especially if he knew the other person. But he was always ill at ease speaking to a group.

It was particularly difficult for him to speak on radio or television. He would crawl into a shell of shyness, which masked his true personality. He was sensitive and ashamed of his lack of education and of his inability to express himself. He needn't have been. In baseball matters he expressed himself simply but effectively. And in other matters he displayed rare insight and an innate intelligence.

On a visit to Chicago, Berra was asked to do a radio tape with a local sportscaster. Naturally, he agreed, since he realized that public relations is part of a manager's job and because he is not the kind of man who can say no. The interview covered a wide range of baseball topics, and eventually the announcer asked Berra his opinion of Little League baseball.

"I think it's wonderful," Yogi exclaimed. "It keeps the kids out of the house."

The press conference was called for 11:15 A.M. on Thursday, October 24, 1963, in the plush Crystal Room of New York's Savoy-Hilton Hotel. All was in readiness, the kleig lights beaming and the tape recorders droning and the pencils poised on pads, when Bob Fishel, director of public relations for the Yankees, made the historic announcement. "The Yankees are pleased to announce that for the 1964 season the team's manager will be Yogi Berra."

When an announcement of such local importance is made, it is usually followed by a brief moment of silence and immobility as if those in the audience are waiting for the full import of the announcement to penetrate. Then, suddenly, there is a bustle of activity as reporters race to telephones to call their desks in an effort to get the story in the day's late editions.

This was a surprise. Only in the Newark *Star-Ledger* had there been so much as a hint that Ralph Houk would be out and Yogi Berra would be in. Berra carried the secret with him for more than seven months and never spilled a word.

"It was," said a startled Phil Rizzuto, one of Yogi's closest friends, "the best kept secret I ever heard."

The announcement over, the flurry of activity subsided, it was time for Berra to face the press, to answer their probing questions.

"What will be your biggest problem next season, Yogi?"

"If I can manage."

"How have you prepared yourself for this job?"

"You observe a lot by watching."

Houk admitted it was his idea to give Berra the job. He had made the decision back in spring training, when he knew Roy Hamey was planning to retire and Houk was asked to move up into the general manager's chair. It was then he had begun thinking about his successor.

"A lot of names started going through my mind," he said, "And I always came back to Yogi."

Berra had had other offers to manage. At least, there were rumors of other offers and Yogi heard them all.

"People used to say I was going to Boston or to Baltimore to manage," he said. "Maybe I was interested, I used to say, but I was just keeping doors from closing. In my heart I didn't think I would leave the Yankees. Seventeen years, you get used to a place. Besides, it's expensive to move."

Houk thought about how it would be for a rookie manager with the great Yankee teams. He had been in that position himself and had survived. The man who hired Berra was, naturally, his biggest booster.

"He knows baseball. He knows the Yankee players. He's been well-liked by the press. He's been well-liked by the fans. Another quality that should rank high is that he's all baseball and all sports. Because of this his successful businesses won't interfere with the job of managing where I've seen them interfere with other men.

"My problems were quite different from Yogi's because I started in the minors. I had to formulate my ball club, set up my spring training camp, cut the squad down, get to know the press. Here that will not be a problem for Yogi. He pretty much knows who his personnel will be. We're not going to break up the Yankees. He already knows the press. His problems, as I see them, will be formulating his pitching plans, and it will be up to him to make decisions on young players—those who can be kept and those who will be better off playing in the minors.

"Yogi has been an outstanding catcher. He's made a specialty out of studying pitchers, and I'd say that gets him off as an expert in the most important angle of managing a team. A manager has to know when to change a pitcher, when to leave him in. This is a big thing for a manager, and Yogi's got a running start in this department."

Houk remembered that when he offered the job to Berra, Yogi's first remark was, "I wonder what Carmen will think."

"Talk to her," Houk suggested. "Don't give me your answer now."

They talked. "It's wonderful," Carmen said. "But what happens if we lose after all these years of winning?"

"I told her I felt you got to take chances," Yogi said. "That's what convinced her that I should try."

His first press conference as manager of the Yankees ended and Yogi went to work. He spent the next few months going over rosters, checking statistics, looking at minor league prospects, discussing possible trades, and making an endless string of personal appearances. He agreed to do a radio interview with his good friend Joe Garagiola and promised to show up at the NBC building at 4:00 P.M. He arrived at 4:15 and was admonished for his tardiness by Garagiola.

"Gee, Joey," Berra argued. "That's the earliest I've ever been late."

On another occasion he was honored by the Catholic Youth Organization as Sportsman of the Year at a black-tie dinner at the Waldorf-Astoria. Among those in attendance was His Eminence Francis Cardinal Spellman, who met the guest of honor at a predinner reception. Until then, the only cardinals Berra had ever met were Stan Musial, Enos Slaughter, and his buddy Joe Garagiola.

"Congratulations on your wonderful life," His Eminence said in greeting. Then, almost as an afterthought, he asked, "How is your bowling alley doing?" The cardinal also congratulated Berra on his new job as Yankee manager and added, "I also congratulate the Yankees on their choice."

Asked if he had any advice for Berra, His Eminence replied: "What could I tell him?"

Yogi posed for pictures accepting his award from Cardinal Spellman and in an offhand gesture was caught by photographers with his finger pointing to his temple.

"What is that, Yogi, a signal to slide?" His Eminence asked.

Yogi laughed and said something about it being a balk.

"A balk?" asked the Cardinal. "I didn't know a catcher could make a balk. I thought only pitchers balked."

"Oh, no, Your Eminence," Yog pleaded. "Interference by the catcher is called a catcher's balk."

Having dispensed with this little baseball lesson, Berra beamed down at his plaque, which read:

TO LAWRENCE BERRA FOR OUTSTANDING ACHIEVEMENT IN PROFESSIONAL BASEBALL WHILE MAINTAINING A HIGH STANDARD OF EXEMPLARY CONDUCT WORTHY OF EMULA-TION BY THE YOUTH OF AMERICA.

Almost immediately, Berra ran into problems as a manager. Before he even left for spring training, he lost the services of his pitching coach, Johnny Sain, who submitted his resignation. The reason cited was money; the Yankees refused to meet Sain's demands for an additional $2,500 per year and a two-year contract.

Behind the scenes, however, was the suspicion that Sain re-garded Berra as a clown, unworthy of the job he was asked to fill, and Sain chose not to work for him. To fill the vacancy, Berra put in a call to an old friend in Lake Success, New York.

"I had just returned home from a skiing trip in New Hampshire," said Whitey Ford. "The telephone was ringing as I opened the front door. Yogi asked me if I wanted to be his pitching coach in addition to pitching. I threw the phone to Joan [Mrs. Ford] and told her, 'Here, talk to Yogi while I get my wits about me.'" Ford took the job and became the first pitcher-coach in baseball.

Berra had his critics even before he made his first move as a manager. In a sense it was not so much that they were critical of Berra, for they sympathized with him for the spot he was in, for the rap he was being asked to take. Bill Veeck, that old Yankee hater, expressed that point of view in his book, *The Hustler's Handbook*. Veeck wrote:

The decision to make Yogi Berra, of all people, the manager of the Yankees was admittedly one of the more moonstruck episodes in baseball. So moonstruck that nobody will ever be able to convince me that Yogi was ever anything more than a handy stopgap Houk latched onto in order to boost himself up in the front office.

It was Veeck's thesis that Houk used Berra as his dupe, selling him to Dan Topping and Del Webb as the ideal choice for manager, which would clear the way for Houk's elevation to general manager. Veeck believed Berra was there to take the blame when the Yankees faltered, as Houk knew they would, and to be the scapegoat for their failure. By firing Berra, Houk would save himself. Veeck went on to say:

While he has no capacity for public relations and even less interest in it, Ralph was also very well aware, if only from reading the papers, that he was no match for Casey Stengel of the Mets in the battle for newspaper space which everybody had become concerned about. When the opportunity arose, Houk was there to suggest or to quickly agree that Berra was just the man to compete with Stengel. Actually, Houk couldn't have cared less who became manager, just so long as there was a logical reason for removing himself from the line of fire.

Now, pitting Yogi against Stengel was the worst mismatch in history. No boxing commission would have allowed it. Yogi is a completely manufactured product. He is a case study of this country's unlimited ability to gull itself and be gulled. Yogi had become a figure of fun originally because with his corrugated face and squat body he looked as if he should be funny, and because when he turned out to be a great ballplayer in spite of his odd appearance a natural feeling of warmth went out to him, as to the ugly duckling who makes it big in a world of swans. It pleased the public to think that this odd-looking little man with the great natural ability had a knack for mouthing humorous truths with the sort of primitive peasant wisdom we rather expect of our sports heroes.

Besides, there was that marvelous nickname. You say "Yogi" at a banquet and everybody automatically laughs, something Joe Garagiola discovered to his profit many years ago. Not that Yogi had ever been heard to say anything funny. But by then he didn't have to. Everytime Yogi hiccuped, he was answered by gales of laughter. Boy, you said to yourself, nobody can hiccup as funny as that Yogi.

Veeck depicted Berra as a lovable dupe and remembered playing cards with him in St. Louis when Veeck ran the Browns and Berra returned home each winter. "He talked just about the way any guy would talk while he was involved in a friendly game of chance, like you or me or Adlai Stevenson."

As a rookie manager, Berra made plenty of mistakes. But his baseball sense, his knowledge of the game, and his ability to judge pitchers stood him in good stead in the early going.

There was nothing especially exciting or memorable about his first clubhouse meeting. He was talking to friends, and he kept his remarks brief, as he always did. He never enjoyed making talks in front of a group and preferred to speak to players individually. Even then, he would grope for words, but with a veteran team there was little that needed to be said, anyway.

It was true the Yankees were in a panic because they were losing ground to the upstart Mets in their battle for New York City. Playing in a temporary home, the old, dirty, dingy, and dilapidated Polo Grounds, the Mets drew 1,080,180 fans with the worst team in baseball in 1963—their second year of existence. In that same year, with a pennant-winning team, the Yankees drew 1,308,920 at home.

Now, in 1964, the Mets were moving into a beautiful, new home—Shea Stadium in Flushing, near the site of the World's Fair, surrounded by huge parking lots that would accommodate thousands of cars. The Yankees knew they were in danger of falling behind the young team in attendance, and that was part of the reason they chose Berra, hoping his reputation would help them in their fight with the Mets.

On the night of Monday, June 15, Berra and Stengel met in a showdown, the annual Mayor's Trophy Game played between

New York's two major league teams. After a terrible start, the Yankees had begun to play better and, in fact, entered the game with a winning streak.

After dressing in the visitors' dressing room, the Yankees wandered out to the dugout. It was raining and the field was covered, canceling batting practice. Berra spotted Stengel across the field in the Mets' dugout and ventured across to see his former manager, making the first move in deference to Stengel's age and experience.

"If I had lost the last five games instead of winning them, I would have waited for you to come and see me," Berra chided.

"You done all right, yes, sir," Stengel said. "How'd you get those fellers to start hittin'? You tell 'em to copy you? You had a pretty good idea. It just wasn't one party. Most of them commence comin' in all at once."

The rain was coming down harder, and Berra suggested the game be called off.

"Who's gonna call it?" Stengel asked.

"The mayor, I guess," Berra said.

"Can't call it," Stengel objected. "They said you was gonna catch tonight."

"Not that I know of," Berra said with a shrug.

"What if you played and you break a leg," Stengel went on. "Then you gotta go take pitchers out on crutches. . . . You never got nervous when you lost some games, hah, Yogi? You haven't tore up the clubhouse?"

Berra reached for a cigarette.

"Hey, I thought you quit smoking," somebody said.

"When you see the bases loaded and no outs and you don't score, then you start smokin' again."

"Hey, Case," a photographer yelled. "How about you and Yog posing under an umbrella?"

"I'm outta the umbrella business. I've had the umbrella thing done 100 times. Take Yogi's picture, he's on a winning streak."

"Where ya been all day?" the old man asked Berra. "All the clubs were callin' you. They wanted to trade with you but they said they couldn't find you because you won six games. I want to make a deal with you to cinch it for you."

Tom Sturdivant, a former teammate of Berra's, came by to say hello. "Is he still throwin' the knuckleball?" Berra asked after Sturdivant left. "You should throw him at us. We just got through beatin' Wilhelm twice."

"How ya doin' with Wilhelm?" Stengel asked. "Do you hit the first pitch on him?"

"Yeah," Berra said. "He never throws his hard knuckleball until he's ahead of you."

"I got a good shortstop now," Stengel said out of the blue, "but he almost got his leg broke. Well, what do ya think of our ball park? If you come out here to run a football team, you'll have to watch. They move the stands here. They generally put ya up there on the scoreboard in color, but I don't think they got ya picture."

"I took one," Berra said. "I even had to shave for it."

They never did play the Mayor's Trophy Game that night, the rain coming down harder and the game eventually being called off, postponing an historic event—Yogi Berra matching wits with the master, Casey Stengel.

June was a big month for the Yankees. When May ended, they had a record of 21–17 and were in fifth place, 4½ games behind Baltimore, and there were grave doubts about Berra's ability to manage. But in June they rallied and won 21 out of 32 and jockeyed with the Orioles for first place. In July they won 19 out of 29 and moved into first place by percentage points, and all around the American League people threw up their hands in surrender.

It was the same old story. The Yankees had let others have their run, now they were beginning to play ball. They had surged into first place, and if history was repeated, they would win the pennant going away.

But history didn't repeat. On August 7 the Yankees were shut out by the Orioles and fell out of first place. They lost the next day, too, then they beat the Orioles, but lost three straight and fell 3½ games behind.

They lost both ends of a day-night doubleheader to the White Sox, but Berra took the double dip in stride. He was in his dressing room, adjacent to the main part of the Yankee clubhouse where players sat in front of their lockers, mumbling curses under their breaths, holding chins in their hands, just sitting there looking into space and feeling miserable.

Berra had emerged from the shower, and dripping wet, he lathered his face, reached for his razor, and began to attack his tough beard.

"Lousy razor," he mumbled, and as he turned away from the mirror to reach for a towel, there was a small trickle of blood dripping from a gash on his right cheek.

"Look," he announced. "I cut my throat."

He laughed, and somebody asked him why he didn't yell, why he didn't throw things, get angry, swear, shout, anything?

"What do you want me to do, flip?" he asked softly.

On his desk was a replica of a one dollar bill and in place of the picture of the father of our country was a picture of Yogi, the father of Larry, Tim, and Dale. Under the picture was the question: "What, me worry?"

That was precisely Berra's attitude. Why worry? What good would it do? While others saw a pennant flying out the window, he remained calm, patient. At the time, it was taken as a sign that he had no answers for the problem. In future years it would prove to be his style.

"Will you have a meeting?" somebody asked.

"What for?" he asked back. "They know they're lousy. They know they're not hitting. What good would it do to yell at them?

There's still time. Didn't we go through the same thing in 1949? All we gotta do is start hittin'."

Berra put his hand in his pocket and fished out a white envelope. "I ate good today, and look, I even got paid. We'll snap out of it tomorrow."

He was confident—or was it a pose? Around him there was growing doubt. Some of his players thought he was in over his head, that he could not control the players and he could not think with the other managers. They cited an example.

As the second game was about to start on the night in question, Phil Linz was standing at shortstop. Suddenly, Tony Kubek dashed out and Linz returned to the bench.

"I made a mistake," Berra admitted later. "I wanted to rest Tony and I put Phil's name on the lineup card that was taped to the dugout wall. By mistake I put Kubek's name on the official card, the one that goes to the plate umpire. That meant that Tony was officially in the game. I didn't realize it until just before the game was about to start, and I had to start Tony or waste him for the game. It was a mistake. You know how it is, you get in the habit of putting a guy's name on the card."

His players didn't know how it was. To them it was a grievous error, an indication that Yogi's head wasn't in the game, that he wasn't the man for the job. Most of them said the same thing. "Houk would never have made such a mistake."

Soon after, the Yankees rallied. They won four of their next five games and that took the heat off. But they were still 2½ games behind Baltimore as they started a four-game series in Chicago. It was to be a crucial four games.

The Yankees lost the first game, 2–1. They dropped the second game in ten innings. They lost the third game and were shut out in the fourth game. Just like that, they were in third place, 4½ games behind the White Sox with 43 games to play. The Yankees, everyone said, had had it. Berra would never be able to bring them back.

And then came the now famous Harmonica Incident. There have been many versions of what happened. Here's the official version, as recalled by Phil Linz, one of the principals in the piece.

"We had just lost our four straight to Chicago and were feeling pretty bad. We got on the bus that was going to take us to the airport for a flight to Boston. There was a big crowd outside, and we had to wait.

"I was sitting there in the back of the bus. I had a coat draped over the back of the seat. I had a harmonica and a learner's sheet that I had just bought that day. I began to play, "Mary Had A Little Lamb." Just then, Yogi walked on the bus.

" 'Hey, Linz,' he said, 'take that harmonica and stuff it.'

"I didn't hear him, so I kept playing. Now he started toward me.

" 'Hey, Linz, I said take that harmonica and stuff it.'

"I flipped the harmonica to him and said, 'Do it yourself.' He caught it and threw it back at me and it hit Joe Pepitone in the leg. First there was silence, and then all hell broke loose. Pepi is limping around and yelling that he's injured, and I jump on the back of the seat and begin shouting.

" 'Why are you yelling at me? I give you 100 percent all the time. Why pick on me? Why not pick on some of these other guys who aren't hustling?'

"I don't know why I did it," Linz said later. "I was uptight. I had been benched after I had a ten-game hitting streak and I broke my neck for him whenever I played. I don't know. The harmonica was there and I just did it. It was an hour after the game. I didn't think it was so terrible."

According to Tony Kubek, an eyewitness, the harmonica was lying on the floor and Mantle picked it up.

"Well, gang," Mickey said, "that's it for our manager. From now on, I'm the manager. Here's the signal for a bunt . . . *toot!* . . . Here's the signal for a steal . . . *toot, toot!*"

By now everybody in the bus was laughing, including Berra, and that was that. The incident was over as quickly as it started . . . until the papers had their fun with it the following day.

In Boston the next day Yogi called Linz into his office.

"I'm sorry, Yog," Phil said. "I shouldn't have done it. I was wrong. You know I always give 100 percent."

"Okay," Yogi said. "But I gotta fine you."

"I know."

"It's going to cost you $200."

"That's fine with me, sure."

"And that was all there was to it," revealed Linz. "It was over, forgotten, just like two friends having an argument and forgetting about it. I never had any problem with Yogi before or after that incident. He was always very nice to me. When I was a rookie, he used to take me out to dinner. He was a fantastic guy, but I guess he had his problems as a rookie manager and trying to manage guys he played with and the club going bad. He was under a lot of pressure.

"Later, when I joined the Mets and he was a coach, we often kidded about the incident, and we even posed for pictures with me playing a harmonica. There never have been any hard feelings. That's the kind of guy Yogi is. He did what he had to do and it was forgotten."

The following winter, Linz signed his contract for a healthy raise and a bonus of $200.

"For harmonica lessons," announced general manager Ralph Houk.

7

"Mr. Topping Wants to See You"

The bus was parked outside Yankee Stadium waiting to take the Yankees to the airport for the trip to St. Louis and the start of the 1964 World Series. Everything was ready, players and equipment all on the bus. Only Bob Fishel was missing. The dapper and energetic director of public relations for the Yankees had dashed into his office to try to dig up another World Series ticket for pitcher Jim Bouton.

Finally, Fishel hopped aboard, slightly out of breath. He was carrying a manila envelope, which he handed to Bouton.

"Boy, are you lucky," Fishel said. "This was the last one."

"What?" exclaimed Yogi Berra. "You mean they're outta them manila envelopes already?"

If the Yankees had continued their tailspin, if they had gone on to lose the pennant in Yogi Berra's rookie year as manager, the famed Harmonica Incident would have been proclaimed the turning point, the final straw that tore the team apart, divided it, and caused its downfall.

Instead, the Yankees went on to win the pennant, and the Harmonica Incident became the rallying point, clearing the air, putting everything out in the open, relieving the tension, and permitting the Yankees to get down to the business at hand.

If the incident had been truly divisive, however, the Yankees could not possibly have won. If it was a rallying point, they would have gone out the next day and begun their comeback. They didn't. Going from Chicago to Boston, the Yankees went from frying pan to flame. They lost the first two games of a four-game series to the Red Sox. Some rallying point! That stretched their losing streak to six and left them six games out of first place with 41 games to play, hardly an enviable, advantageous, or attacking position.

And then suddenly, and for no apparent reason, everything changed, the whole season turned around. There was no one thing that did it, no rallying point, no clubhouse meeting, no change in personnel, no "Win-One-For-The-Gipper" speech by Berra. It just happened, as Berra kept saying it would.

There were little things. A rookie right-hander named Mel Stottlemyre came up from Richmond to win nine games down the stretch. Pedro Ramos was purchased from Cleveland on September 5 and became the ace of the Yankee bullpen, appearing in 13 games, saving seven, and winning one without losing a game.

The Yankees didn't exactly take command all at once. They won three straight, then lost a pair; they won four in a row, then lost two; then they ripped off five straight victories and trailed Baltimore by only a game, and you could almost see the Orioles looking over their shoulders, listening for those same old familiar footsteps.

Mickey Mantle spent much of the time on the injured list, but Roger Maris was moved to center field and carried the team through the last weeks, and around the American League people knew it was just a matter of time before the Yankees would claim their rightful possession—the pennant.

Johnny Pesky, manager of the Boston Red Sox, had said right along that the Yankees were the team to beat. In late August, when it looked like they would not make it, Pesky remained as persistent as Berra was optimistic.

"I stick with my original choice," Pesky said. "With all the problems they've had, they're still in it. I keep expecting them to win eight or ten in a row and take over."

It was a prophetic remark, made on August 30. Sixteen days later, the Yankees did, indeed, take over. They went on an 11-game winning streak. When the streak started, they were one-half game behind. When it ended, they were four in front with only eight to play. Like champions, like the thoroughbreds they were, the Yankees had come through in the stretch, whipping and driving to win the race going away. They beat the Indians two straight and clinched the pennant on October 3, the next-to-last day of the season.

Even the blasé Yankees, accustomed as they were to winning pennants, celebrated this pennant wildly. It was especially sweet because it was so unexpected. The champagne spilled all over the plush carpet in the Yankee clubhouse, and they tossed Berra in the shower and somebody handed Phil Linz a harmonica and he played something resembling "Mary Had A Little Lamb," and it was music to Berra's ears.

The World Series was anticlimactic. The Cardinals had won in the National League in a fight to the finish among four teams when the Phillies blew a ten-game lead in the final month.

The Series opened in St. Louis on October 7 with Ray Sadecki beating Whitey Ford, 9–5, in a battle of veteran left-handers. Trailing 4–2, the Cardinals rallied for four runs in the sixth and went on to take the opener.

The following day rookie Mel Stottlemyre, who had saved the Yankees all year, saved them again. He hooked up in a pitching duel for eight innings with St. Louis ace Bob Gibson. But Gibson, pitching on short rest after winning the next-to-last game of the season and saving the last game in relief, was removed for a pinch-hitter in the eighth. With Gibson gone, the Yankees scored four runs in the ninth for an 8–3 victory, and the Series was tied, one game apiece, when the two teams shifted to New York's Yankee Stadium.

Game number three was the most thrilling of the Series. Tied

1–1 in the ninth, the Cardinals removed starter Curt Simmons for a pinch-hitter and brought in knuckleballer Barney Schultz, the Cards' ace relief pitcher, to pitch the last of the ninth. He made one pitch. Mickey Mantle drove it deep into the right-field seats for the game-winning home run, a blast Mantle later called "the greatest thrill I've ever had in baseball."

The Cardinals evened the Series by winning the fourth game, and a well-rested Gibson came back in game five to set the Yankee power hitters on their ears, striking out 13 and winning a 5–2 decision that gave the Cardinals a 3–2 lead in the Series. Now they needed to win one out of two at home to beat the Yankees and capture their first world championship in 18 years.

Yankee power exploded in game six. Mantle and Maris homered, a familiar occurrence, and Joe Pepitone blasted a grand slam in the eighth as the Yankees won, 8–3.

It all came down to one game, Stottlemyre versus Gibson. The Cardinals struck early on home runs by Lou Brock and Ken Boyer and raced to a 6–0 lead. Pitching with only two days rest, Gibson began to tire but held on to strike out nine and register a 7–5 victory. The Yankees scored two in the ninth, but the rally fell short, and the Cardinals were world champions.

If he had had to go another inning, it is doubtful Gibson would have made it, and the Yankees might have won the championship. But it was no disgrace losing to Bob Gibson in the seventh game of the World Series, and Yogi Berra could take consolation in a great year. He had brought the Yankees back from oblivion. He had rallied them from fifth place, from six games back in August. He had carried the Cardinals to the maximum seven games and lost the championship of baseball by a mere two runs. It had been a most rewarding season, a fantastic season for the rookie manager, and Yogi Berra went home knowing he had done an outstanding job.

The events that followed in the next few days are mysterious. They have been replayed and analyzed and placed under microscopic scrutiny. Experts and nonexperts have expressed their theories, but only a few people know for certain exactly what happened, and they're not talking.

What is known is that somewhere between St. Louis and New York, on an airplane carrying the Yankees home, Ralph Houk said to Yogi Berra: "Mr. Topping wants to see you in his office tomorrow morning at ten."

Berra did not indicate he knew what Mr. Topping, the Yankee owner, wanted. He did not indicate he thought it strange that Mr. Topping wanted to see him so soon after the Series, so early in the morning. Why couldn't it wait? Berra dismissed any further thoughts and said he would be there.

The 1964 World Series ended on Thursday, October 15. On Friday morning, October 16, Yogi Berra awoke early and drove to the team's offices at 745 Fifth Avenue in New York to keep his date with Dan Topping.

Later that day the Yankees called a press conference. It seemed a routine thing. The press figured it was being assembled to hear that Yogi Berra had been rehired for 1965, maybe for 1966 and 1967, at a substantial pay raise. Instead, the Yankees announced that Yogi Berra would not be back as manager in 1965. It was stunning news.

Coincidentally, half a continent away, in the office of the owner of the St. Louis Cardinals, Johnny Keane was telling Gussie Busch, the beer baron, that he would not accept a new contract to manage the world champion Cardinals.

During the season, when the Cardinals were going bad, Busch had humiliated Keane. Not only did he refuse to give Johnny a new contract or a vote of confidence but he openly negotiated with Leo Durocher to be the Cardinals' manager in 1965.

But Keane fooled everybody. He won the pennant and beat the Yankees in the World Series. He was a local hero and Gussie Busch came crawling, contract in hand. Johnny Keane, a gentle man who had thought of studying for the priesthood as a youth, politely told Busch to stick the contract in his beer barrel. Four days later the Yankees held another press conference and announced that Johnny Keane would succeed Yogi Berra as their manager.

Some say that Yogi told friends a week before the seventh game of the World Series that he had the feeling he would not be back as Yankee manager in 1965 despite winning the American League pennant.

Whitey Ford is one of Berra's closest friends, and he was also Yogi's pitching coach. His opinion on the subject is something of value.

Whitey recalls the plane ride home from St. Louis after the seventh game. "I was sitting in the back, and Yogi was sitting in the front. He came back and took a seat next to me.

" 'Will you come back and coach again next year?' he asked me.

"I didn't like doing both jobs, but I couldn't say no to him, especially after we had won the pennant. I said I would. I'm not saying he would have told me if he thought he wasn't coming back the next year, but I doubt if he would have asked me to coach if he didn't think he'd be back."

The decision to fire Berra had been made before the World Series. Ralph Houk made it clear that Yogi was not being faulted for losing the seventh game. Actually, the defeat saved the Yankees considerable embarrassment. It was bad enough to fire a pennant-winning manager; it would have been shocking to fire a man who had just won a world championship.

According to Bill Veeck, writing in *The Hustler's Handbook,* the decision to replace Berra was made before the seventh game. It was made in August.

When the Yankees won the pennant, the most astonished person in the country was Ralph Houk. Houk . . . had quit on his team . . . [he] decided in August that (1) the Yankees were going to lose; (2) that it was all Yogi Berra's fault and (3) that Yogi would therefore have to go. When they fooled him and won, he went ahead with his plan just as if they hadn't. Ralph Houk's ability to adjust his thinking is so slight that he could not bring himself to admit that having been wrong in August, he might do well to draw up a new set of plans in October.

Houk's decision to replace Berra, if Veeck is correct, was not based solely on the standings, although he obviously believed Berra incapable of coming through and winning the pennant. Veeck's account continues:

> The players came to his office to cry that Yogi was a poor manager and notably lacking in the essential qualities of gentlemanly behavior and inspiring leadership as enunciated by the YMCA. It would seem far more probable that they departed with the distinct impression that they wouldn't have to put up with Yogi's crudities for another year since, as the season progressed, the players felt increasingly free to express their complaints to newspapermen.
>
> To be fair about it, though, I could be doing both Houk and the players an injustice. These were players who had become accustomed over a period of years to bringing their troubles to Houk. Ralph himself is accustomed, by background and by nature, to listening to the troops and distrusting everyone else. It was natural enough, perhaps, that the players would influence him all out of proportion to their intent. It was perhaps inevitable that he would see massive indictment in what they only meant as mild complaint.
>
> After that has been said, however, it is still clear enough that it was hardly any service to Berra to permit the players to come around behind the manager's back and weep on his ready shoulder.

According to Jim Bouton, one of Berra's players in that fateful summer of 1964, Veeck is right about the players complaining to Houk. "The biggest gripers were Elston Howard, Clete Boyer, and, surprisingly, Tony Kubek, who also spoke for Bobby Richardson. Mantle and Ford kidded about Yogi, but I don't remember them ever complaining. It was beneath them. And I never heard of Houk kicking the whiners out of his office, either.

"Yogi's problem was not himself, but the players. Houk, the master psychologist, the smoke blower, was our pacifier, and when he was taken away we reacted like babies. The players never respected Yogi. He was always 'good old Yog,' who was thought to be in over his head even as a coach."

Kubek's story is slightly different. Tony says he didn't go to Houk, Houk came to him.

"It was on a cross-country airplane trip," Kubek recalls. "We were going bad and Houk decided to make the trip with us to see what was wrong. On the plane he asked me about Yogi and I told him. It wasn't exactly a gripe session, but I let him know how I felt as honestly as I could. I didn't think what I said was so terrible. Certainly nothing that would suggest I thought he should be replaced."

As he looks back, Kubek realizes now that Berra was on a spot, being asked to manage men he had played with, socialized with, lived with.

"It was a difficult position for him," Tony emphasizes. "He had been the butt of our jokes for so long, and then he was our leader. We respected him for his knowledge of the game, and he really didn't have any trouble with the older guys. But the young guys, well, we had a few free spirits and I guess they ran all over the place. The older guys wouldn't do it to him.

"The new guys who met him for the first time in spring training probably came away with the idea that he wasn't too bright. That really isn't true. Yogi is a complex person who is very compassionate for the problems of others. The one thing I remember most about him as a manager is that he never panicked. At least he never showed panic. He'd just hang in there and say we'll get 'em the next day. Just like he did with the Mets."

Phil Linz was one of the younger guys in 1964, one of the free spirits Kubek talks about, but his only problem with Berra was the Harmonica Incident.

"As a manager, he had all the faith in the world," Linz recalls. "He never gave up heart. We'd lose a few and he'd always say, 'Okay you guys, we'll get 'em tomorrow.' He had great faith. He might not have been articulate, but he knew baseball and he always impressed you with his knowledge of the game. His opinion was valued even before he became manager. They would always consult him before they made a decision on keeping or cutting a rookie pitcher, and he wasn't often wrong in his judgment."

The reason for Berra's dismissal? Houk wouldn't say, but there were enough innuendoes. Yogi was being dismissed because he was considered incapable of handling men. There had been a rash of stories in the press, stories attributed to Bobby Richardson and Tony Kubek, among others, that Yogi could not handle the players.

"The afternoon Yogi was fired," Kubek remembers, "my telephone rang. It was Carmen Berra. She said, 'Yogi would like to talk to you, but he can't. He feels bad. He's heard the stories about you saying he couldn't handle the players, and he wants to know if they are true.'

"I told her I never said that. I told her about the talk I had with Houk on the plane and that was the extent of it. She seemed satisfied, but I felt bad. The reason Yogi couldn't come to the phone, Carmen said, was that he was too broken up. Not about getting fired, about the idea that the players had said those things about him. She said he would feel much better when she told him what I said."

It still didn't explain why Berra was fired. Perhaps it was because he had taken a veteran team, the same team that had won three straight American League pennants under Ralph Houk by eight, five, and ten games, and had barely won by a game. That was cutting it too close. They might have felt he was lucky to win and that his luck was about to run out.

And maybe Bill Veeck was right. Maybe the decision to fire him was made in August when the Yankees were 6½ games out of first place and it looked like they would never catch up.

Rumors abounded about secret deals made in August, when it appeared certain the Yankees would be unable to turn their season around and win the pennant. One of the most popular theories was that Houk decided in August that Berra must go and he dispatched emissaries to St. Louis to inquire if Cardinals manager Johnny Keane would be interested in coming to New York in 1965 to manage the Yankees.

According to this theory, Keane, upset with the constant criticism, second-guessing, and back-biting in St. Louis, agreed to take the Yankees job and the deal was set. To the embarrassment of all parties, Berra's Yankees and Keane's Cardinals turned their seasons around and wound up as rivals in the 1964 World Series. It could have been even more embarrassing for Houk and the Yankees. Berra's Yankees could have beaten Keane's Cardinals and then, having made a commitment, Houk would have had to explain why he was firing the winning manager of the World Series and replacing him with the losing manager.

It was not possible to evaluate Yogi Berra as a manager immediately after the 1964 season. He made mistakes—plenty of them—but he did some good things. He used Mel Stottlemyre and Pedro Ramos perfectly. And he disagreed with management over one young pitcher. The front office wanted to keep Tom Metcalf. Yogi insisted on keeping Pete Mikkelsen. Berra won out and Mikkelsen won seven big games in relief; Metcalf was never heard from again.

But the true evaluation of Yogi Berra as a manager came later. He won a pennant with the Yankees in his first year as manager. In the next five years, without Berra, the Yankees failed to finish higher than fifth.

8

"If You Can't Imitate Him, Don't Copy Him"

Old and obsolete Crosley Field in Cincinnati was not long for this world. Already, plans were in the works to get the Reds a new, modern ball park, and progress was interfering with the grand old game. A new freeway, Interstate 75, had been built behind the left field fence in Crosley, causing havoc to hitters. The lights from the passing cars and the overhead lights illuminating the freeway shone in the eyes of hitters, practically blinding them and putting them in danger of being hit with a 90-mile-per-hour fastball.

To remedy the situation, the Cincinnati management had a wooden barricade erected atop the left field wall. Its purpose was to block the light, but it also created a small problem. It meant a ball that hit the wooden barricade was a home run. But one that hit the concrete was in play.

One night Ron Swoboda came to bat for the Mets with the bases loaded and hit a tremendous smash to left. It hit either the wooden barricade or the concrete wall and bounced back onto the field. Certain the ball hit the barricade for a home run, Swoboda broke into his home run trot. But the umpire ruled the ball hit the concrete wall and was in play.

The Mets were livid with rage, and the most outraged of all was first base coach Yogi Berra. He argued so long and so loud he was eventually ejected from the game.

Later, talking with reporters, Berra swore he was right and the umpire was wrong, that the ball had hit the wood barricade, not the concrete.

His argument was as basic as his logic: "Anybody who can't tell the difference between the sound of a ball hitting wood and a ball hitting concrete must be blind."

The houselights were dim and the crowd of 1,500 had its attention turned to the stage where a spotlight caught a lone shadow. From somewhere offstage came a voice: "Here comes Yogi, now."

The solitary figure walked across the stage pushing a wheelbarrow and stopped in the center of the stage, in front of a microphone, and the spotlight stopped with him. He wore a clown's uniform, and there were dollar bills—stage money—spilling out of every pocket of his jaunty costume.

The date was Sunday, January 31, 1965, and this was the New York Baseball Writers' dinner and show, an annual ration of corn and ham placed on a harpoon by a group of frustrated actor-singers.

The music started and the clown on stage, played by Leonard Koppett of *The New York Times,* began to mouth words that were coming from an offstage microphone, sung in the operatic tenor voice of Arthur Rubin, an island of professionalism in a sea of amateurs.

The tune was familiar. It was "Vesti la Giubbe" from Leoncavallo's *I Pagliacci.*

> Be a clown! That's the role that they expected!
> They wished I could be funny—and smart—like
>   Casey,
> So attendance would improve! Ha!
> But I was a man!
> And won a pennant. . . . Ha, ha, ha, ha, ha, ha . . .

Put on the shin guards,
Buckle on the protector.
The Yanks discharged me, so back I go to play.
They said I'm not
The right kind of director,
Laugh, good old Yogi, be nice . . . but go away.
Be happy with some sort of phony title,
Don't rock the boat, don't complain, don't be upset.
Laugh, good old Yogi, though your heart may be
      broken.
Laugh through the tears, as you become . . . a Met."

The parody brought the house down, for as he finished, Koppett (Yogi) sprinkled play money all over the stage. Even Yogi Berra could be seen laughing, probably because it hurt too much to cry.

When the Yankees fired him as manager and gave him some meaningless job with a title to match, Berra did what he would have done had he not been fired—he went to play golf. His semiretirement lasted less than a month. In November 1964, the Mets signed him to a contract as a player-coach.

It was an obvious public relations stunt. The Mets, new to New York and fighting for attention and attendance with an established ball team and a winner, did everything they could to attract attention. And they loaded up with ex-Yankees.

George Weiss, former Yankee general manager, became the president of the Mets. Casey Stengel, after a one-year retirement, became their first manager at the age of 72. As a manager, his skills were questionable. As a public relations man for the Mets and baseball, he was without peer.

Now the Mets were about to pull off perhaps their greatest coup in signing Berra, a favorite of fans, who had been dismissed unjustly, most people thought, as manager of the

Yankees. Yogi's fans were legion, and many of them followed him from the Yankees to the Mets.

Whatever Berra's future role was with the Mets, what Yogi himself thought his role was going to be isn't known. But some assumed he believed he would eventually step in and manage the team when Stengel retired—if Stengel retired. Others had different ideas, including, presumably, the Mets. And Bill Veeck. In his *Hustler's Handbook,* Veeck expresses his views:

> With the Mets, Yogi will be the space-catcher the Yankees hoped he would be for them, because while Yogi can't play the comic lead, he makes an excellent second banana. With Stengel there to bounce his jokes off him, Yogi will seem to be funny again. And don't think the Old Man doesn't know how to do it. Casey could give public relations lessons to BBD&O—and all the rest of the alphabet, too. Casey's decade of unparalleled success with the Yankees seduced us all into forgetting where his real talents lie. Casey doesn't really care whether he wins or loses, just so long as the turnstiles keep moving.
>
> For Berra, it might be a foolish move. Unless he had a sudden and highly unlikely feeling of revulsion at the way he had permitted the Yankees to treat him, he would have been far better off staying right where he was. The Yankees, to put it baldly, were stuck with him. Yogi could have sat there for ten or fifteen years, drawing down an annual $35,000 or so for playing golf.
>
> Yogi apparently thought he had a chance to become the manager of the Mets after Stengel departs. His chances aren't that hot. He apparently thinks that with Weiss and Stengel around, he can draw on past associations and loyalties to take care of him. Unhappily for Yogi, Stengel and Weiss will both be gone very soon, and neither Grant nor Mrs. Payson nor Bing Devine owes Yogi Berra a thing. He was a public relations coup for them, nothing more.

The public relations coup was to include Yogi Berra crouching behind the plate again, swinging a bat again. Put him out there; he couldn't hurt the Mets. Yogi gave it everything he had. He trimmed down, got in shape, and went through a torturous spring training. He actually got into four regular season games in 1965, came to bat nine times, and lined two singles. He wouldn't have been the Mets' worst hitter had he played all year.

But he was 40 years old and he had missed an entire season of active competition and he just didn't have it anymore. Even the Mets, anxious to have the Berra name in their lineup, conceded that, and Yogi retired to become their first-base coach and hitting instructor.

As a hitting instructor, Berra provided some memorable moments. There was, supposedly, the time Ron Swoboda sought Yogi's advice.

"I think if I stand up close to the plate, I'll be able to handle the outside pitch better," Swoboda said.

"Nah, they'll jam you," Berra disagreed.

"But Frank Robinson does it," Swoboda argued, "and they don't jam him. He gets out in front of the ball."

"He's Frank Robinson and you're you," Berra protested. "That's his style of hittin'. If you can't imitate him, don't copy him."

Still it was a memorable year that 1965 season. The Mets finished last again with a 50–112 record, but they had fun. Stengel had his assistant manager, Yogi Berra, to kid around with once again and to add to his storehouse of Yogi Berra memories. And what a memory Casey Stengel had. For example:

"Yogi Berra worked for me a long time, and when he started, he had a wonderful career because he lived in St. Louis, which I was familiar with because I lived in Kansas City when I went to dental college and he was living in Kerry Patch[1] because all the Irish was there, then in come the Italians like Graziola and Berra and they commenced makin' more money because they worked in the factory and if it wasn't a factory they kept busy and everybody worked and they brought the beer back in a bucket or

---

[1] The section in St. Louis where Berra grew up, now called The Hill, was known as Kerry Patch in earlier days when it was inhabited by Irish immigrants.

whatcha call a pitcher that they filled because it was very hot in St. Louis like you wouldn't believe, next to hell, and the fellows was very tired in the factory and finally they got started with the ball club and most of the players like Howard[2] lived there and for 30–40 years they played ball in three or four parks[3] when the National League had it.

"Now Berra became very well known when the war started because Phil Rizzuto was in the navy in Portsmouth and immediately Berra went and joined, and this is when I wasn't there, he wanted to sign up with the Yankees and he came to see the business manager and if you went there you had to go through two or four secretaries, but he had four or five things that he could do which wasn't funny to me in my life with his antics. He was very nervous when he was there and young and now he has raised three kids that are taller than he is every one of them, when he had a way of walking around, you know, like a bear and they forgot that he could bat like Graziola did. And you could look it up that he went up there and he didn't care about signs if you tell him to bunt and he swung and hit some of them home runs and you can't catch home runs.

"McDougald and Simmons everybody thought had peculiar stances[4] if you were a first-year player in life they'd say how could you stand like that but I always thought he was graceful because few of them made good like Berra was a very good hitter and I thought he had a good year after he talked with people all over the country, they wanted to know, some of them, why you didn't get with Mr. Rickey and they didn't give ya a big

[2] Former Yankee catcher Elston Howard was also a native of St. Louis.

[3] The St. Louis Browns joined the American League in 1902 and left in 1954. The St. Louis Cardinals have been in the National League since its inception, playing home games in several ball parks, including Sportman's Park and Busch Memorial Stadium.

[4] Former Yankee Gil McDougald and Hall of Famer Al Simmons were noted for their unorthodox batting stances.

bonus because he wanted to go back to Kerry Patch and say he got more than Graziola or at least as much.

"In the World Series they put him in right field and when he was in right field he used to have the best alibi guy which was DiMaggio and he would say 'Isn't that so, Joe?' if he went to a banquet that he led the league in three or four departments he commenced partying because some of the owners were there and they took in outstanding people or an actor or singer not like New York which takes only baseball people[5] and they called on him to talk, but how ya gonna interview him about hitting the ball sideways on the golf course,[6] now in time he got up to speak and Braven Dyer[7] said if you want to make that man talk you gotta ask him questions like how in the world did you sign so fast they thought you should hold out like Babe Herman used to say if you hold out they automatically pay you $1,000 to sign, but he signed at a banquet in New York because he thought he was the maitre d' he used to always be around Topping and Weiss[8] until they said why don't you come into the office and he said I do but you're never around and leading in three or four things how in the world can you sign the contract so soon and why wouldn't you hold out and he hemmed and hawed and he said, well he knew Del Webb was sitting there listening, and he said to tell you the truth I figured it out and I asked for $10,000 and they give me $10,000 more than that.

[5] The Los Angeles Baseball Writers annual dinner, unlike that in New York, is often attended by Hollywood celebrities.

[6] ? ? ?

[7] A former Los Angeles sportswriter.

[8] The Yankees always had a World Series victory party in a Manhattan hotel, and it was Berra's custom to stay near team owner Dan Topping and General Manager George Weiss. As the drinks flowed and the elation built, Topping would invariably ask Berra, "How much do you want next year?" Yogi would tell him and Topping would say, "Okay, come in tomorrow and we'll draw up the contract." It was Stengel's contention that Yogi therefore got a better contract than he would have had he waited.

"After that he talked about him with Brownie,[9] who did wonderful in life and he even studied in spring training and now he's a big doctor with all them big doctors and he's done wonderful and everybody talked about the funnies[10] because they used to say if you owned a paper and you didn't use the funnies you couldn't sell the papers but it's not like that anymore and very seldom did you ever see Mr. Berra in a fight and with our pitchers they said he couldn't catch and handle pitchers and if you count them they have a lot of catchers with that there club. Let's see, Scheffing, Walker, Pignatano and himself, all catchers if you look it up, and which one is right on how they catch. I think the greatest coach was Dickey and he was wonderful against Cochrane and men who were real outstanding catchers if you owned them.

"One year he had stopped hitting, not stopped, but he had bad luck and he coulda led the league in home runs except he pulled the ball too much[11] they slowed up on him and I'd jump out and I'd say, '*Ohhhhhh,* it's foul but it will be a home run,' and he had beautiful brilliance with writers about why he hit bad balls for home runs you better not throw the ball over the plate to him. 'Yeah,' I said, 'I'd like to see 'em throw the ball over the plate, too, he'd do pretty good.'

"I always thought he worked good with young pitchers. That's why he could beat that Cleveland club 18 times without ever losing a game if you look it up. Now when you talk about Ford, he was the best pitcher we ever had for a left-hander, and they used to say he didn't think good and I said, 'Huh, huh,' but he hits good and he rearranged the Dodgers and they were scared

---

9 Bobby Brown.

10 A reference to Berra's predilection for reading comics.

11 A reference to Berra's habit of repeatedly pulling balls foul into the right field seats in Yankee Stadium.

to death that he would hit to left field and they made a great catch and there went Mr. Stengel.[12]

"When he was managing I've heard about on the bench all the arguing, the umpire did this and the umpire did that. 'Huh, huh,' he'd say and he'd go like this with that and one thing he was generally right. When Reynolds pitched the no-hit game you must be pitching pretty good when Williams hits a pop fly and even if he got his toe stepped on, who would have thought he would do it again which only proves that baseball must be honest because who would do it again except a guy who hits .110 and him one of the greatest hitters of all time if you look it up and Del Webb with all his troubles because the market ain't so good and he said when he went and faced the Great Man above he hoped he got a second chance like that.

"Well, now, he was always a pleasant feller and he would never snitch on a ballplayer even when they got into some trouble in New York in a night club[13] that they had made a date 30 days ahead because it was a off day and they wuz takin' him out because it was Martin's birthday. Now it came up rain and we had to play but they still filled that engagement. I said, 'You was with them,' and he said, 'No, I went home early,' see he never snitched on anybody. He led a very good life off the field, I mean he liked a lot of people but he liked sports. You know, he

---

[12] In the 1955 World Series, Berra crossed up the Dodger strategy by hitting the ball to left field, but Dodger left fielder Sandy Amoros made a spectacular catch of a Berra drive down the left field line that looked like a certain double. Amoros, instead, turned it into a double play, killing a Yankee rally that cost them the game and the World Series.

[13] A reference to the famous Copacabana Incident, during which Berra, Whitey Ford, Mickey Mantle, Hank Bauer, and Johnny Kucks took Billy Martin out for his birthday. During the course of the evening an argument developed between the Yankee players and people at another table. The groups continued their disagreement in the lobby of the night club where Bauer was alleged to have punched a member of the other party. The person sued, but Bauer was found not guilty. He was, however, fined by the Yankees (as was every other player in the party) for their shameful behavior.

thought they were really playing hard those women playing hockey,[14] can you believe it?

"He had good instruction from Dickey and he got better. He's an awkward man, but he's fast. When we beat them in Brooklyn and they had all those good managers like Dressen and Durocher, he's the one went out and got the ball and they called him out, but he could go out and get the bunt. Another thing he did when he was playing, he never showed he was going crazy on the field, you never saw him tearin' up a uniform, did you? But to tell you the truth, he'd talk to them players. I heard him this fall. He had a line of bull this fall, but they caught 'em. He did a good job in certain ways. They missed one or two pitchers[15] and I thought the shortstop[16] was great for him when he played and another thing, he reported to the ball club on time. He wasn't a good base stealer, but he was a fair base runner, but I don't want to tell you too much about him because then you'll have 5,000 pages."[17]

[14] Roller derby, presumably.
[15] Tug McGraw and Jon Matlack were injured or ineffective for a good portion of the season.
[16] Bud Harrelson.
[17] You'd better believe him.

9

Mr. Lucky

Those who can, do; those who can't, teach.

It's an old axiom, especially true in professional sports. The best teachers (managers, coaches) are often men who were not much more than average players themselves.

The great players, the superstars, are often failures as teachers. Their ability comes naturally and they have little patience with those who do not have comparable ability. They can't explain how they threw their curve ball or hit the fast ball—they just did it, naturally.

When a young player asked the great Stan Musial how to hit the slider, Musial's reply was to climb into the batting cage, ask the pitcher to throw a slider and say, "Like this . . . wham!"

Yogi Berra was much the same. He could hit the curve ball, get out in front of the fast ball, and wait on the knuckle ball, but he could not transmit that skill to others with less natural talent.

As a coach for the Mets, it was Berra's job to work with the hitters, to help them solve their problems, help them improve. One such hitter with a problem was Ken Boswell, a young left-handed hitting second baseman known for his good hitting stroke.

"Hey, Yog," said Boswell, "I can't seem to break this slump."

"What's the matter?" Berra asked.

"I'm in a rut," said Boswell. "I can't break myself of this habit. I keep swinging up at the ball."

Yogi contemplated the problem for a moment. Finally he had a solution.

"Well," he said, with impeccable logic, "swing down."

Nobody knew how much Yogi Berra wanted to get another opportunity to manage a baseball team. He kept it all within him and went along doing his job while the Mets repeatedly passed him up when it came time to find a new manager.

When Casey Stengel broke his hip in a fall at West Point late in the 1965 season, it was Wes Westrum, not Berra, the old man suggested as his temporary replacement. And when Stengel finally retired at the start of the 1966 season, it was Westrum, not Berra, who was selected to be his successor as manager of the Mets.

When Westrum was fired on September 21, 1967, Berra was passed over once again and Salty Parker, another coach, was chosen to finish out the season. Yogi, presumably, was among those under consideration to be named manager in 1968, but once again, he was bypassed, and Gil Hodges became the team's manager for the new season. Through it all, through the triple bypass, Berra said nothing.

"Why would he?" some people asked. "He has the best job in the world."

While it was true that Berra had the perfect job—an estimated $35,000 per year, probably for life, just to be a first base coach—how could they know of Yogi's secret desire to manage again when he never spoke of it?

In retrospect, Berra was probably lucky not to be tabbed to succeed Stengel. Westrum did and was fired. He was lucky, too, not to be asked to fill in when Westrum was fired. Parker did and he, too, was fired. But, then, Yogi was always lucky.

Berra proved that repeatedly in business and in sports. He got into the bowling business before the boom and got out before the crash. He bought stock in a buyer's market and sold in a seller's market. He lent his name to the Yoo-Hoo Chocolate Drink firm and wound up as a vice-president of the company. As a Yankee player once said, if God had to make somebody who looked like Yogi, the least he could do was make him lucky.

"Not only is he lucky," points out Whitey Ford, "he's never wrong."

Yogi proved that, too. If there was some question among the Yankees as to how a certain hitter should be pitched, they consulted Yogi. If Yankee players argued over a play that occurred weeks, months, even years before, Yogi settled the argument. Picking the winner of Sunday's football game, Yogi had it. Movie trivia? Baseball trivia? Yogi.

In March 1971, when Muhammad Ali met Joe Frazier in New York's Madison Square Garden in what was billed as Super Fight I, a battle of unbeaten fighters both claiming the heavyweight championship of the world, the New York *Daily News* conducted a poll of celebrities asking them to predict the outcome of the fight. In all, 100 celebrities were polled, from Frank Sinatra to Tiny Tim, from Rod McKuen to Jacqueline Susann, from Dr. Michael de Bakey to Mae West, from Senator Hubert Humphrey to Jackie Gleason, and a group that could have represented a Who's Who in Sports.

If they cared to, the celebrities were permitted to embellish their selections and give details about what they thought would happen in the fight. The final tabulation could not have been closer. Joe Frazier was chosen to win by 46 people, Muhammad Ali by 45, with nine voters unable to decide on a winner. Most of them predicted a knockout by one fighter or the other; many had Ali winning by a decision; but only one person predicted that Frazier would win by a decision, obviously the least likely result.

"Frazier by a decision," said Yogi Berra. "Clay laid off too long."

On March 8, 1971, Joe Frazier scored a 15-round decision

over Muhammad Ali to win undisputed possession of the heavy-weight championship of the world. Yogi Berra was right again.

"The players always felt that having Yogi around was like having a good luck charm," said Jim Bouton. "Once we were on a plane that was bouncing through a thunderstorm. Lightning was dancing off the wings. Everyone was afraid, of course, but it was nothing like the chill we all felt when some wise guy remembered that Yogi had stayed back a few hours and taken a later flight. We said we could all see the picture of Yogi the next day with a sad look on his face as he was reading a newspaper headline that read:

YANKEE TEAM KILLED IN PLANE CRASH

BERRA LIVES—CATCHES LATER FLIGHT

Former Met coach Joe Pignatano says good things are always happening to Berra. One incident he remembers happened in St. Petersburg one spring training. There was a laundry out on St. Pete Beach, Pignatano says, that offered one-day service. So the Met coaches would drop off their laundry in the morning on their way to the ball park and pick it up when they returned.

"We go in to pick up the laundry," Joe says. "There are four of us. Me, Yogi, Rube Walker, and Gil Hodges. Gil gives the girl his ticket, gets his laundry, and pays his bill. Rube does the same and so do I. Now it's Yogi's turn. He gives the girl his ticket, gets his laundry, and hands her some money. As he does, she rings the cash register and a star comes up.

"'There's no charge for you, sir,' she says. 'Every thousandth customer gets his laundry free. That's what the star means.'

"The three of us looked at each other. We weren't really surprised. That kind of thing could only happen to Yogi."

Several years ago, Berra and his three sons were asked to do a television commercial for an underwear company. It was a profitable venture, but it was almost a costly one. One of the boys, Tim, was playing college football; another, Dale, was playing high school football. There was some question whether the commercial jeopardized their amateur standing.

An investigation proved that Yogi was the only one of the four Berras to get paid and the boys' amateur standing was preserved.

"Hell," said Whitey Ford, "I could have told them Yogi got all the money. He always does."

10

A Second Shot

It was an off day on the road, one of those rare occasions in the life of a professional athlete, a day to do whatever it is that turns you on. For the Met coaches, the thing on this day was going to be deep-sea fishing because Yogi Berra had a friend. Yogi Berra always has a friend.

This friend invited Yogi, who in turn invited the other coaches, Joe Pignatano, Eddie Yost, and Rube Walker.

"Nothin' doin'," drawled Albert Bluford Walker of the Lenoir, North Carolina, Walkers. "Me and those boats don't exactly hit it off too good."

"You mean you get seasick?" Berra asked.

"Do I ever," Walker replied.

"On water?"

It was one of those few memorable days in one's lifetime that can never be forgotten; for as long as you live you would remember exactly where you were when you first heard the sad news about Gil Hodges. Yogi Berra was visiting friends in Miami Beach when he heard about Gil Hodges. It was April 2, 1972, Easter Sunday.

The night before, the baseball players of the major leagues had struck. The start of the season was in jeopardy. All remaining exhibition games would be canceled. The Mets made plans to return to New York on Monday, April 3. That made Sunday a completely free day for manager and coaches.

Berra and Carmen took the opportunity to see friends in Miami Beach. Had he not gone visiting, Yogi no doubt would have been right there with Gil and the others, playing golf.

Gil Hodges, so big, so strong, so seemingly indestructible, was struck down by a heart attack. It was his second attack, and it was fatal. He had recovered remarkably from the first heart seizure two years earlier. Under doctor's orders, he had lost a considerable amount of weight, and his new figure was streamlined—trim, but hard—and he had done a lot of walking.

Golf was ideal. It provided the walking exercise the doctor prescribed. Besides, it was fun and satisfied the competitive drive that was within him. Accordingly, when the game with the Braves was canceled by the strike, it gave Gil and his coaches, Joe Pignatano, Eddie Yost, and Rube Walker, a day of golf.

They shot 18 holes and because it was still daylight when they finished, they shot another nine. They finished up, had a beer, and prepared to return to their rooms, adjacent to the golf course, to shower and dress for dinner. The four of them had agreed to meet later that evening.

The ninth green and the lobby of the Ramada Inn in West Palm Beach are separated by a sidewalk, perhaps 100 feet long. Gil Hodges was on the sidewalk, walking to the hotel lobby. He had just said something to Pignatano—"What time are we meeting for dinner—seven-thirty?" The words had no sooner left his lips when he toppled over backwards—fell "like he was shot," Pignatano remembered—and his head struck the concrete. Gil Hodges never felt the blow. He was dead by the time his head hit the concrete, dead from a coronary.

Yogi Berra heard the news later that night by way of a telephone call from Bob Scheffing, general manager of the Mets. Scheffing asked Yogi to meet with him and M. Donald Grant, chairman of the board of the Mets, in West Palm Beach the following day.

The season was scheduled to open in four days (because of the strike, it would actually open 13 days later). There wasn't time to go looking for a new manager. And Yogi Berra was the only Met coach with managerial experience. Scheffing and Grant offered him a two-year contract.

"I'm going to take it," Berra told Carmen.

"What do you want it for?" she asked. "You've got a good job."

"I thought about it," Berra said later. "It was home. It would be different if it was another town."

At first, even Joe Garagiola thought his childhood pal would be a fool to take the job.

"Why take it?" Garagiola asked. "You've got the best job in baseball. Managers come and go, but you could be a coach forever."

His strongest arguments, Garagiola soon realized, were falling on deaf ears. Somehow, Yogi was able to convey to his friend what was deepest in his heart—that despite the insecurity, the anxieties, the problems, the sleepless nights, the criticism, despite the roller coaster ups and downs, he had to take this job. He wanted to manage again and he might never get another opportunity.

"When the Yankees fired him," Garagiola recalled, "he was very bitter and also very hurt. Now I realized he wanted to prove something; he wanted to prove he could manage. So I told Carmen, 'We have no right to ask him not to take this job, to deprive him of this chance. He's got to find out if he can manage.'"

Four days after the death of Gil Hodges, Yogi Berra was named manager of the Mets.

"I don't like the way the job came," Yogi said later, "but I want to prove I can manage."

If Gil Hodges had been able to handpick his successor, it is very unlikely he would have chosen Berra. The two men were friendly enough, had respect for each other's ability as players and knowledge of the game, and they worked well together. But with Hodges around, there was never any doubt who was boss. They weren't close friends—more like business associates. Gil was the boss and Yogi was a guy punching a time clock. Berra was there when Hodges came to the Mets in 1968. The other three coaches were Gil's own. He brought Rube Walker, Joe Pignatano, and Eddie Yost with him from Washington. Berra was there, a fixture with the Mets. Whoever came along, for years, would inherit him. He had more security than any manager; he could have survived any administration, any purge.

But now Berra was the manager, and the contrast between the two men—Hodges and Berra—was stark and startling. Where Hodges was quiet and aloof, Berra was affable and outgoing; where Hodges gave the impression of austerity and cold efficiency, Berra seemed bumbling and uncertain; where Hodges was confident and direct, Berra often groped for words when talking with players and press. It was simply a matter of style. They couldn't have been more different, yet Berra admitted he took something of Hodges with him into his new job.

"I think Gil was very patient," he said, indicating he would attempt to emulate Hodges' patience. "He gave each guy a square shot. He believed once you take your 25 with you, that's your best 25 men and they have to do it for you."

As different as their styles were, that's how different was their acceptance by the players they managed. Comparisons were inevitable, and some players couldn't help thinking, when a move of Berra's backfired, that Hodges would have done it another way. Was it to be the Yankees and Ralph Houk all over again?

Actually, to many of his players, Berra benefited by being compared to Hodges. He presented a pleasant alternative to the man of steel. Not everybody believed Gil's way was the only way—or even the best way. Some people found his aloofness irritating and his stolidness discomforting. These men were more at ease with Berra.

On the other hand, there were some who were turned off by Yogi, found him to be a buffoon because of incidents such as the one that happened one night in Shea Stadium. Tom Seaver was running in the outfield, doing wind sprints. He was scheduled to run for 15 minutes. After awhile he asked Berra a question.

"Hey, Yogi, what time is it?"

"You mean now?" Berra replied.

Yet there were others who found Yogi compassionate, warm, friendly, outgoing, and always willing to listen to problems. That, too, was a stunning contrast to Hodges.

"Yogi opened an avenue we didn't have before . . . or we didn't think we had," said one veteran Met. "The players like it. We're not cold steel."

Under Berra, the Mets won 25 of their first 32 games and forged into first place right from the opening gun. That made them believers. And Yogi made them believers, too, because he executed all the right moves and drew the approval of the boss—general manager Bob Scheffing, the man who hired him.

"He's been a helluva manager since he took over," Scheffing said. "And he couldn't have done it under worse conditions. But he doesn't lose his cool. He might not sound too good when he talks, but his actions tell you something, and the players are responding to him. He's got Cleon Jones hustling the way I never saw him before. All of them, in fact."

On May 11, 1972, the front office made things more difficult for Yogi. The Mets purchased the contract of Willie Mays from the San Francisco Giants. He was nothing more than a plaything for the owner, Joan Payson. She had admired Mays when he was a Giant in New York, she was a stockholder of the Giants, and when the opportunity presented itself for the Mets to buy Mays, Payson jumped at the chance.

She was bringing Willie Mays back to New York, bringing him

home to finish out his illustrious career. Willie Mays was a legend—an old legend at 42, but a legend nonetheless. He was also one more problem Yogi Berra didn't need. Not at this time, in his first year as manager. Mays' presence and his reason for being a Met made things difficult and touchy for Berra. He knew Payson liked Willie. He also realized that she signed the checks. Mays played when he wanted to play and sat when he wanted to sit and Berra had to accept it. It was the price Yogi had to pay for the job he wanted so desperately.

In the beginning, though, he didn't accept it. Yogi refused to be a foil for the charade. In Mays' first game in a Met uniform, the Shea Stadium crowd wanted him, begged for him, implored Berra to use him.

"We want Willie, we want Willie," they chanted, rocking the huge stadium, and Berra could not have failed to hear.

They never got him.

"Good for Yogi," Scheffing said. "He's going to be his own man."

By June 3, the Mets had won 31 of 43 games, and they were five games ahead of the pack in the National League East. Then things changed as they moved into July and August, the dog days.

Suddenly everything went bad for the Mets. Shortstop Bud Harrelson strained his back and missed 47 games. Catcher Jerry Grote missed 98 games with bone chips in the elbow. Jim Fregosi, obtained from the California Angels to give the Mets some batting punch at third base, had broken a thumb and missed the entire exhibition season; he wound up playing in only 101 games and batting a meager .232. Rusty Staub, obtained from the Montreal Expos for three prospects, broke his hand and missed 96 games. And Cleon Jones was out for 56 games with an elbow injury.

It was that kind of year. The Mets slipped out of first place on June 13, losing five games in the standings in just ten days. By

July 10 they were 4½ games out. By August 16 they were ten games out. They won only 52 of their last 113 games and finished the season in third place, 13½ games out of first.

Had Yogi Berra's lifetime of luck finally run out? He had one year left to get it back . . . one year left on his contract.

11

In Distinguished Company

It was a very hot day, a day in the nineties in St. Petersburg, a town where many of the residents are in their nineties. Standing outside Al Lang Field, waiting for a friend, Yogi Berra was the picture of sartorial splendor. He was attired in cream-colored slacks, a tan polo shirt, and white loafers.

Two of the town's typical female citizens walked by, saw Berra standing there, and instantly recognized the famous face.

"Good afternoon, Mr. Berra," said one grandmotherly type. "My, you look mighty cool today."

"Thank you, ma'am," Yogi replied. "You don't look so hot yourself."

The town is a typical, sleepy, upstate New York town, the kind Washington Irving depicted in his classics, *Rip Van Winkle* and *The Legend of Sleepy Hollow.*

Cooperstown, New York, may well be Sleepy Hollow. It sits up there in all its summer beauty and winter cold at the southern end of Otsego Lake in central New York State, 70 miles east of Syracuse, 60 miles west of Albany, 200 miles northwest of New York City.

From the heart of the city, from the hustle and the bustle and the traffic, it is a pleasant and lovely five-hour drive on a summer's day up the New York State Thruway to exit 23, then west on Route 20 for 60 miles, and finally south on Route 28 for 10 miles.

Huge fields stretch out as far as the eye can see on both sides of Route 20, a stark contrast to the overpopulation of the city. The water is a deep blue in the many lakes that abound in the area, and the trees, in full bloom, are a lush green.

Route 28 is a two-way, two-lane highway, and the ten-mile drive may take 30 minutes or more if you are unfortunate enough to get behind a native of the town driving at the customary, leisurely pace of about 12 miles per hour. The driving speed of the natives of this town, which was named for Judge William Cooper, father of the great American romance novelist James Fenimore Cooper, typifies the pace of the town. On every day of the year except one.

For 364 days a year, Cooperstown just sits there ruminating— a pleasant, little, country town out of a storybook and as quiet as the library where the storybook may be found. On the 365th day it comes alive with an infusion of thousands of people. The 365th day is Hall of Fame Day.

The Baseball Hall of Fame and Museum was formally opened on June 12, 1939. It was the brainchild of Ford C. Frick, then president of the National League and later commissioner of baseball. It became a reality with the financial backing of the late Stephen C. Clark, a native of Cooperstown, which also happens to be the birthplace of Abner Doubleday, alleged to be the originator of baseball.

The first players were voted into the Hall of Fame in 1936, and new members have been inducted every year since in an impressive and moving ceremony at the National Baseball Library in Cooper Park, directly behind the Hall of Fame and Museum.

The day of Yogi Berra's inauguration was August 7, 1972. He had been elected in his second year of eligibility. He had missed making it in his first year by only a handful of votes, but he made it with votes to spare in his second year.

The telephone rang in the Berra home on Tuesday evening, January 18, 1972. It was Jack Lang, secretary of the Baseball Writers Association of America. The Hall of Fame ballots had just been tabulated, the results were in. Yogi Berra had been expecting the call all day. In or not, Lang had promised he would call.

Now Berra calmly returned the telephone to its cradle and turned to Carmen.

"Whew, I made it," he said.

Larry Berra, Jr., went around the house shouting, "I'm the son of a Hall of Famer." Dale Berra went to school the next morning with his head in the clouds. The middle one, Tim, took it in stride. He had been studying his dad's records the day before and came to one conclusion. "He's a cinch to make it."

Cinch or not, Yogi Berra was a Hall of Famer, one of eight enshrined on August 7, 1972. The eight were: Lawrence Peter Berra, Joshua Gibson, Vernon Louis Gomez, William Harridge, Sanford Koufax, Walter Fenner Leonard, Early Wynn, and Ross Middlebrook Youngs.

"Sure I'm excited," said Larry Berra, Jr. "Looking at all those names, all those great players, I'm excited that dad is going to be in there with all those guys. There are only 130 in there out of how many—seven thousand?"

Soon there would be one more plaque on the wall. It would read:

LAWRENCE PETER BERRA

"YOGI"

NEW YORK, A.L. 1946–1963
NEW YORK, N.L. 1965
PLAYED ON MORE PENNANT-WINNERS (14) AND WORLD
CHAMPIONS (10) THAN ANY PLAYER IN HISTORY. HAD

358 HOME RUNS AND LIFETIME .285 BATTING AVERAGE.
SET MANY RECORDS FOR CATCHERS, INCLUDING 148
CONSECUTIVE GAMES WITHOUT AN ERROR. VOTED A.L.
MOST VALUABLE PLAYER 1951–54–55. MANAGED
YANKEES TO PENNANT IN 1964.

The ceremony began shortly after ten o'clock on a warm, muggy, overcast morning and would continue on a collision course with the hot, midday sun that would burn the clouds away as it threatened to melt the audience.

First, there was a program of speeches, presentations, dedications, and introductions. Then came the induction ceremony— short, simple, but elegant. It ran the gamut of emotions. The new Hall of Famers were humble and proud, confident and dignified, comical and emotional. They were a mixed bag of men from varied backgrounds and varied generations.

It was incongruous to see Sandy Koufax, so young, so fit, sitting there on the same dais with old Ross Youngs. He was sleek and handsome, the youngest man ever inducted into the Hall of Fame. At 36, he should have still been pitching. He was too young to be an immortal, too young to have been retired for five years, too young to be a museum piece.

"How lucky I feel to be in such distinguished company," he said.

Buck Leonard, out of the Negro Leagues and accorded the recognition in the twilight of his life that he didn't get in the prime of his life because of the color of his skin, made a promise: "I will do everything in my power to honor and uphold the dignity of baseball," he said.

Early Wynn, the hard-as-nails right-hander, showed emotion at the microphone that he never showed on the mound. "I just wish I could have been better than I was," said the man who won 300 big league games and was better than he thought he was. "Everytime I played in a game, I wanted to be an all-star, play in a World Series, and be elected to the Hall of Fame . . . and I have."

Lefty Gomez lent a much-needed air of levity. "I want to thank my teammates who scored so many runs and Joe DiMaggio, who ran down my mistakes."

Josh Gibson, Jr., accepted the award for his late father, the star of the Negro Leagues, whose skin color also kept him out of the major leagues. He brought chills to the crowd, and a sea of handkerchiefs suddenly washed up on Cooper Park. "I want to say something personal to my father," he said, then turned his eyes heavenward and said, "Wake up, dad, you just made it in."

In introducing Lawrence Peter Berra, Max Nichols of the Minneapolis *Star* and president of the Baseball Writers Association of America, couldn't resist his own Berraism: "I needed a first edition story one day in 1964, when Yogi was managing the Yankees," he related. "The Yankees had flown into Minneapolis early that morning, and when I called the hotel at nine o'clock, Yogi sounded like he had just awakened.

"I said 'I hope I didn't wake you up.' And he said, 'Nah, I had to get up to answer the phone, anyway.'"

It wasn't true. But nobody cared. They all laughed. They thought it was true. They wanted to believe it was true. And Yogi Berra laughed, too.

Then he was on his feet, accepting his plaque, ready to make his speech. He took a piece of paper from his inside jacket pocket. It was his speech. Carmen had written it for him the day before they left for Cooperstown. She had written it in pencil on a plain, white piece of paper. Then she rewrote it.

He reached into his breast pocket. "I have to put on my glasses," he said nervously. "I guess the first thing I ought to say is that I thank everybody for making this day necessary."

There were chuckles from the crowd. And then silence.

"Since this is the most important day of my life, I want to get it right, so I'm going to read it."

Haltingly, crudely, he read, and although he was reading from a piece of paper, it was obvious the words were coming from his heart.

"Thank God, I made it," he said. "I have to mention Bill Dickey and, of course, Casey, who had the confidence to play me every day. Also George Weiss, who gave me my first contract with the New York Yankees. Being with them was a dream come true . . . now the Hall of Fame.

"My only regret," he continued, "is the people who didn't live to see this day. My mother and father, who died a few years ago, and my brother John."

He paused. His voice cracked, and there were tears in his eyes as he struggled to gain control of his voice. Moments passed that seemed like hours, and then he continued in a hoarse voice.

". . . My brother John, and Gil Hodges, who died this year. I hope they are proud of me today. Last of all, I want to thank baseball. It has given me more than I could ever hope for. I hope when I leave this game, I will put something back."

Photo courtesy of the New York Yankees.

Strike zone? What strike zone! Yogi could hit off the peak of his cap as well as off his shoe tops. *Photo courtesy of UPI.*

(From left to right) Yogi, Mickey Mantle, Doris Day, and Roger Maris—who all appeared in the film *A Touch of Mink*. *Photo courtesy of Universal Pictures.*

Playing left field in the 1961 World Series, Yogi misjudged a fly ball. As he said, "It gets late early out there." *Photo courtesy of Wide World.*

Yogi makes his acceptance speech after being named Yankee manager in 1963. Dan Topping is seen to his right. *Photo courtesy of the N.Y. Yankees.*

(From left to right) The Father of the Year Awards luncheon in 1964 saw Yogi honored as Sports Father of the Year, Sargent Shriver as Father of the Year, and Bert Lahr as Theatrical Father of the Year. *Photo courtesy of the N.Y. Yankees.*

General manager Ralph Houk and Yogi had the lead roles in the summer of 1964. *Photo courtesy of the N.Y. Yankees.*

Former President Eisenhower joined managers Gil Hodges of the Washington Senators and Yogi Berra of the Yankees before a 1964 game. Eight years later Yogi succeeded Hodges as manager of the Mets when Gil died. *Photo courtesy of UPI.*

Sandy Koufax and Yogi at a press conference in New York, January 1972, at which it was announced that Koufax, Berra, and Early Wynn had been elected to the Hall of Fame. *Photo courtesy of UPI.*

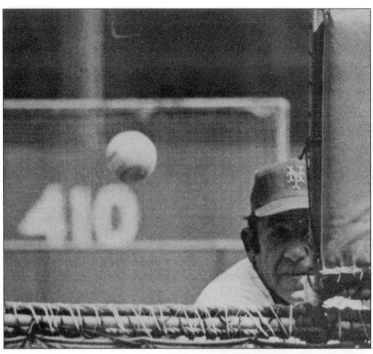

Yogi stayed in shape working
out with the Mets at batting
practice. *Top photo courtesy of
the N.Y. Mets; bottom photo
courtesy of UPI.*

Tom Seaver (right) was pronounced fit to play in this game, the first of the 1973 National League playoffs, against the Cincinnati Reds. There's Yogi looking on. *Photo courtesy of UPI.*

Umpire Augie Donatelli apparently wasn't one of those who believed in the 1973 Mets. The team, with manager Yogi in the middle, lost this argument in Game 2 of the Series. *Photo courtesy of UPI.*

Yogi got a second shot at managing the Yankees in 1984 after George Steinbrenner fired Billy Martin for the third time. Early in 1985 Yogi was gone and Billy was back once more. *Photo courtesy of Wide World.*

Lou Piniella and Yogi in the midst of an animated discussion at spring training. This year, 1984, would prove to be Piniella's last as a player. *Photo courtesy of Wide World.*

(From left to right) Roger Maris, Joe DiMaggio, and Bobby Brown
reunited with Yogi at an Old-Timers' Day at Yankee Stadium in 1984.
Photo courtesy of Wide World.

Infielder Dale
Berra meets his
new manager
in 1985.
*Photo courtesy of
N.Y. Yankees/
Sports Photo
Source.*

Yogi hits to the infielders as an Astro coach in 1986. *Photo courtesy of Wide World.*

Rusty Staub making a presentation to the ex-Mets manager in a Hail to Yogi Night at Shea Stadium in 1986. *Photo courtesy of Wide World.*

"Houston has never seen anyone like Yogi," said Astros owner John McMullen. *Photo courtesy of Wide World.*

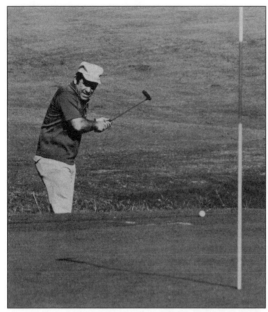

In and out of the trap with Yogi; golf was one of his great loves. *Photo courtesy of American Airlines.*

The University of Massachusetts held a Salute to Yogi at halftime of its 1973 game against Vermont. No. 42, standing with Mom and Dad, is Tim Berra, star flanker at UMass. Dr. Randolph W. Bromery (right) was the school's chancellor. *Photo courtesy of UPI.*

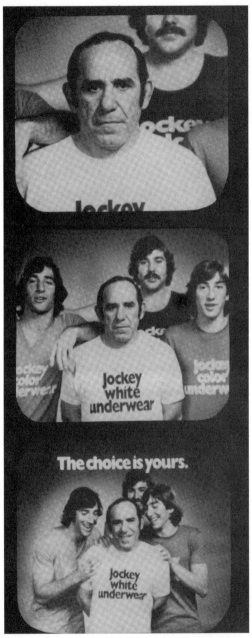

Yogi and his boys in another of his funny TV ads. *Photo courtesy of Jockey International—Levine, Huntley, Schmidt.*

Yogi clowning around with former St. Louis Brown Johnny Berardino, star of ABC-TV's *General Hospital. Photo courtesy of UPI.*

Another one of Yogi's advertising endorsements; here the voice-over is commenting, "Yogi is one of those sissies who uses his wife's hair spray." Yogi laughed all the way to the bank at gentle jibes like this one. *Photo courtesy of Jerry Della Femina.*

Yogi in one of his many commercial spots, here hawking for a cat food manufacturer. *Photo courtesy of the George Lois Collection.*

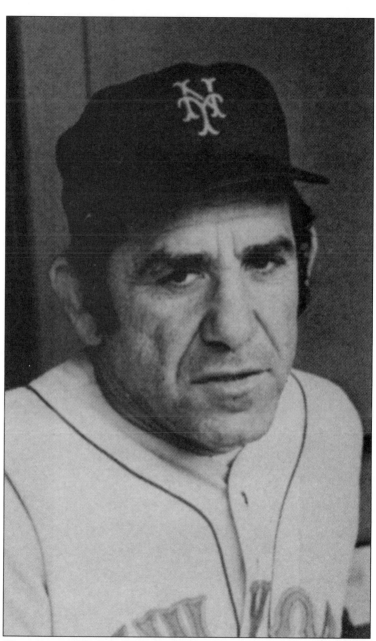
Photo courtesy of Malcolm W. Emmons.

12

"You Gotta *Bee-leeeeve*"

Before a game between the Mets and the Cardinals in St. Louis, Cardinal broadcaster Jack Buck invited Met manager Yogi Berra to be a guest on his pregame show. Berra accepted.

When the interview was concluded, Buck presented Berra with the usual fee for such an appearance—a check for $25.

To avoid delay, Buck carries a supply of $25 checks with him from the sponsor of his show. In this way, he can present his guest with his gift and avoid keeping records or forgetting to pay his guests. However, since he rarely knows in advance who his guests will be, Buck has the checks made "Payable to Bearer."

On this particular night in August 1973, Berra accepted the check from Buck and looked at it.

"Hey," he said to Buck. "How long you know me?"

"I don't know," replied the Cardinal announcer, "maybe ten, twelve years."

"You known me all that time and you still don't know how to spell my name."

To fully appreciate what happened at the end, it is necessary to go back to the middle, back to July and early August, back to all those awful dog days.

With his best team on the out-patient list at Roosevelt Hospital,

135

Yogi Berra stood idly by and watched the Mets tumble to the bottom of the heap in the National League East.

All around him, people were losing their heads. All around him, rumors swirled. One night, as he returned from the mound after removing another ineffective pitcher, Berra heard boos in Shea Stadium.

Boo Yogi Berra? It is like desecrating the flag, like booing apple pie or Mount Rushmore.

Yogi reacted impulsively. He tipped his cap.

"Booing don't bother me," he insisted. "I've been booed before."

Nobody could remember when.

Tug McGraw, the best relief pitcher in the major leagues, couldn't get anybody out. His earned-run average ballooned to almost five per game, but Berra stayed with him.

"He's the best I got," the manager said. "I'm gonna live or die with him."

The Mets couldn't hit, and when they lost shortstop Bud Harrelson for two months, they couldn't field, either. The natives grew restless, and the whispers grew louder. The rumors came more frequently. And the media got more ridiculous.

Just when Berra thought things couldn't get any worse, they got worse. M. Donald Grant, chairman of the board of the Mets, refused to give him a vote of confidence. In replying to the rumors, Grant refused to concede that Berra would not return in 1974.

Then he would return?

"The people will decide that," Grant replied.

If that was the case, the New York *Post* decided, it would help Grant have the people decide. It conducted a poll of its readers: Who should be blamed (i.e., fired) for the failure of the Mets? (1) M. Donald Grant, Chairman of the Board? (2) Bob Scheffing, General Manager? (3) Yogi Berra, Manager? (4) All of the above? (5) None of the above?

If he worried about it at all, it was little consolation to Berra that the poll held him unaccountable for the failure of the Mets. The fans placed the blame first on Grant, second on Scheffing, third on Yogi.

But as low man in the hierarchy of the Mets, it was Yogi who was on the spot. Grant took orders from Joan Payson. Scheffing took orders from Grant, Berra took orders from Scheffing. It gave you a pretty good idea just who would be left holding the bag.

At the same time, *New York Magazine,* with its customary clairvoyance, ran an article under the title: "The Last Days of Yogi Berra."

The writer of the article, from his storehouse of knowledge acquired in three or four visits to Shea Stadium, boldly quoted several equally bold, unnamed sources and concluded that Berra was responsible for the Mets' demise and he would be the one to take the rap. Through it all, Berra never panicked, never flared, never grew impatient. A visit to Shea would find him at his usual stand, behind the desk in his newly decorated office. Pictures of the manager of the Mets, taken during various stages of his career, were on every wall in the room.

"Place looks good, don't it?" Yogi Berra asked. "They've been fixing it up lately. I guess maybe they expect me to be around awhile," he said, and he couldn't resist a huge, toothy grin.

"Have they said anything to you about next year?"

"Not a thing," he said. "Why should they?" We still got a long way to go in this year. It's too early to talk about next year."

"Would getting fired bother you?"

"If they fire me, they fire me," he said. "That's their right. In a job like this, you probably have to get fired sooner or later, but they haven't said anything to me about it yet and I don't know why they would. Not so early."

He scanned the daily statistic sheet and noted that Cleon Jones had missed more than half the team's games, that Bud Harrelson had played in just about half, that John Milner, the team's only serious home run threat, had lost five weeks just when he was swinging a good bat, that Jon Matlack and Jerry Grote and Willie Mays had all spent time on the disabled list.

Someone mentioned the Cubs, who had raced off to a huge lead and then watched it disappear.

"That would bother me," Yogi Berra admitted. "It's a mystery. They haven't even had an injury. If I had my whole team and we weren't doing any better than we are, then I would worry. Then my hair would be gray."

He removed his cap for emphasis. His hair was still jet black.

When historians look back at the 1973 baseball season—more specifically, when they look back at the race in the National League East in 1973—they will pinpoint Friday, August 17, as the day it all turned around for Yogi Berra and the Mets. Up to that point, Berra kept insisting, "We're not out of it, yet."

People would nod their heads politely and then, when his back was turned, they would whisper: "Who does he think he's kidding? Probably himself."

On the morning of Friday, August 17, the Mets were buried in last place in their division, 7½ games behind the first-place St. Louis Cardinals, with a record of 12 games under .500—53 and 65—and with only 44 games to play. They had returned from a trip to the West Coast during which they had continued their spotty play, winning three, losing five. A deficit of 7½ games with 44 to play is not insurmountable under any conditions. But when it means hopping over five other teams, it is a difficult situation, at the very least.

Yogi came home, took one look at the standings, and said to himself, "We can still do it."

Later he explained what he saw that nobody else did. "Everybody was stumbling and fumbling like they didn't want to win. We came back off that bad West Coast trip, but we didn't lose any ground. We were still only 7½ games out. Everybody in our division had some kind of streak except us, and I had my whole team back. I felt if we could go on a little streak, we could make a move."

That night, the night of August 17, the Mets lost a heartbreaker to the Reds, 2–1, in ten innings. It left them 13 games under 500, their lowest point in the season. The next day, Bud Harrelson came off the disabled list and then things began to happen.

One night, the Mets were paid a rare visit in their clubhouse by the boss, M. Donald Grant. "I just thought I should talk to them, to try to get their chins off the ground," Grant revealed. "I told them there was still plenty of time, that they couldn't give up, that if they believed in themselves, they could do it. I told them they had to have faith, they had to believe in themselves."

At that point Tug McGraw, the iconoclastic relief pitcher, climbed on a stool and exhorted his teammates. "You gotta *bee-leeeeve*," he shouted. "You gotta *bee-leeeeve!*"

"I realized later that Mr. Grant might have misunderstood," McGraw said. "He might have thought I was mocking him. I wasn't. I went to his office the next day and told him. The night he made his talk to us, I had been running in the outfield, and I began talking to a group of fans in the right field stands. They kept asking me questions about the team. Did I think we could still win it? I said sure we could. I said we all just had to believe.

"I said it over and over and it kind of stuck with me. 'You gotta believe, you just gotta believe.' And then when Mr. Grant said practically the same thing, it really hit home, and I just got up on the stool and began shouting. Mr. Grant said he understood; he knew I wasn't mocking him."

That became the Mets' rallying cry in August and September. Every big victory was followed by a noisy clubhouse, and Tug McGraw led the chant: "You gotta *bee-leeeeve*, you gotta *bee-leeeeve*."

And there were a lot of big victories in August and September as the Mets made their move and climbed in the standings. By the end of August the Mets were in the thick of the pennant race. They hadn't won anything yet, they hadn't saved Yogi Berra's job, but they were making a good run at it.

"You have to put everything on the scale," said Don Grant. "Right now, there isn't enough to tilt it one way or the other—not enough one way to say you're going to be fired; not enough the other way to say here's another two-year contract.

"When I said the public would decide Yogi's fate, I didn't mean it would be the result of a poll and that their decision would be final. But a decline in attendance, a general lessening of interest, those were things that could influence Yogi's future."

It all went hand in hand; loss of games would mean loss of interest and attendance. But the Mets had turned it around, and Yogi Berra had to be credited with the resurgence just as he had been blamed for the decline. Meanwhile, there was one other thing on which Yogi's fate might have been hanging.

"If he had lost control of the club or anything like that," Grant said, "I wouldn't have had any trouble making the decision. I haven't noticed anything like that."

Win or lose, Berra never changed. He didn't panic in defeat and he didn't gloat in victory.

"He's a lot like Hodges," said Bob Scheffing. "Win or lose, he doesn't blow his cool. I like that in a manager. You've seen managers who are great while the team is going good. Then the team goes the other way and they go the other way. They start rapping the players."

Yogi never rapped. There were some who didn't like his style, but even they had to agree he was always the same Yogi.

"Yogi talks to you individually," said one Met. "He doesn't chew you out in a meeting. Some managers do that. Yogi will come to you when nobody is around in the clubhouse or the dugout, and tell you something you did wrong. Or he'll say hang in there, you can't be a three hundred hitter every day."

"Yogi is Yogi," said another Met, not a big Berra fan. "He's just too nice a guy. He's afraid to hurt anybody's feelings. That's his personality. It doesn't change. I don't think a man can manage and worry about hurting people's feelings. Personally, I prefer stronger leadership."

The Mets came on in September, and there have been any number of theories advanced to explain their resurgence, including the supernatural. In a game with the Pirates, the score was tied in the 13th. Richie Zisk was on first for the Pirates and another rookie, Dave Augustine, drilled a tremendous shot to deep left field. "Home run," was the first thought. But the ball hit the top of the wall, the point of the wood fence.

A fraction of an inch higher, and the ball would have hit and sailed over the fence, into the bullpen, for a two-run homer. A fraction of an inch lower and it would have ricocheted back past left fielder Cleon Jones for an extra-base hit and a run.

But the ball hit the point, shot up a few feet in the air, and landed right in Jones's glove. Cleon took it, whirled around, and threw a perfect strike to Wayne Garrett; Garrett whirled and threw a perfect strike to Jerry Grote and Zisk was nailed at the plate. Naturally, the Mets won the game in the last of the 13th.

"When that ball came right back at me," said Jones, "I said to myself, 'Man, we got a shot at this guy.'"

"When I saw that happen," said Garrett, "I said, 'This is our year. No way we can lose now.' I've seen a lot of balls hit that fence here, but in this park they go out. I've never seen one act like that."

To Harry Walker, scouting the Mets for the Cardinals, there was a simple explanation. "You can't tell me there isn't a man up there pulling the strings," he said.

A few days later, he was convinced, when a ground ball hit a rock, then glanced off the shoulder of Montreal shortstop Tim Foli, permitting the Mets to score the winning run in a game against the Expos.

"You can sense when things start breaking for one team," Walker said. "Things happen that defy explanation." `

Other things were occurring, however, that could be explained. "We got our team back," Berra stated simply. "And no other team stepped out."

Getting his team back meant getting Bud Harrelson to play six weeks of shortstop like it had never been played before; getting Tug McGraw pitching like "the best damn relief pitcher in baseball"; getting Tom Seaver, Jon Matlack, Jerry Koosman, and George Stone to be miserly on the mound; getting Cleon Jones launched on one of his hot streaks.

And don't forget the job the manager did. He brought them back, kept them believing in his own quiet way. It is his style.

"I can be tough if I have to," Yogi insists. "I just don't think yelling at players does any good. I'd rather take a guy over to the side quietly and tell him if he does something wrong."

Jerry Koosman remembered 1972, when he was unhappy and thought he was being mishandled, being yanked too early. "We talked it over like gentlemen," Koos said. "He explained all the things a manager must take into consideration: Tug was strong then . . . the number of pitches I had thrown . . . the weather . . . the manager not only observing my stuff but talking to the catcher. He made me understand that a manager cannot allow his individual feelings to interfere. After that, when he did take me out, I understood. And he understood me a little more. Now, when he takes me out, it doesn't bother me anymore. We learned a lot about each other."

In 1973 there was more understanding—Yogi for the players and the players for Yogi.

"He's got a lot of knowledge and a lot of patience," Koosman continued. "You know with him if you make a mistake he's not going to chew you out. He's going to ask you what you did and he's going to tell you if he thinks you were wrong.

"Some things went on in 1973 that you couldn't believe—the

way we were losing. He might show his emotion by kicking a water bucket, but he'd never take it out on the players. He'd come in the locker room and he'd say, 'Hang in there, we'll get 'em next time.'

"It was natural, at first, for us to compare him with Gil. We got so we knew Gil's moves, but we didn't know Yogi's. When a situation came up where Gil liked to make a certain move, we'd be looking for Yogi to make the same move. But he didn't and we thought he made a mistake. He had his own style and it took us awhile to understand his style. When we understood it, we realized he was right. He has tremendous judgment."

To illustrate, Koosman told about Ron Hodges, a young catcher who came up in the middle of the 1973 season when injuries depleted the Mets' catching corps.

"Yogi had seen him in the instructional league," Koosman recalled. "Nobody had heard of him, but he kept raving about him. When he finally came up, Hodges did a tremendous job, and Yogi was right about him all along. Not only that, but Yogi had seen him only once or twice, yet he described his hitting and catching style perfectly.

"I never saw a man with such concentration. It's tough to be psyched up on every hitter of every game in a 162-game schedule, but Yogi is. He's always deep in thought, 100 percent of the time. He's always in the game. And he talks a lot on the bench. He's completely involved in the game.

"When things were going bad, he always had a smile on his face. He'd shrug his shoulders and say, 'What am I gonna do?' He didn't have much schooling, but he has an education . . . a self-education. There are a lot of people who don't let school interfere with their education. Yogi is one of those people. He erased a lot of doubts by the way he handled himself when we were going bad."

His handling also included getting more out of Cleon Jones than any Met fan had a right to expect. For years Jones had been an enigma for the Mets. Injuries, real or imagined, reduced his extraordinary skills and made him an ordinary player.

Gil Hodges had his problems with Jones and had to embarrass him in 1969, walking all the way out to left field when he thought Cleon showed less than the desired amount of hustle and removing him from the game in full view of a near-capacity crowd at Shea.

Even under Yogi, Jones failed to play up to his potential. He seemed to be operating at half speed most of the time. Yogi's approach was not humiliation but compassion. One day, while the Mets were in San Diego, the manager summoned the left fielder to his hotel room.

"I still feel we have a chance to win this thing," Berra said. "But I'm going to need your help. I need you to hustle, to play all out, every day, to give it your best. If you do, you're the best I've got and you can carry us."

Whatever it was about Yogi's words—his manner of speaking, just the fact that he took the trouble to talk to Jones—it worked. For the last six weeks of the season Cleon Jones was a hitting fool. He carried the Mets on his bat and he played outstanding ball in the field; all this despite painfully sore feet, which have plagued him throughout his career.

"He's hurting," Berra said, "but he's doing a helluva job. In the spring he runs barefoot to toughen his feet. When he got hurt this year, he didn't have a chance to toughen them again, and he's paying the price."

Berra was asked if there was something that could be done, some kind of therapy to soothe Cleon's feet. "I don't know," the manager said. "I wish I could give him two new pair."

Whatever he said to Cleon Jones worked. It worked for Tug McGraw, too, and for Wayne Garrett and Jerry Koosman and Jon Matlack and Harry Parker. It worked for all of them.

On Monday, October 1, the Mets beat the Cubs in the first game of a doubleheader before a handful of chilled fans in

Chicago's Wrigley Field. The victory clinched the title in the National League East, and in the tiny clubhouse, with champagne spurting all around the place and Jerry Grote dumping buckets of ice water on reporters, Tug McGraw climbed on top of a trunk, called for attention, and shouted: "One, two three . . ."

In unison, all the Mets joined in.

"You gotta *bee-leeeeve* . . . you gotta *bee-leeeeve!*"

Yogi Berra was the only one who believed all the time.

"He took the job because he wanted to prove he could manage," said his friend Joe Garagiola. "By God, he proved it. He can manage. He can manage."

13

Family Man

*They tell about the time Carmen Berra returned home from the movies
and was greeted at the front door by an impatient husband.*
"Where you been?" Yogi Berra asked.
"I took Tim to see Doctor Zhivago.*"
"What the hell is wrong with him now?"

It was Saturday, October 6, 1973, game number one of the
National League championship playoffs in Cincinnati's opulent
Riverfront Stadium. In the visitors' dugout Yogi Berra paced the
floor nervously—unusual behavior for the manager of the Mets.

The telephone rang and Berra picked it up on the first ring. It
was Harold Weissman, director of public relations for the Mets,
calling from the press box.

"Massachusetts just beat Rhode Island," Weissman said.

Even from high up in the press box, you could see the smile
on Yogi Berra's face. Now he could stop pacing, stop worrying,
and concentrate on the Mets against the Reds.

It is, perhaps, typical of Berra that he worried more about the
University of Massachusetts football team and the Montclair
High football team than he did about the Mets.

"That's the kind of guy he is," says Joe Garagiola. "Those kids
mean everything to him. He is completely wrapped up in them.

The boys and Carmen. They are the most important things in his life.

"Like the Doctor Zhivago story. He probably never said it, but he could have. And think about why he would have said it. He hears 'doctor' and the first thing he thinks of is that somebody is sick. As a father and a family man, it figures that's the first thing he's going to think of.

"Yogi's got everything a man could want, and his most prized possession is Carmen. And rightfully so. She is a beautiful lady. Not only physically, but in every other way as well."

All three of Yogi's boys have been involved with athletics, and Yogi has always been involved with all the boys. Larry, Jr., the oldest, was following in his father's footsteps. He was a catcher at Montclair State University and later signed with the Mets' organization. But knee surgery ended his career. Tim, the middle one, gained a measure of athletic fame in his own right as a flanker on the University of Massachusetts football team. He set records for pass receiving at the school, and later played briefly with the Baltimore Colts and New York Giants. He had talent, but no interest in baseball.

Dale, the youngest, had the most success of the three. A three-sport star in baseball, football, and hockey at Montclair High, he turned down dozens of offers to play football in college and signed a bonus contract with the Pittsburgh Pirates. He never attained the Hall of Fame success of his father, but Dale had a productive nine-year career with the Pirates and Yankees.

If there was one thing about managing in the 1973 playoffs and World Series that bothered Berra, it was that it kept him from a couple of UMass football games. He kept tabs as closely on the Yankee Conference as he did on the National League.

While it was difficult to engage Berra in conversation regarding his pitching plans for the playoffs or how he would order his pitchers to work on Johnny Bench, it was never any problem getting him to talk about his boys.

"Who does Massachusetts play today?" somebody asked before game one of the playoffs.

"Rhode Island," Yogi replied.

"Oh, an easy one."

"Don't you believe it," Berra said.

"How about Montclair?"

"They play Garfield. If they win this one, they could go all the way."

When the World Series was over, Berra would spend his Saturday afternoons driving up to Amherst, Massachusetts, to see Tim play football. Those were the best of days. He and Carmen would drive up with Mr. and Mrs. Frank Tripucka, their close friends. Tripucka is the former Notre Dame quarterback, and his son, Mark, a quarterback at UMass, was red-shirted in 1973 because of an injury.

On November 3 UMass played Vermont, and it was Salute to Yogi Day. At halftime ceremonies they presented the manager of the Mets with a portrait and a scrapbook of Tim's three varsity seasons.

It was a wonderful day. Tim returned a kickoff 63 yards, caught a few passes, and UMass won, 27–7. Tim Berra didn't score any touchdowns, but he added to his school record for receptions.

"I grew up as a Red Sox fan," said UMass football coach, Dick MacPherson, later the architect of the resurgence of football at Syracuse. "When the Red Sox played the Yankees, the one man I feared was Yogi Berra. In the clutch, the kid's just like his father."

The Berras are a close family. If there is one thing upon which Yogi and the boys disagree, it's the length of their hair. But that doesn't make them any different from any other family.

"He isn't crazy about long hair," Tim says, "but we have no problems communicating. He's concerned about everything we do."

His father, said Tim, didn't change with the NL East standings. He remained the same and continued to express confidence in his team.

"When we [the Mets] began winning," Tim recalled, "all he said was, 'I told you so.'"

His middle son described Berra as "quiet, but not that quiet. We'll laugh at things he says, but my mother really teases him. She'll scold him for saying it and then he'll be careful for a while in public or when she's with him."

In the off-season, when there was no baseball and when he wasn't chasing his boys, driving great distances through snowstorms or rainstorms to watch them play football or hockey, Berra would spend his leisure time at the White Beeches Country Club in Haworth, New Jersey. When weather permitted, he would play a round of golf, sometimes with former Yankee first baseman Joe Collins. If it was too cold for golf, he would play gin rummy at the club.

In recent years, his passion for golf has subsided somewhat, largely because he is too involved with the family business, "Yogi Berra's Health and Racquet Club," in Fairfield, New Jersey. Tim runs the club and Yogi can be seen there every day during the off-season. He'll play a little racquet ball or while away the hours at gin rummy.

"He's an excellent card player," attests former Met coach Joe Pignatano. "He's got great concentration and he can remember every card that has been played."

During his tenure as manager of the Mets, Berra would spend off days on the road playing golf with the coaches or with general manager Bob Scheffing or public relations director Harold Weissman.

"He'll drive you crazy on the golf course," Weissman once said. "He hits right-handed and putts left-handed. At least he's improved. He used to have right-handed drivers and left-handed sand wedges and putters. Now, he only has the left-handed putter."

On the road he would get up early and have breakfast, then return to his hotel room, usually to watch television. "He watches a lot of television," Pignatano said. "He'll watch a test pattern if there's nothing else on. He might take a nap if we have a night game, but we're usually out at the ball park by two or a little later."

At home Berra is much the same. He prefers quiet evenings at home watching television but recognizes his duty to his employer and attends a great many sports banquets in the off-season. Occasionally Carmen can get him to attend the Broadway theater, but mostly he enjoys watching television.

He has trimmed down considerably since his playing days, yet he is hung up on Italian food and considers himself something of a gourmet when it comes to that subject. If you ask him to recommend an Italian restaurant in New York City, he will mention Romeo Salta. Yet he prefers to stay closer to home in New Jersey, and in that case, he will tout Villa Cesare in Hillsdale with all the enthusiasm of a satisfied gourmet.

While he ignores kidding, Carmen once told Joe Donnelly of the Long Island newspaper *Newsday* that he "can hardly take offense to it when he's quite a needler himself. If they get on him, he reminds them they're bald, fat, or have a big nose. They get what's coming to them and so does he.

"Yogi is so much more interested in people than he used to be years ago. He's grown. Maybe not in world affairs. I'm involved in political research in my district. The other night I was kidding a friend, 'I won't speak to you unless you vote for McGovern.' Yogi comes in and says, 'Who the hell is McGovern?' Can you imagine that? But don't paint him a simple man. Maybe he is not involved with world affairs. But he loves to listen and learn from his educated friends."

And Yogi has thousands of friends, educated or not. He is the kind of man who inspires friendship because he comes across as a kind, humble, likable human being.

On the night Mickey Mantle and Whitey Ford were voted into the Hall of Fame, the New York Baseball Writers Association held an annual party. The guests of honor were Lee MacPhail, departing Yankee general manager, and Ralph Houk, departing Yankee manager, but no speaker could very well ignore the presence of Ford or Mantle or Berra, the successful, pennant-winning manager of the Mets.

When he was called on to speak, Mickey Mantle spent his time discussing MacPhail, Ford, and Houk. When he returned to his chair, Mickey asked the man next to him, "Did I mention Yogi?"

He was told he hadn't.

"Damn," he said. "I wanted to, but I get so nervous standing up there, I forgot what I wanted to say. I wanted to tell Yogi what a great pleasure it was being his teammate for so many years, and especially what a great thrill it was being his friend for so many years. I hope I get a chance to see him later. I want him to know how I feel."

In all likelihood, Yogi Berra already knew.

14

"Mr. Grant Wants to See You"

The relationship between Frank Scott and Yogi Berra goes back many years. As road secretary for the Yankees, Scott was responsible for the comfort of Berra and his teammates. Later, as the first of sports agents, Scott helped Berra and others supplement their baseball income with endorsements and personal appearances.

With this long-standing relationship, Frank Scott was among the privileged few who felt free to ask Berra for World Series tickets.

"Okay," said Berra, "but no checks. You gotta have cash, and you gotta pick the tickets up at my house. I'm not goin' in the ticket business."

Scott agreed and waited until Berra called him one day.

"Your tickets are here," Yogi said. "Come pick them up."

As he was leaving his home, Scott's daughter asked him to look after her dog while she was away.

"Okay," said Scott, "but I'll have to take him with me to Yogi's house."

Scott put the dog, a big beautiful Afghan show dog, in his new Chevrolet Camaro and drove off to pick up his World Series tickets at the Berra home. When he arrived, Yogi was practicing putting on his front lawn. Scott parked his car, rolled down the window of his Camaro slightly so his daughter's Afghan could get some air, and went to conduct his business.

Berra produced the tickets. Scott produced the cash and then noticed Yogi staring at his car.

"Oh," said Scott, "what do you think of my daughter's Afghan?"
"Nice," said Berra. "I was thinking of getting a Vega myself."

What happened when the Mets got to the 1973 World Series was really of minor importance, because getting there was so much fun and totally unexpected.

The same may be said for the league playoffs. When the Mets came through to win the title in the NL East in the closest race in memory, they had done enough to ensure a successful season and to save Yogi Berra's job. Nobody counted on them to beat the powerful Cincinnati Reds in the playoff, and there would be no shame if they didn't. But they had momentum going for them, and superior pitching, which is always a great advantage in a short series.

Even when Jack Billingham outpitched Tom Seaver, 2–1, in the first game, the Mets were still alive. Seaver struck out 13 Reds and had them shut out until Pete Rose homered in the eighth to tie and Johnny Bench homered in the ninth to win.

Young Jon Matlack rekindled the dream with a two-hit shutout in the second game, and the Mets returned to Shea Stadium tied, one game apiece, in their drive for a pennant.

The Mets exploded early and Pete Rose exploded late in game number three. The Mets won on the lusty hitting of Rusty Staub, while Rose aroused his teammates and incurred the wrath of Met fans by going in hard against Bud Harrelson at second base and coming up swinging. Met fans showered Rose with debris as he stood in left field and Cincinnati manager Sparky Anderson pulled his team off the field until order could be restored.

Yogi Berra and Willie Mays led a delegation that went to left field to plead with the fans to cease and desist. It worked, and the game went on. And Rose's maneuver worked, too. He had inspired his teammates, and the following day drilled a 12th-inning home run to lead the Reds to a 2–1 victory that tied the series at two games each.

Now the pennant—an entire season—rested on the outcome of one game. And the Mets had Tom Seaver going for them once again, plus the incalculable advantage of their home field.

In the last of the fifth, the Mets broke a 2–2 tie with a four-run rally, and when Seaver loaded the bases in the ninth, Tug McGraw came in to get the last two outs, and the Mets were champions of the National League.

"You gotta *bee-leeeeve*," shouted Tug McGraw. "You gotta *bee-leeeeve!*"

Now the Mets were in the World Series against the Oakland A's, a team that had pitching plus power. They also had Charles O. Finley and the most remarkable collection of beards and mustaches this side of a 1920s saloon. And they were defending champions.

"I don't know too much about them," admitted Yogi Berra. "I don't know anything at all about that Blando [third baseman Sal Bando] and Campanis [shortstop Bert Campaneris]."

As anticipated, the first game in Oakland, left-handers Ken Holtzman versus Jon Matlack, was a pitchers' duel. What was totally unexpected was the outcome, the Mets losing, 2–1, on an error by their most reliable fielder, second baseman Felix Millan.

Game two was one of those incredible phenomena that occur in a World Series and would be recalled and replayed for decades. It lasted four hours and 13 minutes, and it wasn't particularly well played, but it was a stomach-churner.

The Mets broke a 6–6 tie with four runs in the top of the 12th and won, 10–7, but not until George Stone put down a 12th-inning Oakland uprising by getting Campy Campaneris on a ground ball to shortstop with the tying runs on base.

Berra distinguished himself in the Series, as he had all season, by making a move and sticking with it; not panicking under pressure, not changing for the sake of change.

"Were you apprehensive in the 12th inning?" someone asked Berra in the postgame interview.

"No," said the manager of the Mets. "But I was scared."

The Mets ran into an outstanding pitcher in game three—a young man named Jim Hunter, called Catfish, because once, when he was a boy, he left home to go fishing and when his worried parents found him, he had a mess of catfish. Once again, it was Tom Seaver's misfortune to be pitted against an outstanding opponent. Tom struck out 12 in eight innings, including slugger Reggie Jackson three times, but lost, 3–2.

Jon Matlack made things right again in the fourth game, beating the A's, 6–1, on a five-hitter as Rusty Staub drove in five of the Met runs.

When Jerry Koosman and Tug McGraw combined for a three-hit shutout in game number five, the Mets had a 3–2 lead in the Series. They returned to Oakland needing just one victory in two games to complete their latest miracle, to accomplish the impossible.

All things considered, what happened in those final two games in Oakland on Saturday and Sunday, the 20th and 21st of October, are of little importance to the saga of Yogi Berra and the Mets. Tom Seaver failed again and was beaten by Catfish Hunter for the second time, and Jon Matlack had nothing when he tried to pitch the seventh game with only three days' rest. Campaneris and Reggie Jackson slammed him for homers, and the A's went on to win their second straight world championship.

There was no reason for the Mets to be ashamed of their showing in the World Series, no reason for Yogi Berra to have any regrets or to second-guess any of his moves. He managed in the playoffs and the World Series as he had throughout the entire season, and almost pulled off a great victory against overwhelming odds.

It was a great finish to a strange year; Yogi Berra would be rewarded, and handsomely. On the charter flight back from Oakland, General Manager Bob Scheffing slipped into a seat next to Berra and said, "Take a day off tomorrow and rest up, then Mr. Grant would like to see you the following day at 9:30 in the morning."

Berra couldn't help flashing back nine years, to another charter flight after another disappointing defeat in the seventh game of the World Series when another general manager had slipped into the seat next to him and said the boss wanted to see him back in New York. That time, when he kept his appointment, Berra had gotten the shocking news that he would not be rehired. This time it was different.

He arrived for his meeting with Mr. Donald Grant a few minutes before 9:30.

"We had a little coffee and we talked," Grant said. "He asked for a three-year contract, and I asked him if he wouldn't be just as happy with two. I said I could go to the board of directors and recommend either two or three years. I thought two was best, but I wanted him to be satisfied."

"New York is my home, now," Yogi replied. "I don't want to go no place else."

That was all there was to it. The meeting broke up before ten, and Grant went to meet with the board of directors of the Mets. He recommended three years, and the board approved it. And Yogi was signed for three years at $75,000 per year.

"We were just showing Yogi that we'd like to have him around awhile," explained Bob Scheffing.

There was no big press conference in any fancy New York hotel to announce the news. The Mets made the announcement by telephoning the local papers and radio stations and wire services. While Harold Weissman and Matt Winick were making their calls, the manager of the Mets was on the golf course of the White Beeches Country Club in Haworth, New Jersey.

15

Home Again

Billy Martin was visibly distressed. The manager of the Yankees had locked his keys inside his new Lincoln Mark V with no way to get them out. A wire coat hanger could not be forced inside the air-tight window. Martin was stymied and greatly concerned as he arrived at the Yankees' training facility in Fort Lauderdale early one spring morning.

Yogi Berra noticed that Martin was particularly irritable and he attempted to be solicitous of his old friend.

"What'sa matter, Billy?" Berra asked.

"Aw, I locked my keys in my car," Martin replied. "I don't know how I'm going to get in there."

"That's easy," Berra decided. "You gotta call a blacksmith."

The first time was a shock because it was so unexpected and because he had won a pennant and extended the St. Louis Cardinals to the seventh game of the World Series. The second time was not so shocking.

It's never easy being fired as a manager, the first time, the second time, or the fifth time, but there are degrees of pain. Yogi Berra had no inkling of impending doom and unemployment when he was summoned to the office of the Yankee co-owner Dan Topping that October morning in 1964. When the Mets relieved him of his managing duties on August 5, 1975, and replaced him with Roy McMillan, he was not surprised.

Rumors had run rampant for weeks that Berra's days as manager of the Mets were numbered. After their dramatic and miraculous comeback in 1973, the team sputtered and fizzled, finishing a well-beaten fifth in 1974. And when there was no appreciable improvement in 1975, Berra was fired with the Mets in third place in the National League East with a record of 56–53. For the first time in 33 summers, Berra was home in Montclair, New Jersey, playing golf during the baseball season instead of being in uniform.

His unemployment lasted only a few months. One day, Yankee manager Billy Martin placed a telephone call to his old friend.

"Yogi," Martin said, "I want you to be one of my coaches next season."

At first, Berra was reluctant. The hurt of his firing by the Yankees 11 years earlier still lived within him. But Martin was persuasive.

"Yogi," Martin argued, "you're a Yankee. You belong here. Come back where you belong. The people who fired you are gone. There are new people running the team now. Come back. Be with me."

Eventually, Berra agreed. He would return as a coach with the Yankees. They would unpack his familiar No. 8 and he would return to Yankee Stadium, the scene of his greatest accomplishments.

It was a triumphant return, almost MacArthur-like. Yogi Berra was back in Yankee pinstripes where he belonged; all was right with the world. And as luck would have it—Berra Luck—in his first season back, the Yankees won their first pennant in a dozen seasons, since Berra himself had led them to their last championship in 1964. The Yankees followed their 1976 pennant with their first world championship in 15 years, then won another world championship in 1978. Three seasons as coach, three pennants, two world championships. Berra Luck was in force once more.

The fans loved having him back, the players enjoyed having

him around, and the sportswriters and story tellers had a field day with him.

Once, during spring training, a writer traveling with the Yankees noticed that each evening, Berra would be wearing a different colored sweater. One night it was dark blue, the next night light blue, a third night red, a fourth night yellow.

"Hey, Yog," the writer remarked. "How many of those sweaters do you have? You must have every color they make."

"Nah," he said. "I got every color but navy brown."

It was a time of turmoil and turbulence with the Yankees. Controversy swirled around the team almost daily because of the volatile mix of personalities, a *dramatis personae* that consisted of George Steinbrenner, the egomaniacal, meddlesome, and demanding owner; Billy Martin, the feisty, combative, and competitive manager; Reggie Jackson, the opinionated, loquacious, braggadocio superstar slugger; and Thurman Munson, the stubborn, sensitive, and insecure captain and catcher. Hardly a day elapsed in which one, two, three, or all of these individuals did not create some controversy. In addition, there were minor role players who contributed to an atmosphere in the Yankee clubhouse that prompted pitcher Sparky Lyle to refer to it as "The Bronx Zoo."

As veteran third baseman Graig Nettles wittily explained, "When I was a kid, I always wanted to do two things—play in the major leagues or join the circus. I've been lucky. I got to do both."

While controversy and discontent permeated the Yankees in the seventies, Berra remained immune to it all. Good, old, lovable Yogi, everybody's friend, took it all in stride, avoided the eye of the hurricane, and went about his business with a smile on his face.

Even when managers and coaches were coming and going like so many gypsies, the one constant in pinstripes was Berra. He was the hero and the legend, an untouchable.

For eight years, Berra watched Yankee managers come and go

while he retained his place in the dugout, impervious to any purge. There were nine manager changes in eight seasons, until finally Berra could be overlooked no longer. When finally there was no one else to whom George Steinbrenner could turn after Billy Martin failed in his third stint as Yankee manager, Berra was asked to take over for the 1984 season.

He was no babe in the woods. He had seen more than one Yankee manager crumble under the relentless pressure of the involved owner. He knew he could not escape, that it would be no different for him than it was for any of the others. Yet something made him accept the job. The competitive fires within him had not been extinguished. The excitement and challenge of managing had not quite vanished.

"I want to prove I can manage," Berra told Joe Garagiola, who pleaded with Yogi not to take the job. At a packed press conference, George Steinbrenner introduced his new manager, a popular choice. The owner talked of Yankee tradition and pride and of loyalty, and reflected on the triumphs of the Hall of Fame catcher. It was a wonderful day for Yankee fans, a proud day for Yogi Berra.

The honeymoon did not last very long. The pressure mounted early. The disenchantment set in almost immediately, in spring training, even before Berra had managed a game that mattered. The owner was displeased with losing certain exhibition games. He openly criticized Berra's lack of preparation, assailed his training methods, second-guessed his decisions.

As difficult as spring training was for him, Berra still managed to get off a few accidental *bon mots* to be added to the Yogi legacy of malaprops. On one particularly blistering hot and humid day in Fort Lauderdale, Berra came off the practice field and fell into the chair in his office, exhausted and parched from the morning's activity.

"Hey, Nick," he shouted to clubhouse custodian Nick Priore, "bring me a diet Tab."

The 1984 season would be Yogi Berra's purgatory. The sniping and meddling got to be so unbearable, Berra returned to smoking, a habit he had quit for several years. By the start of the season, he was practically chain-smoking Lucky Strikes as his job seemed to be on the line with every game, the scale tipping with each victory or defeat.

The Detroit Tigers broke quickly from the gate in one of those perfect seasons when everything comes together. Meanwhile, Berra's Yankees started slowly and floundered through the first two months of the season. On June 1, Berra's job hung by a thread. The Yankees were already well back in the race and at least one newspaper reported that Berra was about to be fired and replaced by none other than Billy Martin.

Somehow Berra managed to escape that tight spot, extricating himself from a situation that seemed unconquerable, even for a Houdini. He rallied his team for a second-half comeback that enabled the Yankees to finish a respectable third with a record of 87–75, and he showed his baseball acumen and his willingness to gamble by converting Dave Righetti from a starting pitcher to a reliever. Righetti saved 31 games in 1984 and, to Berra's everlasting credit, the left-hander became the premier relief pitcher in the American League.

Berra's reward for his good deeds was the renewal of his contract for the 1985 season and the promise of fidelity from his boss. On February 20, 1985, the day spring training opened for the Yankees in Fort Lauderdale, George Steinbrenner publicly endorsed his manager and vowed his loyalty to Berra.

"Yogi will be the manager this year, period," Steinbrenner announced. "I said the same thing last year and I stuck to my word. A bad start will not affect Yogi's status either. In the past, I have put a lot of pressure on my managers to win at certain times. That will not be the case this spring."

Yogi Berra was fired on April 25, 1985, after the Yankees had played only 16 games of a 162-game season.

The sad part of his firing is that Berra had looked forward to this season probably more than any other. During the winter, in need of a spare infielder, the Yankees had made a trade with the Pittsburgh Pirates to acquire Dale Berra. Yogi had long dreamed of having his youngest son on a team he coached or managed and now that dream had come true.

Some people criticized the move, suggesting it would be a difficult situation for father or son, or both, one that would lead to problems, especially with other members of the team. The person who knew the principals best predicted there would be no problems.

"The only problem will be in the minds of other people," said Carmen Berra. "You have to know the individuals involved. You have to know that with Yogi, the most important thing is the team. Winning comes first. And he's not going to favor Dale at the expense of the team just because he's his son.

"And you have to know Dale. He idolizes his father. He's not going to do anything to jeopardize Yogi's job. I do know this about Dale. If Yogi is fired and Dale is still there, he'll play as hard for the next manager as he did for his father."

Dale was asked how he would address his father/manager during the season. His reply was direct and logical, befitting the son of Yogi.

"I'm not going to call him 'Skip,'" Dale said. "That would be silly. Who would I be kidding? Everybody knows he's my father. So I'll call him what I've always called him. 'Dad.'"

But it was Yogi who put things in their proper perspective when asked how he planned to use Dale and what advantage Dale would derive from being the manager's son. Never one to waste words, Berra's reply was succinct and simple.

"If he hits, he plays," the manager said. "If he don't hit, he sits."

Steinbrenner's promise not to harass Berra during spring training proved to be so many hollow words. When the Yankees lost certain exhibition games, the criticism began. By the time the Yankees broke camp and headed for New York, the rumors were flying again that Berra's job was in danger.

The rift between owner and manager widened over the wisdom of holding a team workout on a day off in New York. Steinbrenner wanted the team to work. Berra thought his players would benefit more from rest than work. As a compromise, a workout was scheduled, but it was to be voluntary, not mandatory. When only six players showed up, Steinbrenner had more ammunition to use against his manager, and the rumors of Berra's imminent dismissal became a loud report.

"That shows the respect his players have for their manager," Steinbrenner said. "They have heard the rumors that his job is on the line, yet only six of them showed up to help save him."

The last straw was a three-game sweep by the White Sox in Chicago, the final game of the three being lost on a bases-loaded walk in the bottom of the ninth inning. But Steinbrenner had already made up his mind. He dispatched club representative Clyde King to Chicago with orders to inform Berra that he was being replaced. The new manager would be Billy Martin—for the fourth time.

Players reacted angrily to the news; the same players who failed to show at the voluntary workout. Veteran Don Baylor overturned a trash basket when he heard of Berra's firing. Don Mattingly read the press release, then crumpled it and tossed it against the wall.

Naturally, no player took the news any harder than Dale Berra. He went immediately to the manager's office and, with tears in his eyes, threw his arms around his father and hugged him.

"Don't you worry about me," said Berra with customary class. "I've done everything in baseball there is to do. So don't worry, I'll be all right. But you're still young. You have a future. Billy's a good man. Play hard for him. I'll be watching."

The Yankees would pack their gear and head for the airport and their trip to Texas. Berra would pack his gear and also head for the airport, but his destination was New Jersey. He asked the clubhouse attendant to call for a taxi. But Clyde King insisted that he ride the team bus and be dropped off. Berra accepted.

When the bus pulled up at the terminal, Berra was the first to get off. He walked to the front of the bus and turned and waved to his players, who applauded him spontaneously.

The next day, in Arlington, Texas, Martin assumed the reins of the team. The first thing he did was call a team meeting. He had something to say.

"You say you liked Yogi, then why didn't you show him you liked him?" Martin said. "Why didn't you play for him? If you had played for him, he would still be here and I'd be off somewhere fishing and we'd all be happy. I didn't get Yogi fired, you did because you didn't play for him."

Then Martin's gaze fell on Dale Berra, sitting glumly by his locker, his head in his hands. Martin had known Dale since he was a baby and he had something special to say to Berra's youngest son.

"Dale," Martin said, "I want you to know that your father and I have been friends for years. Changing jobs is not going to change that."

A few days later, Berra finally spoke with the press. He was at home in Montclair, enjoying the spring weather, catching up on his golf, when he took the time to be interviewed. It can be considered significant that he never mentioned George Steinbrenner by name.

"Hurt?" he said. "Yeah, I'm hurt a little. But what the hell. You get fired, you get fired. I'm a big boy and he's the boss. He can do whatever he wants. And you can't say I didn't have an inkling."

Time would prove that Berra was hurt more than just a little.

He would resist all efforts by Steinbrenner and his aides to get him back to the Stadium to discuss a job with the organization.

His public posture was noncommittal, not vindicative, but Berra would not return for the annual Old Timers' Day and he would not be seen in Yankee Stadium. Privately, he vowed never to go to Yankee Stadium again.

16

"Most Everybody Knows Me by My Face"

One night, Yogi and Carmen settled down after dinner to watch television. A movie buff with a particular penchant for westerns, Berra had talked for days about seeing this particular flick, The Magnificent Seven, starring Steve McQueen.

"He made that picture before he died," Berra explained.

Every attempt to entice Yogi Berra back to the Yankees failed. Lou Piniella tried, asking Berra to be his bench coach after he was named manager for the 1986 season. Billy Martin, acting as agent for George Steinbrenner, tried. Berra stubbornly and steadfastly refused all offers, put off all overtures. That's how hurt he was over his latest firing.

The thought of Berra not being in a baseball uniform when spring training began was inconceivable. Except during the war, he had not missed spring training since he was 18 years old. His name was synonymous with baseball. He had so much to offer the game.

It was Berra's close friend and Montclair neighbor, Dr. John McMullen, who came to Yogi's rescue.

McMullen was the principal stockholder of the American Shipbuilding Company, of which George Steinbrenner is chairman of the board. When Steinbrenner assembled a group to buy the Yankees from the Columbia Broadcasting System in 1973, he asked McMullen to join him as a limited partner. It was years later that McMullen said, "Nothing is more limited than being a limited partner of George Steinbrenner."

Bitten by the baseball bug, McMullen purchased the Houston Astros from Judge Roy Hofheinz and continued as an absentee owner, running the team from his New Jersey home. Later, he would add to his growing sports empire by purchasing the New Jersey Devils of the National Hockey League.

Berra is an avid hockey fan and he often attended Devils' games as the guest of McMullen. It was at one of these games that McMullen broached the idea of Yogi going to the Astros as a coach. It wasn't New York, but it was baseball, and Yogi belonged in baseball.

Confident that he could work for a close friend, who would look after him, Berra accepted the offer with the stipulation that he be accepted by whomever would take over the then-managerless Astros.

No manager in his right mind would object to having the legendary Yogi on his coaching staff, especially in light of Berra's close relationship with the Astros' owner. But when Hal Lanier was named as manager, his approval and endorsement of Berra was genuine. Hal's dad, Max Lanier, had pitched for the St. Louis Cardinals when Berra was breaking into pro ball and they spent time together in St. Louis during the off-season. Besides, as a rookie manager, Lanier recognized the value of having Berra's years of experience and knowledge from which to draw.

"He'll be a big asset to our club," Lanier said. "Yogi has been exposed to every aspect of the game. He has coached first base and third base as well as managed."

At the press conference announcing his appointment, Berra modestly admitted he was widely recognized around the country and denied that he was the author of many of the quotes attributed to him.

"Most everybody knows me by my face," he admitted. As for all those quips and one-liners?

"I really didn't say everything I said," Berra insisted.

He went off to spring training—his 41st consecutive spring training, but the first one in which he was not wearing a uniform that belonged to a team from New York—and visitors found it strange when they saw him in the Houston uniform. The face was familiar, the only one like it in the world. The No. 8 on the back was familiar. But the uniform looked like somebody had left a box of crayons in the pocket when it was put in the washer and the colors splattered all over.

Mention that to him and Berra would smile that familiar, toothy, Ernest Borgnine smile. If you were looking for complaints, if you thought you would get grumbling and finger-pointing, then you had come to the wrong place and to the wrong man.

Even in the uniform of the Houston Astros, Yogi Berra was a contented man. It is his rare gift that he can be at home in any place, in any situation; that he holds no grudges.

It would have been so easy to be bitter. The firing was sudden, unwarranted, after only 16 games. It stung him deeply. So did some remarks attributed to Billy Martin that seemed to impugn his managerial ability and his preparedness. But Berra would not retaliate. That was never his way. His way is to see the good in all people or to see nothing at all.

"We're gonna score some runs," he said, switching the conversation to baseball.

The positive approach, always positive. He might have talked about the Astros' defensive deficiencies or the thin pitching.

"Wait 'til you see this kid at first base," Berra said. "His name is Glenn Davis, just like the old Army football player. Big. Strong. He can hit. Had three homers the other day."

To Yogi Berra, loyalty was not a one-way street, so when John McMullen asked him to come aboard as a coach, he agreed. But he would not manage.

"Never again," he said. "I told John that."

Perhaps McMullen thought he was doing Berra a favor, giving him a job, keeping him in uniform. Perhaps Berra thought he was doing McMullen a favor, bringing his famous countenance and his name to Houston. It might sell some tickets or he might help get a rookie manager over the hump. It doesn't matter who was doing a favor for whom. With friends, it never does. And Yogi was just happy to be back in the game.,

"I'll get to go to St. Louis," he said. "I haven't been there in years."

There were still friends there, and family.

"I'll get home to New Jersey when we play in New York and Philadelphia," he said. "One good thing about playing in the Dome, you can make plans. You know you're not going to be rained out. And when there's a day off, you know you're gonna be off."

That was a veiled reference to George Steinbrenner's penchant for turning days off into mandatory workouts, and it was the closest Berra would come to putting the knock on the man who fired him.

He would continue to follow the Yankees, Berra said, because his son Dale was still held hostage there, because he liked Lou Piniella and because, no matter what, in his heart he would always be a Yankee. It is not surprising that the first thing he asked when he spotted a visitor from New York was, "How are things over there? How is Lou doing?"

His advice to Piniella? "Tell him to let it go in here [pointing to his left ear] and come out here [pointing to his right ear]. And one other thing," he said. "Win. Don't lose two games in a row."

But that was in the past. He was an Astro now and he had made the transition surprisingly comfortably.

"We play the Mets in May," he said. "Carm is going to stay home and then come down when we go back to Houston. We got a nice place, right near the Galleria shopping center. I hope she doesn't spend all her time shopping."

He had turned 60 and he did not have to work another day if he chose not to. But he could not stay away from the game that had been his life for almost half a century.

"I love it," he said. "Maybe it's because I always did, all the way back to American Legion ball. And in the Navy, I traveled a lot."

He is a person of such simple tastes, it never took much to make Yogi Berra happy. A uniform. A ball game. A feeling of being wanted.

He would go around spreading sunshine and joy that year, goofing with kids younger than his own. They respected him, idolized him, and liked him—and it was genuine.

"It's just great having a Hall of Famer on the team," said pitcher Charlie Kerfeld. "My dad talks about him all the time. Sometimes, I feel sorry for him. Whenever we get off the team bus, he gets mobbed. The thing I like best about Yogi is he's so down to earth. He's such a good person. He's always there if I need to talk."

Astros general manager Dick Wagner recalled that the Astros wanted Berra to bring the lineup card out to the umpire before games so that fans could get a glimpse of the legend. Yogi was uncomfortable about it.

"He didn't want to take anything away from Hal or the other coaches," Wagner said. "He's outgoing but quiet and he worries about upstaging other people. That's the way he is. That's just Yogi."

The 1986 season passed quickly for Berra. He was right on target about the young Astros' first baseman, the kid with the same name as the old Army football player. Glenn Davis hit 31 home runs and drove in 101 runs. And the Berra mystique continued. So did the Berra Luck.

Organized as an expansion team in 1962, the Astros had never won a division championship until 1986, the season Berra joined the team. It figured. They won the National League West, but were beaten by the New York Mets in the Championship Series. What do you want, everything at once?

17

"Thank You for Making This Necessary"

The well-groomed, rather matronly woman engaged Yogi Berra in conversation at a cocktail party, and the talk got around to Yogi's activities outside of baseball. He mentioned that, among other things, he was vice-president of the Yoo-Hoo Chocolate Drink Company.
"Yoo-Hoo?" the woman inquired. "Is that hyphenated?"
"Lady," Berra replied, "it ain't even carbonated."

The poll was conducted in 1974 as an independent survey by the Alan R. Nelson Research Company. Some 2,500 men were asked to rate well-known sports personalities under four categories: 1) awareness of the person; 2) admiration and respect for the individual's ability or talent; 3) how well they liked the person; and 4) how much they trusted the person's endorsement.

The results were somewhat surprising. In the awareness category, Willie Mays was first, followed by Joe Namath, Muhammad Ali, Mickey Mantle, Arnold Palmer, Howard Cosell, and Yogi Berra. In admiration and respect, Berra was 11th. In likability, Musial was first, then came Johnny Bench, Mays, and Berra. In trust for a person's endorsement, Musial was first, Mantle second, Berra third.

The last category was considered the most important because it suggested to Madison Avenue which sports personality would be the most effective for an ad campaign. In advertising, believability converts to effectiveness, and Yogi Berra was totally believable.

"The reason he's believable," said Jerry Della Femina, president of the ad agency Della Femina, Travisano & Partners, "is because of all the stories that have been written about him through all the years—stories attributed to him to make him seem dumb. The American public has heard those stories for so many years, they believe them, and the stories make it impossible to believe that Berra is smart enough to do something evil. The public associates intelligence with evil. A person who is smart can be devious. A person who is not smart cannot be devious.

"In this respect, even though these stories are not true, they have helped Berra's credibility. So when he tells you to use this product, it gives that product believability because Berra has believability."

There was, said Della Femina, an opposite reaction to Joe Namath. "He has been painted as a guy who makes wise remarks, and that destroys his believability. The image Berra conveys is that he's not capable of lying. If a man says funny things accidentally, it means he doesn't stop to think before he talks. To lie, to have to stop and think before you talk. You know Yogi isn't stopping and thinking, therefore you believe he's telling the truth at all times. I believe I can sell anything with Yogi Berra."

As a case in point, there was the hair spray commercial that Della Femina created when he worked for another agency.

"We had this hair spray account," Della Femina recalled. "Sales were slipping, and it was our job to boost them. In talking with friends, I found out that a lot of men were using their wives' hair spray, but on the sly, as if it was something to be ashamed of. This was before there were men's hair sprays on the market and it became a common thing for men to use hair spray. I figured we could get a jump on the male market by doing a commercial showing that you don't have to be a sissy to use your wife's hair spray. We decided to use athletes, immediately creating the impression that these men are virile and masculine, and if they could use hair spray, so could anyone. But we didn't want just any athletes. We wanted sports figures that looked the part."

They chose three, for three different reasons. One was Joe Pepitone, who had the reputation for being a playboy and who had already been getting attention because he was using hair dryers and hair spray in the Yankees' dressing room. Another was Hank Bauer, whose face had been described as "looking like a clenched fist." He wore his hair in a crew cut, but no matter. The point was that nobody would dare call Bauer, a tough-looking ex-Marine, a sissy. The third was Berra, for his image, his believability, his visibility, and because he looked like the average working guy.

None of the three said a word in the commercial. They merely sprayed their hair while a voice said, "Joe Pepitone [or Hank Bauer or Yogi Berra] is one of those sissies who uses his wife's hair spray."

The commercial won awards and, more importantly, boosted sales.

"That commercial was shot in 1966," said Della Femina. "To this day, I still have clients and colleagues who remember it. They refer to it as the Yogi Berra Hair Spray Commercial. They have long since forgotten the name of the product [Ozon] or the two other guys in the commercial, but they remember Yogi. That's believability, recognizability, whatever you want to call it.

"Incidentally," Della Femina added, "Berra is supposed to be dumb, but he got more money than the other two, and he didn't even have an agent."

Years later, an agency called Levine, Huntley, Schmidt was working on a campaign for Jockey underwear. Their campaign was built around the theme that there are two different kinds of people in the world—the white underwear people and the colored underwear people. Because they were successful playing Bart Starr's Mr. Straight to Paul Hornung's Mr. Swinger, they decided to use another sports personality.

"Yogi was Mr. Straight, Mr. America, Mr. White Underwear," said Howard Levine. "Now we needed somebody to play off him. Somebody remembered that he had three sons, so we decided to see what they looked like. They were perfect. They were three good-looking kids, with long hair, very mod. They were colored underwear types, and to use them with their father was perfect in those days of the generation gap."

There still were two minor problems. One was that Yogi's Mets were in last place when the idea was conceived.

"He might get fired before the commercial runs," said somebody at Levine, Huntley, Schmidt.

"So what?" said another. "Everybody knows Yogi and likes him. He's a great guy, a lovable fellow. That's not going to change even if he does get fired."

The other reason was that the people of Jockey International, back in Kenosha, Wisconsin, might think the Berra and Sons idea was too regional, too New York. It turned out to be no concern at all.

"The client loved the idea," Howard Levine said. "They convinced me that Yogi was a national personality. Not only did he transcend New York, he transcended sports."

They shot the commercial and it was a hit—Yogi singing the praises of white underwear, the boys expressing their preference for colored underwear. "Where did I go wrong?" Yogi Berra asks as the commercial ends.

The answer is that he didn't . . . neither with his boys nor with himself. As a matter of fact, Yogi Berra has done just about everything right. In some cases, the best thing he has done is nothing at all—nothing except being his own lovable, believable, recognizable self.

"It's incredible," said Joe Pignatano, a coach for the Mets under Berra. "Wherever he goes, people recognize him. In airports, at hotels, on the street. People don't give him a moment's peace. It was that way not only when he was a manager, but also as a coach."

In St. Petersburg, on Ash Wednesday, 1971, Berra went to St. Mary's Church to receive ashes on his forehead, an annual ritual of the Catholic Church. The church was crowded with worshipers and there were lines of people waiting to have ashes administered by a priest. Yogi got in the line and awaited his turn as the line moved up slowly. Finally, he was face-to-face with an elderly priest who looked up, saw that familiar face, and put out his hand.

"Hello, Yogi, how are you?" said the priest, who proceeded to engage Berra in conversation. A woman behind Berra began to grow impatient as the priest and ex-ballplayer talked.

"Wait just a minute, Madam," said the priest. "Can't you see I'm talking to Yogi Berra?"

Another time at Sunday mass in Atlanta, the priest delivered his sermon from the pulpit, then paused to make a special announcement.

"Forgive me for getting personal and for being a little excited," said the young priest. "But I grew up in New Jersey, in the shadow of Yankee Stadium, and I was a great Yankee fan. I would like you all to say a special prayer for one of my old heroes, Yogi Berra, worshiping with us here today."

Pignatano remembered another incident in Atlanta.

"Yogi and I went to the movies," he recalled. "I walked up to the booth, paid my money, and got my ticket. When Yogi got to the booth, the cashier said, 'Oh, no, Mr. Berra. There's no charge for you.'

"I told him, 'Next time you go first, and if they don't charge you, tell them I'm with you.'"

That story reminded Pignatano of another. He had a friend in the clothing business who invited him to come down and pick out some clothes at a wholesale discount. Piggy took advantage of the offer and invited coach Eddie Yost and Yogi Berra to go with him.

"We picked out some clothes," Pignatano said, "and when it was time to pay, I paid wholesale. Eddie paid retail. And there was no charge for Yogi."

Pignatano never resented the attention Berra got. He rather enjoyed it. "He's good people," said Joe. "He's an honest man. You can't ask any more than that of anybody."

Mets' general manager Frank Cashen remembers attending the Mardi Gras in New Orleans one year with Berra.

"Yogi was with some pals," Cashen said. "I was with some pals. Glen Campbell was supposed to be the King of Bacchus that year. But you know what? Yogi was the king of the Mardi Gras. It was unbelievable. At breakfast, on Bourbon Street, in the saloons, they just all wanted to talk to Yogi. I never forgot that. In baseball, out of baseball, I've never met anyone who does not like this man."

Perhaps the best example of Berra's far-flung fame came from George Theodore, once a young prospect in the Mets' farm system. In January 1972, Joe McDonald, director of minor league operations for the Mets at the time, received a letter, instead of a signed contract from Theodore, who was "entrenched in boredom, regression and stagnation."

Included in the letter were Theodore's five contract demands, in addition to his desired salary:

1. A pair of athletic glasses.
2. Models of bats, different styles and weights, for experimentation.
3. Met emblem stickers; I need about a dozen.
4. The address of the Players Association; I owe them two years' back dues.

5. I have been a Met almost three years and I'm ashamed to say I've never met Yogi Berra.

McDonald met Theodore's first four demands and promised he would do his best to take care of the fifth when the opportunity presented itself. It came that spring on Payson Field in St. Petersburg. Berra had come to see his son, Larry, Jr., then in the Mets' farm system, and McDonald asked Yogi if he would do him a favor.

"There's this kid named George Theodore," he said. "He's a pretty good prospect and I promised him I'd introduce you to him."

"All George said was, 'I'm very happy to meet you,' then he trotted off happily," McDonald said.

There is no reason to believe the events are related, but as a postscript to the story, Theodore caught Berra's eye in spring camp the following season and was kept with the big club all year, although few thought he had a chance to make the big leagues so soon, if ever.

"I like him," Berra explained, "because he makes contact. He don't strike out a lot."

For as long as anyone can remember, Yogi Berra has been attracting attention. It was for this reason he was asked to do an episode on the popular daytime soap opera, "General Hospital." This was back in 1963 when Yogi was a player-coach with the Yankees and "General Hospital" was a struggling infant on TV. The show's star, Johnny Berardino, had played 11 seasons in the big leagues with the St. Louis Browns and Cleveland Indians in the American League from 1939 until 1952 with time out for military duty, part of his career overlapping with Berra's.

Berardino used his baseball background to get famous ballplayers to make cameo appearances. It was, Berardino freely confesses, an attempt to give the show a push in its early days.

"We got a lot of mileage out of having Yogi on the show,"

Berardino admitted. "And that's exactly what our intention was. I wouldn't say I was a good friend of his, but I knew him as an opposing player and a little bit before that when he and Joe Garagiola would come around and work out with the Browns.

"Yogi and I had one other thing in common. He is the only catcher in baseball history to make an unassisted double play. That makes me the only batter in history to hit into an unassisted double play by a catcher. When we asked Yogi to be on the show, he was delighted to do it."

Berardino vividly remembered the role Berra played on the show. Who could forget? But he doesn't remember whose idea it was to have Berra play the part of a brain surgeon. Yogi had about five lines to deliver, but the scene Berardino remembered most vividly took place in the cafeteria of General Hospital.

"I walk in with my nurse just as Yogi is about to leave. He's paying his check as we walk in, and we pass each other. Then we both stop and do a double take. He's at the exit looking at me, and I'm at my table looking at him.

"What's wrong, Steve?" asks the nurse.

"There's something about that man's face. . . ." Steve says.

Whether it is his face or his personality or whatever, there's something about Yogi Berra that moves people. When the Mets were driving toward their 1973 pennant, it moved people to write to him—more than 1,500 letters per home stand, which is usually a little less than two weeks.

"Sometimes it was a little heavier than others," said Regina Cassell of the Mets' Special Services Department, whose job it was to answer the mail. "Usually, it's heaviest when the team is doing well."

Most of the letters were requests for autographed pictures. Some offered suggestions on how the Mets could be improved. Others included good-luck charms, such as Indian Head pennies and Italian charms in the shape of bell peppers.

"When the team won the pennant," recalled Cassell, "he got a lot of mail thanking him for giving them such a wonderful season, so much fun and enjoyment. I was really impressed with the tone of the mail. And it came from people in all walks of life."

Berra's popularity never diminished with the years. It never waned when he was no longer in the high profile position of manager. If anything, the legend grows with each year. More than a quarter of a century after he retired as an active player, his schedule was as busy as ever; he was as much in demand for commercials, endorsements, and appearances because of that old Berra charm and believability.

Miller Lite included Berra in its successful television commercials. He is sitting in a tavern surrounded by a group of men drinking beer. Berra begins to extol the virtues of Miller Lite beer.

"It's got a third less calories than I probably thought it didn't have, and it's less filling than it would have been if it was more filling than they didn't want it to be."

Recently, Berra took on a new career: film critic. A syndication service produced and distributed a series of shows, "Yogi at the Movies." These were some of his observations:

> *Platoon*—"Didn't see it."
> *The Godfather*—"Saw it on TV. Good movie."
> Favorite actor—"Spencer Tracy."
> Favorite actress—"Green [*sic*] Garson."

He said he also liked Bette Midler "in that movie where they buried somebody and they come back." He enjoyed *Fatal Attraction*, with "that Glenn Cove [Close]," and as a kid he liked comedies. "My favorite," he said, "were *The Four Stooges*."

Yogi Berra's life is a very simple one and easily defined by the changing of the seasons. In the spring and summer, and into the fall, there is baseball. In the winter, he can be found most days at his thriving and popular "Yogi Berra's Health and Racquet Club," run by his son Tim.

Whitey Ford, Berra's old batterymate with the Yankees, said that once Berra found himself in a golfing foursome with former president Gerald Ford. As they played the round, the talk drifted to a variety of subjects, racquetball included.

"Do you play racquetball, Mr. President?" Berra asked.

"No, I never have," replied Ford.

"It's a great game, Mr. President," Berra said. "You must try it. If you're ever in New Jersey, I'd like to have you come and play at my club."

With that, according to Whitey Ford, Berra handed the former president a card indicating that the bearer was welcome to play at the club as a guest.

"When President Ford turned the card over," Whitey said, "stamped on the back was, 'Good Tuesdays.' "

Yogi Berra's reign as the master of the malaprop, the father of the *faux pas*, continues, but that isn't the strongest aspect of his character, or the most important. Those who have been associated with him, or have associated with him over the years, know him, simply, as a good guy.

And they say thank you for making Yogi Berra necessary.

Glossary of Berraisms

On the Mets' chances in the 1973 National League East pennant race: "It's not over 'til it's over."

Explaining declining attendance in Kansas City: "If people don't want to come to the ball park, how are you gonna stop them?"

Why the Yankees lost the 1960 World Series to the Pittsburgh Pirates: "We made too many wrong mistakes."

Why he thought he would be a good manager: "You observe a lot by watching."

On becoming a good defensive catcher: "Bill Dickey is learning me all his experience."

Explaining why he wasn't dancing at a Yankees' victory party: "I got rubber shoes on."

His theory on baseball, a thinking man's game: "Ninety percent of the game is half mental."

When fellow coach Joe Altobelli turned 50: "Now you're an old Italian scallion."

When a friend said he was afraid it was too late to get into a popular Fort Lauderdale restaurant: "Well, why did you wait so long to go now?"

When a Yankee player walked into the hotel bar and said he was waiting for Bo Derek to meet him: "Well, I haven't seen him."

Explaining his variety of sweaters in assorted colors: "The only color I don't have is navy brown."

When Billy Martin locked his keys in his car: "You gotta call a blacksmith."

To Carmen, about the movie, *The Magnificent Seven,* starring Steve McQueen: "He made that picture before he died."

To the clubhouse man after a workout on a hot, humid day: "Hey, Nick, get me a diet Tab."

To a sportswriter complaining that the hotel coffee shop charged $8.95 for a breakfast of orange juice, coffee, and an English muffin: "That's because they have to import those English muffins."

His theory on golf: "Ninety percent of the putts that fall short don't go in."

When Ken Boswell of the Mets said he was having trouble at bat because of a propensity to uppercut the ball: "Well, swing down."

Giving telephone directions to Joe Garagiola, who called to say he got lost driving to the Berra home in Montclair, New Jersey: "You ain't too far, just a couple of blocks. Only don't go that way, come this way."

About a popular Minneapolis restaurant: "Nobody goes there any more, it's too crowded."

On the shadows in left field at Yankee Stadium in the fall: "It gets late early out there."

When he was honored at "Yogi Berra Night" in Sportsman's Park in St. Louis: "I want to thank all those who made this night necessary."

On how he was able to drive in 23 runs in a doubleheader when he was in the minor leagues: "Every time I came to bat, there were men on base."

After his roommate closed his medical school text with a thud just as Berra finished his comic book: "How did yours come out?"

To wife Carmen when she said she had taken their son Tim to see *Dr. Zhivago*: "What the hell is wrong with him now?"

Asked by a player for the correct time: "Do you mean now?"

When Cardinals broadcaster Jack Buck presented him with a check made out payable to "Bearer," after Yogi appeared on a pregame show: "You known me all that time and you still don't know how to spell my name."

Why he approved of Little League: "It keeps the kids out of the house."

Describing his new house in Montclair: "Wotta house. Nothin' but rooms!"

Why he refused to buy new luggage: "You only use it for traveling."

Jim Bouton had asked Yankee public relations director Bob Fishel for a ticket to the opening game of the 1964 World Series in St. Louis. As the bus was leaving for the airport, a breathless Fishel appeared with a manila envelope and told Bouton,

"You're lucky, this is the last one." Said Berra: "You mean they're outta them envelopes already?"

To a young player who was emulating the hitting style of a veteran player without much success: "If you can't imitate him, don't copy him."

Arguing with an umpire that a drive to the outfield hit the concrete and should have been a home run instead of a double: "Anybody who can't hear the difference between a ball hitting wood and a ball hitting concrete must be blind."

When Mets' coach Rube Walker refused to go deep sea fishing because he gets sea sick: "What, on water?"

When an elderly woman said to him that he looked very cool in his slacks and polo shirt: "Thank you, ma'am. You don't look so hot yourself."

To the woman who inquired if his soft drink, Yoo-Hoo, was hyphenated: "Lady, it ain't even carbonated."

When asked what he does on the afternoon of a night game: "I usually sleep for two hours, from one o'clock to four."

Upon seeing a well-endowed blonde woman: "Who's that, Dagwood?"

When his son Larry answered the door bell and said the man was there for the Venetian blind: "Well, go in my pocket and give him a couple of bucks for a donation and get rid of him."

On his recognizability: "Most everybody knows me by my face."

Disputing the veracity of much of the above: "I really didn't say everything I said."

ESEA IV-B 1977/78   8.95

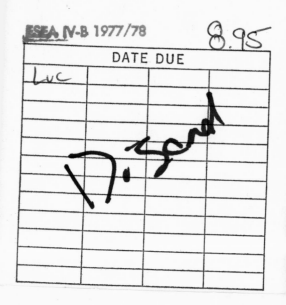

DATE DUE			
Luc			

0109

South Dakota

A Bicentennial History

John Milton

**Golden Sierra
High School Library**

W. W. Norton & Company, Inc.
New York

American Association for State and Local History
Nashville

Published and distributed by W. W. Norton & Company, Inc.
500 Fifth Avenue
New York, New York 10036

Library of Congress Cataloguing-in-Publication Data

Milton, John R
  South Dakota.

  (The States and the Nation series)
  Bibliography: p.
  Includes index.
  1. South Dakota—History.   I. Title.   II. Series.
F651.M5   978.3   76–57677
ISBN 0-393-05627-9

Printed in the United States of America
2 3 4 5 6 7 8 9 0

Contents

Illustrations

Invitation to the Reader

IN 1807, former President John Adams argued that a complete history of the American Revolution could not be written until the history of change in each state was known, because the principles of the Revolution were as various as the states that went through it. Two hundred years after the Declaration of Independence, the American nation has spread over a continent and beyond. The states have grown in number from thirteen to fifty. And democratic principles have been interpreted differently in every one of them.

We therefore invite you to consider that the history of your state may have more to do with the bicentennial review of the American Revolution than does the story of Bunker Hill or Valley Forge. The Revolution has continued as Americans extended liberty and democracy over a vast territory. John Adams was right: the states are part of that story, and the story is incomplete without an account of their diversity.

The Declaration of Independence stressed life, liberty, and the pursuit of happiness; accordingly, it shattered the notion of holding new territories in the subordinate status of colonies. The Northwest Ordinance of 1787 set forth a procedure for new states to enter the Union on an equal footing with the old. The Federal Constitution shortly confirmed this novel means of building a nation out of equal states. The step-by-step process through which territories have achieved self-government and national representation is among the most important of the Founding Fathers' legacies.

The method of state-making reconciled the ancient conflict between liberty and empire, resulting in what Thomas Jefferson called an empire for liberty. The system has worked and remains unaltered, despite enormous changes that have taken place in the nation. The country's extent and variety now surpass anything the patriots of '76 could likely have imagined. The United States has changed from an agrarian republic into a highly industrial and urban democracy, from a fledgling nation into a major world power. As Oliver Wendell Holmes remarked in 1920, the creators of the nation could not have seen completely how it and its constitution and its states would develop. Any meaningful review in the bicentennial era must consider what the country has become, as well as what it was.

The new nation of equal states took as its motto *E Pluribus Unum*—"out of many, one." But just as many peoples have become Americans without complete loss of ethnic and cultural identities, so have the states retained differences of character. Some have been superficial, expressed in stereotyped images— big, boastful Texas, "sophisticated" New York, "hillbilly" Arkansas. Other differences have been more real, sometimes instructively, sometimes amusingly; democracy has embraced Huey Long's Louisiana, bilingual New Mexico, unicameral Nebraska, and a Texas that once taxed fortunetellers and spawned politicians called "Woodpecker Republicans" and "Skunk Democrats." Some differences have been profound, as when South Carolina secessionists led other states out of the Union in opposition to abolitionists in Massachusetts and Ohio. The result was a bitter Civil War.

The Revolution's first shots may have sounded in Lexington and Concord; but fights over what democracy should mean and who should have independence have erupted from Pennsylvania's Gettysburg to the "Bleeding Kansas" of John Brown, from the Alamo in Texas to the Indian battles at Montana's Little Bighorn. Utah Mormons have known the strain of isolation; Hawaiians at Pearl Harbor, the terror of attack; Georgians during Sherman's march, the sadness of defeat and devastation. Each state's experience differs instructively; each adds understanding to the whole.

The purpose of this series of books is to make that kind of understanding accessible, in a way that will last in value far beyond the bicentennial fireworks. The series offers a volume on every state, plus the District of Columbia—fifty-one, in all.

Invitation to the Reader

Each book contains, besides the text, a view of the state through eyes other than the author's—a "photographer's essay," in which a skilled photographer presents his own personal perceptions of the state's contemporary flavor.

We have asked authors not for comprehensive chronicles, nor for research monographs or new data for scholars. Bibliographies and footnotes are minimal. We have asked each author for a summing up—interpretive, sensitive, thoughtful, individual, even personal—of what seems significant about his or her state's history. What distinguishes it? What has mattered about it, to its own people and to the rest of the nation? What has it come to now?

To interpret the states in all their variety, we have sought a variety of backgrounds in authors themselves and have encouraged variety in the approaches they take. They have in common only these things: historical knowledge, writing skill, and strong personal feelings about a particular state. Each has wide latitude for the use of the short space. And if each succeeds, it will be by offering you, in your capacity as a *citizen* of a state *and* of a nation, stimulating insights to test against your own.

James Morton Smith
General Editor

Preface

OUTH Dakotans do not dislike large metropolitan complexes, nor do they stay away from them deliberately, but they can get along without them. Tall buildings prevent a man from seeing the full sky, or from finding a horizon, and if he is from Dakota he is accustomed to seeing weather systems (or feeling them) while they are still hours or even a day in the distance. Weather affects the plains dweller, and he is aware of nature's moods and habits, as various as they may be. The long look across open land gives him a sense of humility (the land is clearly bigger than he is) and a surge of freedom, independence, and pride which both reinforce the humility and build upon it.

The prairie is no Garden of Eden, even though many writers seem to have pictured it as such. It is moody, consistent only in its inconsistency. The landscape appears to be neatly geometric, especially as divided by section lines, fences, county roads, and the remnants of railroad tracks; but it is full of surprises. Coloring changes with the movement of the sun and clouds, and shadows make abstract patterns on the grasses. Variable winds bend the grass, which sometimes undulates like ocean waves and at other times stands straight up as though peering for rain. The weather is predictable only in terms of change. Because of its central location, South Dakota is subjected to weather systems from all directions. If it is true that the people have been slow to change to the newer ways of politics, education, economics, and cultural fashions, it is equally true that they had to learn long ago to adapt themselves to the fluctuations of weather and climate.

The land has been a shaping force in the history of the region because of its location on the continent and because of its characteristics. South Dakotans are acutely aware of their piece of earth and the weather patterns which play upon it. They are also relatively unhampered by many of the social or people problems which plague high-density population areas. And so they are usually friendly to each other, and to visitors, all the while keeping one eye on the sky.

As a state, South Dakota is young. It does not have the long history of the eastern states, nor the 400-year-old Spanish traditions of the southwest states, nor even the well-established Indian culture of other parts of the country, since the Sioux themselves are relative newcomers to the Northern Plains. An overview of the state's history reveals perhaps slightly more than a dozen major events: in the eighteenth century, a few French explorers and the arrival of the first Sioux Indians; in the nineteenth century, the Lewis and Clark expedition, the fur trade along the Missouri River and its tributaries, the European visitors writing about the area from the ''comfort'' of river steamboats, early settlement and Indian conflicts, gold discovered in the Black Hills, the beginning of the cattle industry, and heavier settlement, especially by Scandinavians and Germans; toward the turn of the century, statehood and the official end of Indian resistance (the latter at the controversial ''battle'' of Wounded Knee); and, in the twentieth century, continued homesteading, the Dust Bowl of the 1930s, the growth of agribusiness following World War II, and, finally, an attempt to ''catch up'' in education, culture, and the arts, all of it dependent still upon the weather and crops, although federal assistance has made possible some improvements which the state could not have made by itself.

While such events, capable of being placed in historical or chronological order, are important in the construction of the portrait of South Dakota, they must be seen as actions played upon a stage, and the stage and the players are also an essential

part of the portrait. Which is to say that this book is not history
in the normal sense, although sections of it follow certain events
in their chronological order. My concern is with the portrait,
with the spirit of the place and of the people, who either visited
it or settled down on it, making this particular place their home.
Because the portrait demands more than a listing of people and
events, I have adopted a method of organization which is neither chronological nor topical altogether, which allows a circling of the subject even while proceeding toward a somewhat
unorthodox conclusion through some attention to the progres-
sion of historical events.

In preparing this bicentennial book, this essay of interpreta-
tion, I have had the opportunity (for which I am grateful) to take
another look at the continuity of the land and to review some of
the adventures and achievements of the people who traveled
across it or stayed to become a more permanent part of it. In
some respects the land is a myth, the place more a part of the
imagination than of literal reality. This condition is a result of
the glamor attending Deadwood and gold and Lt. Col. George
A. Custer and the Sioux Indians, all accepted willingly by distant eastern readers as manifestations of the romantic frontier
image which brightened their lives with excitement for a while.
The other side of the image, associated with weather and climate rather than with events, is based upon reports of the extremes of climate rather than the average. The extremes are of
psychological importance, but they do not prove South Dakota a
desert, or a Siberia, or a paradise.

It may be that the state is all of these and that its true soul, or
spirit, lies nestled in the point of tension between several sets of
extremes, just as the state lies physically between Midwest and
West. Because I first saw South Dakota as western, I am still
inclined to think of it that way. Born and reared in the Saint
Paul-Minneapolis metropolitan area, I was occasionally guilty
(in those days) of big-city snobbery toward the surrounding agricultural regions. If my memory is correct, I first set foot on the
soil of South Dakota in June of 1960 while driving from North
Dakota to Denver. The place was Buffalo, in the northwestern
corner of the state. This fact will bring no distinction to Buffalo,

but it is important to me. Coincidentally, this trip also provided my first intimate acquaintance with the interior West, all previous crossings of the Great Plains and Rockies having been made by train. For several years, while driving back and forth between North Dakota and Colorado and New Mexico, my view was from U.S. Highway 85, which went through the Black Hills, or from 83, which ran roughly parallel to the Missouri River down the center of the state. In 1963, when I moved to Vermillion and the University of South Dakota, I dodged pheasants on highway 281, farther east, and eventually I used the more heavily traveled 81 and I-29 at the eastern edge of the state. These are the major north-south highways in South Dakota and my introduction to the state proceeded from west to east as I changed highways. Somewhere in the eastern half of the state the elusive word "west" changed into the equally elusive word "midwest," but my first impression of the westernness of South Dakota remains with me.

In writing this essay, or series of essays, about South Dakota, I have acquired various debts which are difficult to repay. Herbert Hoover, professor of history at the University of South Dakota, gave me a strong nudge when I was reluctant to take on this project, and I hope that he will not regret his actions. Gerald George continually encouraged me at just the right times. Max Leget made life in the university library much easier for me. Prof. Joseph Cash allowed me to pick freely from his book on the Homestake Mine, and Joseph Stuart, director of the South Dakota Memorial Art Center in Brookings, gave me the same privileges with his catalogue, *The Art of South Dakota*. Bob Lee, John Barstow and The Rapid City Society for Genealogical Research, Kathleen Norris and *Sunday Clothes* (edited by Linda Hasselstrom), Tom Brokaw, and Herbert Schell have all provided material, whether in writing or in conversation. On another level, but also an important one, I owe thanks to the editor of the *Sioux Falls Argus-Leader,* who, I sincerely hope, will find in this book some justification for his remarks about me; to the English Department at the university for putting up with my absentmindedness while I was writing; to my students from both sides of the river for confirming my feelings about the East River-West River distinctions; and, finally, to my wife, Lynn, and my daughter, Nanci, for allowing me to be busier than usual for what must have seemed a long time.

John Milton

May 24, 1976

South Dakota

1

Divided Images

IN the minds, or imaginations, of the people living on or near the nation's coasts, the Dakotas are very much alike—if they exist at all. Situated halfway between the oceans, and halfway between the North Pole and the equator, landlocked, north of the main travel arteries, out of the way, they are regarded as a mystery not worth solving or still a frontier country unchanged from the romantic and sometimes bloody days of Custer, Crazy Horse, Calamity Jane, and Wild Bill Hickok. To the average citizen outside the general region of the Northern Plains, the Dakotas are a desolate place of blizzards and droughts, the coldest part of the country in the winter and the hottest in the summer except for the Arizona and California deserts. The Dakotas are a North American Siberia. Names such as Fargo, Bismarck, Aberdeen, and Philip appear on the television news, identified simply as the coldest locations in the fifty states—even Alaska does not get this kind of attention. Then Philip often does an extreme turnabout in July and becomes the hottest place this side of Hades.

To make matters worse, television announcers frequently transpose the two states, so that Fargo is put in South Dakota and Sioux Falls in North Dakota. These two cities have at least one thing in common: in any standard atlas where the map of the United States is double-paged, Fargo and Sioux Falls are lost in the crease of the binding. (John Steinbeck, in *Travels*

3

with Charley, noticed this about Fargo; he did not visit South Dakota.) Confusion gives way to astonishment when children several states away, and farther, see Dakota license plates from either state. It is as though they have been suddenly exposed to a foreign country, a place more exotic, perhaps, than France, England, or Denmark. A Danish family arriving in New York in 1975, on its way to visit relatives in South Dakota, talked to an employee in a restaurant in the Big City who knew where Copenhagen was but had never heard of South Dakota. Whether this kind of ignorance is worse than mistaken opinion is debatable among South Dakotans. A few might rise up in resentment, as from pride; many more would shrug politely, or grin smugly, comforted by the fact that their state is not likely to become overcrowded. South Dakotans value their open spaces and their freedom above all else; they are not anxious for a new immigration. And so they can smile easily at such things as the comment made by a character on a television drama when asked if he had run away to avoid having people find out that he had been convicted of manslaughter: "Why else would a New Jersey Italian move to South Dakota?"

Perhaps going back a century to consider this question is not fair. Nevertheless, musician Felix Vinatieri left Italy, landed in New York, and, bypassing New Jersey, settled in South Dakota. He was living in Yankton in 1873 when Custer and his troops arrived on their way to the Indian campaigns. Vinatieri was a composer, a cornetist, and the director of the band which played a concert in honor of Custer. The general (as he liked to call himself, although it was only a brevet rank) was so impressed with Vinatieri that he persuaded him to enlist in the army and become his bandmaster. Together they traveled to Fort Abraham Lincoln, near Bismarck, from where Custer launched his attack against the Indians. Six months after Custer's death, Vinatieri was discharged; he returned to Yankton, from where he traveled extensively to give concerts. It is possible that Walt Whitman, the great American poet of that time, heard of him, because two years after Whitman's 1879 train trip from Saint Louis to Colorado, a poem entitled "Italian Music in Dakota" appeared in the new edition of *Leaves of Grass*. The poem even suggests that Whitman heard Vinatieri perform.

An Italian in South Dakota. The descendants of Felix are still a prominent family in Yankton. Nevertheless, in 1873 Custer himself must have wondered why anyone at all would settle in Dakota Territory. The weather was balmy when he arrived; the sun was shining and the freshets were running. Spring was in the air. Less than a week after the Seventh Cavalry settled in, a blizzard struck Yankton. Custer was outraged, first because of the chaos caused by the sudden change in weather, and also because the Yankton telegrapher refused to accept his message to the War Department concerning the blizzard. It was bad publicity for the territory. Custer then threatened to have him fired from his job, and the message was sent, describing the worst snowstorm Custer could remember and bemoaning the loss of fifty horses and possibly a few men from his command. In trying to describe the storm, Custer finally gave up and simply concluded in his message that he could not possibly give an accurate idea of the severity of the blizzard.

For a time, some people in later years nicknamed South Dakota "The Blizzard State." But others called it "The Sunshine State," and Custer's April week in 1873 must have confused him as much as the two state names confused everyone else in the early years of statehood. Eventually the paradox was resolved when South Dakota was dubbed "The Land of Infinite Variety." It may be that the "variety" was intended to describe the flat prairie, the lakes, the buttes, the Black Hills, and the Badlands, but everyone knows that its real reference is to the weather.

The considerable emphasis on bad weather and hard times provoked a 1962 editorial in the *Minneapolis Tribune*. The remarks were directed at North Dakota because the immediate occasion of the editorial was the publication of Lois Phillips Hudson's novel of the depression there, *The Bones of Plenty*. Nevertheless, in dealing with images, there are not enough differences between the two states to warrant picky distinctions. Blizzards and drought have been shared quite equitably, as have heat and cold and isolation, although the South Dakotan would argue that his state is neither as cold nor as isolated as the state to the north. The editorial questioned whether North Dakotans could consider it worthwhile to try to explain that their state was not really stricken by drought and debt, and covered from one end to the other by broken-down windmills, when the state's own writers continued to create that kind of caricature. Eric Sevareid was quoted as saying, "It was a trial of the human spirit just to live there." The *Tribune* then expressed concern that Hudson's novel would have the same effect, that both writers grew up in Dakota during the depression and moved away afterward, so that they did not deal with a quality of life in Dakota which, though difficult for outsiders to understand, is impressive.

Images, once established, are difficult to change. In a region as young as the Dakotas, memory is still fastened upon the struggles of settlement, upon the hardships of pioneering, and it will take a little longer to examine contemporary benefits and to re-evaluate man's relationship to nature in a time when cities are coming under attack and rural areas are more appealing than they once were. Even in the existing literature of the past century and a half there is a two-sided picture of Dakota, although only one side seems to have left a strong impression. The image has grown in a curious way.

Lewis and Clark, in 1804 and 1805, were quite objective about what they saw and experienced, perhaps because they were under orders from President Thomas Jefferson to write an accurate report on the land newly acquired through the Louisiana Purchase. They commented on both the warm sunny days and the cold windy ones, on both the treachery of the Missouri River and its majestic beauty. Indeed, they set a pattern for later writers by indicating the extremes of the landscape and its climate. These extremes may be more obvious to us now than they were at the beginning of the nineteenth century because certain facts can be proven by weather bureau records. For example, the absolute temperature range record for the Western Hemisphere was set in North Dakota in 1936, with a variation of 181 degrees at the same location within the same year. And while many people are moving to a more moderate climate, especially as they grow older, it is equally true that the fresh air of the Dakotas, relatively uncontaminated by industrial pollution, attracts both visitors and new residents.

Over the years, the experiences and perceptions of the people who came to Dakota seesawed back and forth between gloom and optimism. On George Catlin's first steamboat trip up the Missouri, in 1832, the artist noticed all the details and liked what he saw. But thirty years later, during a series of bad years in the Dakotas, he changed his mind and said that the Dakotas were part of that region known as the Great Plains, "which is and ever must be useless for civilized men to cultivate." Joseph Nicollet, traveling northward along the James River in 1839, first reported that the James "has been deemed by all travellers to those distant regions perhaps the most beautiful within the territory of the United States." Yet, a few days later, somewhere near the present border between the two states, his men became so depressed by the monotony of the land, the heat, the flies, and the lack of animation on the prairie, that Nicollet had to give them bicarbonate of soda to raise their spirits and keep them going.

Moses Armstrong, a territorial delegate to Congress, used the extreme conditions in pleading for statehood and for a railroad. The climate was mild, he said, and the soil fertile; there was plenty of room, and the prairie was excellent for grazing, with fruit and vegetables also growing readily. But, he complained, the towns were isolated, marketing was difficult, and the homesteader dreaded a lonely exile and would almost as soon homestead the moon as pick a place on "the green prairies of the West thirty miles from a tree." When the railroad did go through, later in the 1870s, it advertised the land it was going to serve as a lush, fertile, almost tropical land where everything grew to gigantic size. (Of course, the biblical image here is debased for commercial purposes.) Grasshoppers and drought seemed to put the lie to the railroad from 1874 to 1877, but the territorial Bureau of Immigration continued to send pamphlets east and to Europe following the tone set by the railroad's advertising.

The discovery of gold in the Black Hills at about that same time proved to be a romantic drawing card, but it was also a business venture like the railroad. It was Theodore Roosevelt as much as anyone who helped establish the double image Dakotans have of themselves and their place. He insisted that Dakota had made a man out of him, and a president. The climate, the outdoor life, the vigor from fresh air—these improved his health. He became an important supporter of Dakota. Even so, he was aware of the ruggedness of the land, of the aridity, the desolation, the scanty grass, the low rainfall, the alkali flats (almost little deserts), the endless plains, the bare buttes, and the often ferocious weather. After glamorizing the cowboy, he implied that the cowboy had to be heroic in order to survive. And, harking back to Nicollet's comments on the monotony, Roosevelt said in an 1888 publication: "The country . . . has a wonderful *sameness* of character." It is hard to tell whether "wonderful" was meant to be sympathetic, polite, or ironic.

The business of survival, of settling, of making a living in Dakota had its ups and downs depending upon the weather, the grasshoppers, the national economy, and even upon methods of farming. Few novels were written about Dakota during the crucial period of settlement because most of the people who came west did so in order to establish a foothold on the land, and the few who took time to write about their experiences did it in letters or journals. Not until the turn of the century did professional writers such as Hamlin Garland come to South Dakota, and as the new century grew older the writers looked back and recreated what had gone before them, so that the Dakota image in literature was built largely through historical rather than contemporary fiction. Garland wrote briefly about South Dakota as he saw it, and perhaps the grim passages in his *Main-Traveled Roads,* 1899, were the most influential of all in shaping the Dakota image a decade after the territory was split into two states. From his preface to that book:

> The farther I got from Chicago the more depressing the landscape became. It was bad enough in our former home in Mitchell County, but my pity grew more intense as I passed from northwest Iowa into southern Dakota. The houses, bare as boxes, dropped on the treeless plains, the barbed-wire fences running at right angles, and the towns mere assemblages of flimsy wooden sheds with painted-pine battlement, produced on me the effect of an almost helpless and sterile poverty.

Garland's dark mood, his father's farm, his mother's "imprisonment" on a barren land, and talks with her lonely and poor neighbors all combined to leave him with a deep sense of bitterness. He was hardly able to dramatize these conditions in his later writing. He was simply overwhelmed by the starkness and the dinginess and the hopelessness of it all.

In Rölvaag's *Giants in the Earth* it is the settler-characters who are overwhelmed, not the author, and they are overwhelmed not so much by sheer hopelessness as by the immensity of the land. Ole Rölvaag came to Elk Point, South Dakota, from Norway in 1896 and lived with his uncle on a farm for three years. The setting for the novel is nearer Canton, where he attended school for two years, but the action of the novel takes place several decades earlier and in that respect *Giants* is historical. Its Norwegian immigrants lose their sense of direction in the tall grass on the limitless prairie; they feel "frail and Lilliputian" on this land. In spite of the size of the landscape, it seemed to close in on the people and become a threat rather than an invitation to freedom of movement. And soon the familiar adjectives creep in:

> Poverty-stricken, unspeakably forlorn, the caravan creaked along, advancing at a snail's pace, deeper and deeper into a bluish-green infinity—on and on, and always farther on. . . .

Some of the chapter titles must have stayed with the book's readers for a long time:
"Facing the Great Desolation"
"On the Border of Utter Darkness"
"The Great Plain Drinks the Blood of Christian Men and Is Satisfied."
Since the novel, published in 1927, was immensely popular, one can only wonder how many people began to think that South Dakota was an evil void gobbling up unsuspecting Norwegians.

Variations on this theme have appeared in too many books to count, all of them dealing with the territorial period, roughly from 1860 to 1890, when the greatest influx of Scandinavian, Bohemian, and New England farmers went into the wilderness to settle and to claim homesteads. One constant factor is the land itself. Whether the subject be farmer, soldier, speculator, or wanderer, his depiction in the novels written about him is tied inexorably to the land. And always it seems to be a hostile land, a frightening land. Ernest Haycox, writing of the time of Custer in *Bugles in the Afternoon* (1944), describes Fargo as having no shape, no core, only a few buildings standing gauntly on the dusty prairie.

> The railroad, which gave the town a single pulse beat once a day, came as black ribbon out of emptiness . . . with hurried indifference, and moved away with equal emptiness. . . . There were no trees in this world, no accents, no relieving interruptions; nothing but the gray soil rolling on and a short brown grass turned crisp. . . .[1]

While the description may seem severe, there are many cases of easterners or southerners feeling a deep sense of fear when they left the Minnesota woods while traveling west and suddenly faced the huge and apparently empty land ahead of them in the eastern Dakotas. One such person objected to the term ''frightening'' which he had read in a poem about this experience and insisted that the word should have been ''terrifying.'' Certainly the plains are awesome to the newcomer; there is more land and more sky and more weather than he has probably ever seen before. And the terror is intensified by the occasional storms, especially in winter, as described also by Haycox:

> The storm pounded the earth for three days. It screamed through the town and drove drifts against the windward side of buildings until men were able to walk out of second-story windows. It snapped telegraph lines and stopped trains from St. Paul. It moved out of the northern emptiness like great wild sea waves, higher and higher, more and more violent, until . . . citizens counted ranks and named those who had been caught away from home and knew that death rode abroad.[2]

It is clear that certain images persist in virtually all literature concerning Dakota. Put aside the winter storms and there are

1. Ernest Haycox, *Bugles in the Afternoon* (New York: Bantam Books, 1944), p. 1.
2. Haycox, p. 207.

still the elements from this list, taken from Wallace Stegner's novel, *The Big Rock Candy Mountain* (1943), one of the major fictional accounts of the settling of the West: lack of trees, farms scattered, no hills, turgidly flowing rivers, sod shanties, unpainted shacks, windmills, "nondescript cattle with cowbirds sitting on their hipbones," wind—the wind "kept you tense all the time." The time of which Stegner writes is 1905.

These images have been reinforced by writers who turned their attention to the depression years of the 1930s in an effort, probably, to portray the drama of man against the land. The depression is part of the Dakota experience and should not be ignored; unfortunately, in a novel such as *The Bones of Plenty,* the joys of spring mornings, of birds nesting, of prairie flowers, and of clean air, which are available at least to children even during hard times, are pushed into the background and almost forgotten while the tragedy of the farmer lingers on. One senses that the conditions of the land, austere at best, have helped develop strong hardy grain and strong hardy men—no other could survive. On the other hand, all available energy had to go into the working of the land, and so there was none left over for the appreciation of the arts or the cultivation of the spirit. This is one obvious reason for the lateness of a varied, less one-sided literature in the Dakotas. The rich complexities of the region and its culture—including the important values to be learned from the Indians and their culture—have been slow in working their way up to the recognition which the arts can give them.

It was just as the depressing picture of Dakota reached its lowest depths, following the economic depression, that a curious change began to take place simultaneously. The key novel was Frederick Manfred's *The Golden Bowl* (published in 1944 under the pen name, Feike Feikema), which had all the ingredients of the Dust Bowl—the earth drying up and blowing away, the people struggling to stay alive, the privation and desperation which eventually turned to sardonic humor. All of this culminates in a marvelous anecdote:

"Reminds me," ruminated Pa Thor aloud, as if he hadn't noticed either Ma Thor or Kirsten. "Reminds me. Neighbor Grayson down the road a piece, had a wife ready to give with child. He was worried about her, worried more than most farmers are. Because, you see, she was awful small. So he took her to Sioux Falls. That's where all them rich an' high monkey-monks live. An' while he was waitin' fer the kid to come, another feller came out, an' sat down to wait too. He was a fat rich feller, had all the sugar in the coffee he wanted. An' they set there waitin'. Pretty soon a nurse come out. 'Mr. Jones?' That was the rich feller, an' he sings out, 'Here. Yes?' 'Mr. Jones, you're the father of a nice, fat, eight-pound baby boy.' 'Great guns!' he roars. 'That's wonderful!' He jumps up and down, an' kisses the nurse and offers my neighbor a cigar. 'Here. Take two. Celebrate with me. It's wonderful, having babies! You're waiting too, I suppose?' My neighbor nods a little, nervous, you know. The rich feller says, 'Say, just to show you what kind of a good sport I am I'll wait an' keep you company till you hear from your wife.' So they set there, an' pretty soon the nurse comes out, an' she says, 'Mr. Grayson?' 'Yes.' The nurse was a little nervous an' she acted kinda funny, an' then she said, 'Well, you had a boy.' 'Oh,' he said. 'Oh. An' how much did it weigh?' The nurse wasn't gonna answer him at first, but finally she said, 'Well, it was about a pound.' Grayson thanked her an' started up to go out. 'Great guns!' yells the rich feller, 'only a pound? That's tough luck, feller. Tough!' 'Hell no,' says Grayson. 'That's not tough. Livin' out where I do, in the dust bowl, why hell! we're lucky to git our seed back.' " [3]

They were lucky, also, to discover that a man needs roots, that the land gives him an identity, and that rebirth is possible even in the midst of what seems to be the death of the land. Manfred takes the discoveries further than that as his chief character, Maury, wanders out to the Bad Lands, sees the petrified dinosaur bones, and speculates on his relationship to all the life that came before him. He finds a continuity, a long view which is almost mystical at the moment of recognition but which becomes a practical matter of seeing man not as isolated and desolated but as part of a life force which sometimes seems to sputter and threaten to disappear but always manages to adjust, or leap into

3. Frederick Manfred, *The Golden Bowl* (1944; reprint ed., Vermillion, S.D.: Dakota Press, 1969), pp. 87–88. Used with permission.

a new form, and endure through thousands of centuries. In light of this long view, the Dust Bowl is trivial and temporary.

In similar fashion, Holger Cahill's novel, *The Shadow of My Hand* (1956), chronicles the now familiar elements of flat land—"You could shoot a cue ball from the southern boundary of the state all the way to Canada and halfway to the North Pole"—flirtatious and unpredictable weather, ice, wind, and isolation. But Cahill, like Manfred, sees beyond the actual physical facts of the land and introduces a number of images which border on the mystical. The fact that anything religious, spiritual, or mystical could arise from this prairie had not occurred to most writers of the nineteenth and early twentieth centuries (although Lewis did have a kind of mystical experience with a grizzly bear farther west on the 1804 expedition). And so new insights have begun to show up in the literature of the prairie and plains, even though Dakotans might not appreciate such images as Cahill sees. They, too, have been conditioned to think of their land in a certain way, partly because of the one-sided literature. But let us try this image. The bones of thousands of buffalo killed on the prairie were once shipped east to sugar refineries, and the sugar—containing the elements of the bones which were part of the refining process—was then shipped back to the prairie people who stirred it in their coffee, thereby partaking of the buffalo in what amounts to a natural communion rite. The people took the land back into themselves. And since New Yorkers were putting the same sugar in their coffee, they were absorbing a natural part of the Dakotas and becoming, perhaps, unwitting "brothers" to those stubbornly uncivilized Dakotans. Ridiculous? Perhaps. But who is to say that a similar process cannot be nourished deliberately, even though only through symbols, to help everyone find new ways of being nurtured by the land.

Contemporary perceptions of the region are slowly changing the traditional images. As John Steinbeck drove across the United States in 1960, preparing *Travels with Charley* (1962), he came to Dakota equipped with a pre-established image (he, too, had read the books), but his image was at least partially destroyed as he looked at the land himself, even though he was reluctant to change his opinion. It is not easy to do away with old images and build new ones. Thinking ahead, as he drove westward, Steinbeck's chief concern was that he might be snowbound in North Dakota if he did not hurry. This corresponded to one of his images of the place. He had others:

> Curious how a place unvisited can take such hold on the mind so that the very name sets up a ringing. To me such a place was Fargo . . . a brother to the fabulous places of the earth, kin to those magically remote spots mentioned by Herodotus and Marco Polo and Mandeville.

In other words, the Dakotas are like a foreign country, exotic in the imagination. The only "facts" available to Steinbeck until he got there were his early memories of Fargo (from radio or newspaper reports) as the coldest place on the continent, or the hottest, or wettest, or driest, or most deeply inundated by snow. It was a place of extremes. Driving through Fargo, Steinbeck noticed nothing unusual and the weather was pleasant, but he felt happy over the fact that the real Fargo did not disturb his "mind's picture of it." He reported that "in the war between reality and romance," reality lost.

And yet reality caught up with Steinbeck when he reached the western part of the state, when he ran into the wind, when the "night was loaded with omens," when he felt something mysterious and was afraid. It was "not the gusty, rabbity wind of the seacoasts . . . but a great bursting sweep of wind with nothing to inhibit it for a thousand miles in any direction." Before the night was over he felt unwanted in this strange land, and later he admitted a reluctance to write about it.

This incident, and others, would seem to prove the need of regional writers to interpret and clarify their own land. The outsider cannot do it as well, and the Dakotas have been described for more than 150 years by passers-through, by visitors, some more perceptive than others, of course. But if the Dakotas are to adjust their images, make them more real, more contemporary, more honest, they will have to encourage their own writers to stay in the region and to write about it. Only in this way will a proper understanding of the land come about. It is possible, one admits, to leave and to come back. This may be necessary in order to achieve the right perspective, as long as the initial rootedness holds in the meantime. Since the Great Plains are the same whether they be in the Dakotas or southern Saskatchewan, we can use Wallace Stegner as an example of a talented writer who returned to the place of his boyhood and came to an understanding with it. In *Wolf Willow* he stresses the beauties of the land without ignoring the harshness, and he begins to develop a language of the land, a fresh set of images:

> winter wheat . . . shadowed as if schools of fish move in it . . .
> grass, the marvelous curly prairie wool tight to the earth's skin . . .
> spring wheat bright as new lawn . . .
> primroses as shy as prairie flowers are supposed to be . . .
> a landscape of circles, radii, perspective exercises—a country of geometry.
> wind, a thing you tighten into as trout tightens into fast water.
> grassy, green, exciting wind, with the smell of distance in it . . .
> a light to set a painter wild, a light pure, glareless, and transparent.[4]

As the images cluster, and grow, the individual meanings take on a significance perhaps noticed by earlier writers but not brought to fulfillment:

> The drama of this landscape is in the sky, pouring with light and always moving. The earth is passive. And yet the beauty . . . is a fusion: this sky would not be spectacular without this earth to change and glow and darken under it.
> The very scale, the hugeness of simple forms, emphasizes stability.[5]

There is a great deal more. Much of it is based on the geometry image, with the straight roads, the right-angle fences, the circle of the horizon. The land is brought under the control of the art-

---

4. Wallace Stegner, *Wolf Willow: A History, a Story, and a Memory of the Last Plains Frontier* (New York: The Viking Press), pp. 6, 7. Used with permission.

5. Stegner, p. 7.

ist. This means seeing both the good and the bad, the possibilities of fusion, and when lucky, the actual fusion of the extremes which, taken separately, lead either to sentimentalism and romanticism or to cynicism and despair.

It is the writers who establish the image, not the arguments of local chambers of commerce or any other kind of advertising. And the writers of the past, in South Dakota, have tended to become romantic or defensive in adopting the ''better'' side of the picture, or, at the opposite pole, they have been gloomy and pessimistic in condemning the sterility of the Dakotas. Sterility is certainly the wrong word, because it signifies ''nothing.'' At the worst, there is too much in Dakota—too much sky, too much flat land, too much weather, too much empty space, too many climatic changes, too many extremes. Perhaps it is these extremes that constitute the basic image, that might be the only significant image. In the tensions between these extremes, between the beautiful and the harsh, may lie the source of both art and psychology in South Dakota.

Meanwhile, whenever an old book is reprinted and reviewed, the easy image is revived, as in the case of *Travels in North America: 1822–1824,* in which Paul Wilhelm, duke of Wurtemberg, traveling by boat on the Missouri River through Dakota, said that the summer reminded him of Egypt and the winter of Moscow. So be it. South Dakotans may lament this one-sided view of their region, but they often hope secretly that the force of the image will prevent an influx of outsiders which might eventually spoil the openness of the land and the physical freedom found in low-density population areas. To be honest, some people are comfortably smug about the whole thing.

2

The Romantic Image

N our time we have been busy debunking the myths, legends, and romances of the frontier West (sometimes called ''The Old West''), but in spite of all the ''truth'' we turn up eventually and sometimes proudly there is still—as there always has been—a soft spot for heroes and villains and colorful characters in the hearts of most Americans. At any given time we find our own lives drab and dreary and enjoy turning back to those more exciting times when the West was there for the taking. South Dakota has its share of Old West excitement and legend, some of it the product of the imagination and some of it factual. Many of the people and events of Dakota Territory—and especially the Black Hills region—received international attention and helped establish a romantic image of Dakota which attracted journalists and thrilled eastern readers. The stories were cherished, and usually believed, and some of their relics are still tourist attractions.

The one amazing story which cannot be debunked is less a part of the South Dakota image than those episodes which, a half century later, were reported in the lurid and florid prose of newspaper reporters and the writers of dime novels. Disregarding the Lewis and Clark expedition, which provided some quiet heroics of its own, the first legendary character in South Dakota was the mountain man, Hugh Glass. In his company were other famous plainsmen, trappers, and explorers whose deeds may have nearly matched his own, but Glass is the one most closely associated with South Dakota. Some of his companions, or *companyeros,* were perhaps more famous: Jed Smith, Jim Clyman, Bill Sublette, and Jim Bridger. But none has quite captured the imagination, as Hugh Glass did, with a single act. It is not uncommon to pit man against beast, in folklore or in fiction, but the importance of the Glass story comes not so much from his single-handed battle with a grizzly bear as it does from his act of survival afterward.

Presumably a native of Pennsylvania, and said to have served reluctantly with the famous pirate, Jean Lafitte, Hugh Glass attached himself to the Rocky Mountain Fur Company in 1823. This company, not the first to ply the Missouri River, began with an advertisement in the *Missouri Republican* of Saint Louis, March 20, 1822:

> To enterprising young men. The subscriber wishes to engage one hundred young men to ascend the Missouri River to its source, there to be employed for one, two, or three years. For particulars enquire of Major Andrew Henry, near the lead mines in the county of Washington, who will ascend with, and command, the party; or of the subscriber near St. Louis.

The advertisement was signed by William H. Ashley, who, with Major Henry, was licensed to trade on the upper Missouri just three weeks after the call for men appeared in the newspaper. The company made its first trip upriver, to the mouth of the Yellowstone, in 1822–1823, with Major Henry commanding. Early in the spring Henry sent word to Ashley in Saint Louis that he needed more horses. Ashley enlisted another one hundred men, including Hugh Glass, and left Saint Louis in two keelboats on March 10. It was his intention to get horses at an Arikara village in South Dakota, the Indians having professed friendliness. Edward Rose, however, warned Ashley about the Indians and was ignored. At the village, about forty of the men left the boats and spent the night on land, believing themselves safe. The next day the Arikaras attacked the land force, killing all the horses and half the men in fifteen minutes. The rest, including the wounded Hugh Glass, got back to the boats and drifted downstream to a place of safety. They debated the wisdom of passing the Arikara village in another attempt to proceed upstream.

Most of the men returned to Saint Louis. Thirty stayed where they were. Jed Smith went north by himself, on land, to get help from Major Henry. Early in July 1823, Henry and most of his men joined Ashley near the mouth of the Cheyenne River; Smith, having completed a dangerous journey successfully, went back to Saint Louis. In July and August, Col. Henry Leavenworth conducted a campaign against the Arikaras, the first army campaign against the Indians west of the Mississippi. It fizzled. But by the time it was over—with no clear-cut decision for anyone—Major Henry was at the mouth of the Teton River and starting across the rugged landscape with eighty men in an effort to reach the Yellowstone River. With him were Jed Smith (who never seemed to stop traveling through the wilderness), David Jackson, Ed Rose, William Sublette, Jim Bridger, and Hugh Glass, all to become famous men before the era of fur trapping and trading ended.

Ashley's company was to be highly successful, bringing a quarter of a million dollars worth of furs to Saint Louis over a five-year period. Ashley's success bothered his rival companies, especially the older companies, and fired the imaginations of people who had visions of wealth. His importance in opening the West is undeniable; his men, both as individuals and in small groups, discovered passes and opened trails; his financial success attracted many newcomers. His lieutenants—Smith, Jackson, and Sublette—eventually took over the company and became relatively wealthy themselves. But not Hugh Glass. This man was probably older than the others in the company since he was frequently referred to as "Old" Glass. He was independent and disliked taking orders, a characteristic which almost led to his downfall and then helped him to survive.

As Henry's company was proceeding up the Grand River in South Dakota, late in August 1823, near evening on the fifth day of the journey, Glass went ahead on his own to hunt. He enjoyed being by himself and was impatient when taking orders along with the other men. Perhaps he disliked the assignment of tasks; perhaps he felt uncomfortable with youngsters; or perhaps he was simply a western "loner." The westering experience has always drawn men and women who feel uneasy in crowds. In any case, Hugh abruptly confronted an immense female grizzly bear with cubs nearby. Whether he had no time to "set his triggers," or whether he got in one shot before he was attacked, is not certain. But before help could arrive, Hugh had been mauled, scraped, bitten, and chewed until he was wounded and torn so severely that it did not seem possible for him to live. There was no medical aid available and he could not be moved. Given the various skills of the mountain man, it is at least a fair guess that some of the bleeding may have been stanched by crude stitching with strips of buckskin. However, no one expected him to live. The problem, then, was what to do with him, since Indians in the area made it dangerous to remain there. Major Henry decided that the main party must move on and that two men could stay with Glass, out of decency, until he died. They could then bury him and catch up with the party. Two or three days would suffice since the old trapper was near death.

It took a reward of eighty dollars to induce two men to stay. One of them was Jim Bridger, then a youngster; the other was John Fitzgerald. They were under the mountain man code which placed the greatest premium upon assistance to those members of their group who were in trouble. Yet, after five days, with Hugh Glass hanging on to life somehow, Bridger and Fitzgerald feared the Indians would find them, saw no hope for Hugh's recovery, assumed he would die, took his weapons, and left. They reported to Major Henry that Glass had indeed died and had been properly buried. For this action they have been called "faithless wretches" and deserters, and some admirers of Jim Bridger have insisted that he was not, in fact, one of the men left with Glass. Since mountain men took care of their own, and there is no other reason, before or after the grizzly episode, to assume that Bridger and Fitzgerald were utterly dishonorable, it seems likely that the men detailed to stay with their fallen companion were absolutely certain that he could not survive, that he might, indeed, die at any minute, and that it was foolish to risk their own lives to "save" a dead man.

Whatever the case, Hugh Glass did not die. When he regained consciousness he undoubtedly saw the remains of the campfire, realized that his weapons were missing, and came to the conclusion that someone had stayed with him for a while and then abandoned him. Some accounts suggest that he knew which two comrades had deserted him. The desertion itself was enough to give him a new will to live, a reason to survive—revenge.

How soon Hugh's mind began to work with any clarity we cannot know. For days he must have remained where he was, mending, eating only buffalo berries and perhaps wild cherries, dragging himself painfully to the river to drink. When he finally felt ready—or impelled—to try to reach Fort Kiowa, the fur company's post near the present location of Chamberlain, it was probably instinct that pointed him south toward the Cheyenne River. Because one leg was severely damaged he could not walk. He began crawling, wriggling on his stomach like a snake. His food was whatever he could reach: berries, wild onion and wild turnip roots, grubs, mice, snakes, and once, left-over meat from an animal kill. As he crawled through prickly-pear, through dust, over rocks, always worried about Indians and food and water, newly worried about being alone, he kept one part of his mind focused on the two men who had deserted him. He would survive if only to get revenge.

Now in September, the days were often unbearably hot and the nights cold, the worst combination for a hurt man with no shelter. Hugh's world, like that of a lower creature, was flat on the ground until his leg healed enough so that he could rise to all fours and crawl a little faster, like a slow bear. On he pushed, sometimes over a landscape that would have been difficult for normal walking. He followed the path of least resistance, along valleys, skirting the hills. Somewhere between the Grand River and the Cheyenne River he fashioned a rude crutch from a tree branch and stood upright for the first time in perhaps more than a month. By the time he reached the river he had wriggled, crawled, and hobbled for more than ninety miles. He had also evolved into a man again, standing on two legs, looking up into sky to watch the geese flying over. It was like a spiritual experience, a rebirth, except that it was incomplete because the strong feeling of revenge was still buried deep in his mind and soul.

At the river he built a crude raft and was at last able to rest as he floated downstream. Ironically, in a later time, a small town would be built near the spot where he began his river trip and would be named Bridger. For the next 200 miles Hugh had Jim Bridger on his mind, and Fitzgerald too—down the Cheyenne until it ran into the Missouri, then down the Missouri almost to the present site of Chamberlain, to that location on the west bank where Fort Kiowa and Fort Lookout—trading posts— stood side by side, perhaps sharing the same outer walls. And the amazing journey had ended, in mid-October. As the Lewis and Clark expedition is one of the world's great travel stories, one of the epic journeys, so is Hugh Glass's crawl and survival, alone, one of the great individual achievements.

The story does not end here, of course. For the next eight months, through blizzards and encounters with hostile Indians, Glass looked for Jim and Fitz. By boat and on foot he journeyed upriver to Fort Union (not far from Canada), up the Yellowstone into Montana—where he found Jim—then southeast across Wyoming, northeast across the corner of Nebraska, into South Dakota again, east to the Missouri, and finally downriver to Fort Atkinson (Omaha) where he found Fitz in June 1824. Glass's need for revenge had carried or driven him almost two thousand miles. But he was unable to kill the two deserters when the time came. Perhaps his own survival had taught him a little of the value of life, of the possibility of forgiveness; perhaps the idea of desertion paled somewhat in the light of the practical arguments given him by his comrades. They could, after all, explain that they thought he was dead, that Indians endangered their own lives, that they had saved his gun for him, and also the money they were paid to watch over him while he died. The arguments were confused on some points, but so was the situation itself, and Hugh certainly did not like the idea of his friends being killed along with him. Besides, Jim had grown up into a real mountain man and claimed that he had learned everything from Hugh, while Fitz reminded him of the old brotherhood and of things yet to be done. No one recorded Hugh's answer to Fitz after hearing the case for the defense, but it is likely that Hugh became embarrassed, that he shrugged and turned away, with a few gruff words: "Tell the boy I ain't goin' to kill him either." Mountain men did not fuss over niceties.

Glass was ambushed, killed, and scalped eight years later by his old enemies, the Arikaras. He was operating out of Fort Union at the time, as a hunter, and it has long been rumored that while he was at the fort he told his life story to someone who wrote it down, but the manuscript has never been found. Perhaps the missing facts are unnecessary. Even without them, Old Hugh Glass and his *companyeros* have left a legacy consisting of the dislike of authority, the ability to live off the land, endurance and courage, and the complex problem which is always with us and is totally American, that of the individual in relation to society.

Historians have referred to the Glass story as the greatest of western tales. Only one has spent an abnormal amount of time attempting to discredit the entire story—a biographer of Jim Bridger who bristles at the thought of his being one of the deserters. The Hugh Glass story lives on in two major literary works, John G. Neihardt's epic poem, *The Song of Hugh Glass* (1915), and Frederick Manfred's novel, *Lord Grizzly* (1954). But Hugh never got the kind of publicity that was accorded events of some forty years later, events set in motion by two separate discoveries at just about the time of Hugh's death. In 1826, or thereabouts, the Sioux Indians began to arrive in substantial numbers in the area of the Black Hills, having been forced out of Minnesota by the Chippewa during the previous three-quarters of a century. As they spread westward, they stopped in several places in the land that would become the Dakotas, with some pushing south into Iowa and Nebraska, others angling north toward Canada, and the largest group spreading over South Dakota. The bands that discovered the Black Hills named them "Paha Sapa" for the color of the pines seen from a distance. They made camps in the lower Hills, heard strange noises from the higher Hills, and gradually felt that they were in a sacred place. For the white man, however, the Hills were a place of profane potential, a possible location of gold.

Most information about gold in the Black Hills before 1874 is suspect. The Hills foster mystery. Few of the early explorers went into the area, but all of them willingly reported rumor and hearsay to the extent that some modern historians believe that gold was discovered in the Hills as early as the time of Lewis and Clark. It is likely that the first gold mining was accomplished in 1834 by an isolated party, all apparently killed by Indians. During the next four decades gold may have been found a number of times, but the information was suppressed by the military in order to avoid a rush of goldseekers into the area, thus disturbing the delicate relationships between whites and Indians. It may be, too, that the army knew many of its own men would desert if they knew of the existence of gold. Nevertheless, the rumors persisted until they became well-publicized fact in 1874. Six years earlier the Treaty of Laramie had designated the Black Hills as a part of the Great Sioux Reservation and the U.S. Army was given the task of keeping non-Indians out of the area. Even so, the army was as curious about the Hills as everyone else was who had heard for years the rumors of gold. The most exciting and ballyhooed period of South Dakota history was about to begin.

In January 1873, the Legislative Assembly of Dakota Territory presented Congress with two requests, the first titled "Memorial asking for a Scientific Exploration of that Territory," and the second titled "Memorial in Reference to the Black Hills Country serving as a retreat for hostile Indians." The legislature contended that the Indians were not using the Hills for anything except a refuge following hostilities, and they should therefore be confined to another part of their reservation and the Hills should be opened to white settlement. In the following year Gen. Philip Sheridan obtained permission from his superiors to send an expedition into the Hills. On July 2, 1874, Lt. Col. George Armstrong Custer left Fort Abraham Lincoln (near Bismarck in what is now North Dakota) with ten companies of cavalry and two of infantry, more than a thousand men, and proceeded southwest, reaching the Belle Fourche in sight of the Black Hills in sixteen days. Shortly they were in the heart of the Hills, perhaps the first white men to penetrate this mysterious place. Custer was struck by its beauty. The scientists on the expedition marveled over the geological and botanical specimens they collected. By August, Custer sent two dispatches to Bismarck in which he rather casually mentioned that there seemed to be gold everywhere in the Black Hills. A newspaper correspondent filed a vivid story with the *Inter-Ocean* on August 27, 1874, and *Harper's Weekly* devoted a full page in its issue of September 12 to the same story. As part of Custer's command drew up papers, quite illegally, for a Custer Mining Company, word of gold spread throughout the nation, welcome news in the wake of the panic of 1873.

The War Department, remembering off and on that the Black Hills belonged to the Sioux by treaty, attempted to discourage the first civilian expeditions, but failed. The first party was organized in Sioux City, Iowa, by Charles Collins and T. H. Russell, with Tom Gordon as captain. Leaving on October 6, and arriving near Sturgis on December 9, the party included Annie D. Tallent who, with her nine-year-old son, had decided to accompany her husband. As a result of her 350-mile trek she became known as "the first white woman in the Black Hills." (Twenty-five years later she was to write an early history of the area: *The Black Hills, or, The Last Hunting Ground of the Dakotahs.*) Hundreds of goldseekers followed during the next year. The Sioux were aware that the Laramie Treaty had been violated. They might have wondered about some of the reasons, such as the curious American concept of Manifest Destiny as echoed in the *Yankton Daily Press and Dakotaian,* June 5, 1875:

> That portion of Dakota occupied by the various bands of Sioux belongs not to them, but to the representatives of an advancing civilization. The romance of the Indian right to hereditary possession of all or portion of the domain over which the United States now claims jurisdiction is the veriest bosh. A power beyond

that which takes to itself the right to make and unmake treaties between men long ago decreed that the American continent should be given over to the progress of enlightenment and the temporal advancement of those who are willing to make use of God's best gifts while they are on earth.

While "those who were willing" went after the "gift of gold," the army continued to attempt to dissuade prospecting parties from entering the Hills. One man started legal proceedings which reached the U.S. attorney general and resulted in the startling ruling that "no statutes made a breach of the provisions of the Sioux treaty an offense against the United States." The troopers relaxed and the northern Plains Indians assembled in what was to be their last great council. Present were the seven Teton Sioux tribes—the Brulés, Oglalas, Miniconjous, Hunkpapas, Blackfeet, Two-Kettles, and Sans Arcs—in addition to the Lower Brulés, Santees, Yanktons, and two non-Sioux tribes, the Arapahoes and Northern Cheyennes. The number was estimated at twenty thousand. Here were enough Indians to wipe out every white person in the Black Hills if they so chose. Instead, they listened to government representatives, to offers to sell the Hills—or at least the mining rights—and to reminders that the white man was slaughtering the remaining buffalo and that money would be needed to buy food.

The council could not agree on a solution and a few months later the military came up with their own. From Washington came an order that all Sioux who were not at their agencies by January 31, 1876, would be considered hostile. Because the winter was severe, the message did not even reach all the tribes by that date, but on February 1 the secretary of the interior told the secretary of war that all Indians not presently at the agencies were his to deal with.

In one sense, the mining ventures in the Black Hills were not different from those in California, Montana, Colorado, and Nevada. Similar kinds of people, similar difficulties in establishing law and order, similar incidents arising from greed or difficulty or heroism could be found in all the mining camps and areas. The big difference in the South Dakota gold strike was that it precipitated an Indian war, the largest and most important in the nation's history. The war raged around the Black Hills and, although the Hills were an island of one hundred miles in length (north and south) and sixty miles in width, the feverish mining activities were not untouched by this war. The combination of war and mining attracted people from all over the West, some of the most famous scouts and gunfighters of the time and some others who might have remained unknown except for the flood of publicity given to the Black Hills in—coincidentally—the year marking the 100th anniversary of the birth of the nation. The year 1876 will never be forgotten.

The Sioux are gentle in their naming of bees: *ováte ćek àla,* the "little people." And so it may be an improper simile to use here, but it seemed that household names of people (and places) were clustered in and around the Black Hills like bees around a hive. The list merely begins with these: Calamity Jane, Wild Bill Hickok, Sam Bass, Jack McCall, Poker Alice Tubbs, Whispering Smith, Colorado Charley Utter, Seth Bullock, Preacher Smith, Crazy Horse, Sitting Bull, Gall, Custer, Lame Johnny, Capt. Jack Crawford, Buffalo Bill, California Joe, Persimmon Bill, Texas Jack, Boone May, Ambrose Bierce, Mount Moriah Cemetery, Deadman Creek, French Creek, Deadwood, Hangman's Hill, Deadwood Gulch, Rockerville, and Harney Peak. And there were the mines and saloons, sometimes named and sometimes just numbered, and that famous hand of cards held by Wild Bill as he was killed, the "deadman's hand." Many of the names live more in legend than in fact. The time and the place brought writers of all kinds, but mostly exploiters, purple-prose practitioners, feeders of the eastern appetite for romance, violence, daring deeds, and colorful characters. The Wild West was in the air and the newspaper and magazine and dime-novel writers made it wilder. As a result of the many "literary" promotions it is difficult—sometimes impossible—to unearth the truth. Furthermore, even now, very few people are concerned about the actuality of Deadwood in 1876; the legends are comfortable, the myths are assuring, and the heroes must be inviolable because there are none in contemporary America.

The main hero of the Old West was the hunter-scout-lawman-gunman, usually although not always born in the Middle West and an ex-soldier from the Civil War. Above all, he was an adventurer, ready to change jobs whenever a better one came along, ready to see new country, and ready for anyone who challenged him. The characteristic of bravery, or valor, or righteous courage varied somewhat from one "hero" to another, as did skill with fists or firearms. It was generally conceded, however, that James Butler "Wild Bill" Hickok was the finest pistol shot on the plains, and his arrival in Deadwood acted as a kind of catalyst for the building of a romantic image which is still being commercialized a century later.

Wild Bill was born in LaSalle County, Illinois, May 27, 1837. As a boy he became accustomed to gunfire because his parents operated a station on the Underground Railroad, smuggling slaves out of the South. After working as a towpath driver on the Illinois and Michigan Canal he got the itch to go West, arriving in Leavenworth in 1855 and joining the free-state army in Kansas. Still later, working for a stagecoach line in Nebraska, he got into a fight with David McCanles and two neighbors (the cause was unclear at the time) and killed the three of them. Indications were that Hickok was not at fault, that perhaps he was only protecting the stage line property, and he was looked up to as a new western hero. The story took on color in later accounts, with Wild Bill being attacked by ten men, killing six of them with the six bullets in his gun, knifing the other four in hand-to-hand combat, and walking away when it was all over, "in fair health except for eleven buckshot holes and thirteen stab wounds."

During the Civil War, Hickok was a scout and sharpshooter with the Union Army, reportedly accounting for fifty or more of the enemy. In 1869 he was presented with a pair of ivory-handled pistols which became famous not only in real life but in popular western fiction as dozens of gunfight stories emanated from Hays and Abilene while Wild Bill was marshal from 1869 to 1872. His fame brought him to the eastern theaters where he, Buffalo Bill, and Texas Jack performed badly before unusually appreciative audiences for one season. Apparently it was the lure of gold that pulled him back to the West; he entered the Black Hills in 1875 with two friends, both of whom were killed by Indians as Hickok escaped to Wyoming. The next year he arrived in Deadwood with Colorado Charlie, interested in mining for gold, interested in gambling, and, according to legend, interested in Calamity Jane. By this time he was said to have killed thirty-six men in gunfights. His reputation was impressive, even in the Deadwood described by J. W. Buel in his 1886 book with the long title: *Heroes of the Plains, or Lives and Wonderful Adventures of Wild Bill, Buffalo Bill, Kit Carson, Capt. Payne, "White Beaver," Capt. Jack, Texas Jack, California Joe, and other Celebrated Indian Fighters, Scouts, Hunters & Guides including A True and Thrilling History of Gen. Custer's Famous "Last Fight" on the Little Big Horn, with Sitting Bull; also a Sketch of the Life of Sitting Bull, and His Account of the Custer Massacre as Related to the Author in Person.* Of Deadwood, Buel says:

> Deadwood, like every other big mining town that has yet been located in the West, was full of rough characters, cut-throats, gamblers and the devil's agents generally. Night and day the wild orgies of depraved humanity continued; a fiddler was an important personage, provided he would hire out to saw all night in a saloon, and the concert singer was a bonanza, especially if the voice were clothed in petticoats. The arbiter of all disputes was either a knife or pistol, and the graveyard soon started with a steady run of victims. Sodom and Gomorrah were both dull, stupid towns compared with Deadwood, for in a square contest for the honors of moral depravity the Black Hills' capital could give the people of the Dead Sea cities three points in the game and then skunk them both.[1]

This would seem to be a fitting context for the battles waged by a tall handsome hero like Wild Bill Hickok whose morals were not in question. Yet, Bill had not come to Deadwood to clean it up, as he had done in Hays and Abilene; he simply wanted to make money, like everyone else, and did so by gambling rather than by panning gold. It did not seem to tarnish his reputation, nor did the rumor that he had a love affair with the most colorful—and depraved—woman in the Hills, Calamity Jane.

1. J. W. Buel, *Heroes of the Plains* (Philadelphia: Standard Publishing Co., 1886), pp. 186–187.

Born near Burlington, Iowa, perhaps on May 1, 1852, Martha Cannary, later known as Calamity Jane, was partly a woman of mystery and partly a drunken prostitute. One account of her life (Roberta Sollid, *Calamity Jane,* 1958) opens with the statement: "No career is so elusive to the historian as that of a loose woman." Jane's own story, set down very briefly by a ghost writer around 1896, is a marvel. According to her, she was a remarkable shot and rider as a girl, crossed the mountains many times, scouted for General Custer, performed many dangerous missions in Indian country, rode for the pony express, drove teams with wagon trains, helped build Sturgis, ranched, and married Clinton Burke in Texas ten years after she had made numerous references to Wild Bill as her friend. These generalizations have been embellished over the years by those writers and gossipers who wanted a "heroine of the plains" and who could not resist a love affair between the two most notorious people in the Black Hills. It does not matter that Calamity Jane was shabby, dirty, homely, and thoroughly debased, or that she may have slept with almost as many men as Wild Bill had presumably killed. Nor does it matter that during the smallpox plague of 1878 she ministered to the sick and dying in Deadwood and in Confederate Gulch. (In fact, one somewhat cynical writer has pointed out that smallpox seemed to break out wherever Calamity went.) Whether she was legally Mrs. Burke, or Mrs. Hickok, or whether she did even a tenth of the things attributed to her, she became a legend very quickly and remains one in the hearts of all romantics. She was featured in Nos. 15 and 39 of the "Deadwood Dick Library" of the late nineteenth century. She may be found in hundreds of newspaper stories, pamphlets, magazine articles, and books, some of them trying to keep the myth alive and others attempting to debunk it.

Her fame was made secure by her burial next to Wild Bill Hickok, according to her request, in Deadwood's Mount Moriah Cemetery. However, it was probably enough that she was in Deadwood in 1876. It was a strange year in a strange place. Poetry and murder lived side by side on this island of rock and forest while the surrounding plains echoed with the sounds of war. Consider a sampling of dates from that year:

June 5—The J. B. Pearson party (Pearson located first claim in Deadwood) returned to Yankton with $20,000 in gold dust.

June 8—First issue of the *Black Hills Pioneer* published by two men from Denver.

June 25—George Armstrong Custer and some two hundred men of the Seventh Cavalry killed in Montana, not far from the Hills.

June—The No. 6 mine in Deadwood yielded $2,300 in gold in one day, the largest up to that time in the Hills.

June—Captain Jack left on a trip to Omaha but wrote a poem first.

July—Weekly trips of pony express established between Deadwood and Laramie.

July 17—Buffalo Bill Cody killed Chief Yellow Hand in individual combat just south of the Hills, and a wagon train piloted by Wild Bill Hickok arrived in Deadwood.

July 23—The dramatic troupe of Mr. and Mrs. Jack Langrishe gave a performance in Deadwood.

August 2—Wild Bill shot in back of head, fatally, by Jack McCall.

August 20—Preacher Smith, who prayed at Hickok's funeral, found shot to death on the road to Crook City.

The news of Custer's *faux pas* and disaster reached Deadwood late in July, so that the town had not recovered from that shock by the time Wild Bill was murdered. Yet, when the *Black Hills Pioneer* reported the assassination three days later, it was only one of several events of interest.

August 2. an exciting day in Dead Wood. The fun commenced early this morning by a crowd of 20 armed men excorting a Murderer through Town. This fellow had killed his man in Gay Ville two miles above this. Some three or four weeks ago he was caught at Fort Larime brought back tried yesterday in Gay Ville and turned loose and was guarded through Town this morning. About noon a man was found just a cross the creek Dead cause of Death poor whiskey. Just after dinner Wild Bill was Shot through the Head. Killed instantly. While the crowd was Debating whether to hang the assassin or not Reports came from Crook City that the Indians have Surrounded the Town and that help was wanted. All those that

could get Horses went down to render assistance. Just at Sundown a
Greaser come in with an Indian Head. This caped the climax. Wild
Bill and everything else was thrown in the Shade. The Greaser was
surrounded and carried through Town. when they reached the upper
end of Town there was fuly two Thousand men hooping and
yelling. Such a Sight is Seldom Seen anywhere.

The head was Strung up on a pole put up at auction carried
around to the places of Busyness and the people asked to give the
killer one or five dollars just as he liked a horrid looking thing to
make Some fuss about. It is getting to dangerous here to be healthy.
A man is liable to be Shot here any time by Some Drunken
Desperado and it is not very safe to go out but we have decided to
go tomorrow.

Capt. Jack Crawford wrote two poems to Hickok after the assassination. Jack McCall was acquitted by a Deadwood jury,
but he was soon arrested again by a deputy U.S. marshal, taken
to Yankton for a new trial, found guilty of murder, and hanged
on March 1, 1877. The poker hand Wild Bill held as he was
shot—aces over eights—has itself become a part of the legend,
known as the "deadman's hand."

Even though Deadwood hosted as large a collection of gun-
men as could be brought together at one time, it remained for
another man, Buffalo Bill Cody, connected to Deadwood only
by association with people who were actually there, to give the
Old West its ultimate publicity and commercial use. Cody, born
in Le Claire, Iowa, on February 26, 1846, became a distinguished plainsman in his own right, serving as a hunter for the
military (thus his nickname) and as a scout. After being interviewed by Ned Buntline (Edward Zane Carroll Judson), a writer
of dime novels and magazine articles, Cody found himself lion-
ized in a fiction which left him astounded: Buntline had taken
great liberties with the facts of Bill's life. Buffalo Bill became
so popular as a western character that Buntline talked Cody into
going into business with him and putting on a stage performance
called *The Scouts of the Plains*. It was a poorly-written "play,"
and badly acted by Cody and Texas Jack, with Buntline himself
also on stage feeding lines to the two famous westerners. After
a year of touring, with great popular response and financial suc-

cess, Cody decided to set up his own tour for the following season, 1873–1874. Starring with him in the play this time were Texas Jack Omohundro and Wild Bill Hickok. The three were good friends, and a photograph of them together has prompted some students of the West to place Buffalo Bill in Deadwood in 1876, since the other two were there. Cody was south of the Black Hills at the time he met Yellow Hand in combat and supposedly shouted, "The first scalp for Custer!" He probably never visited Deadwood, but his first stage productions featured Deadwood notables—Capt. Jack Crawford, poet-scout of the Black Hills, in addition to Omohundro and Hickok. The later productions, such as the one that toured Europe and included Sitting Bull for one year, were broader in scope although they frequently made use of Deadwood incidents and characters.

Popular stories of frontier life were being published before Buffalo Bill Cody's Wild West Show toured the cities of the eastern United States and of Europe. Beadle's Half Dime Library, beginning with "Deadwood Dick" by Edward L. Wheeler, had reached 187 issues by 1877. These adventure tales were not limited to the West, although most of them traded upon the names of the western heroes in thin disguise: Jack, Seth, Buffalo Ben, Hurricane Bill, Kit, and Sam, in various combinations suggested Jack Omohundro, Seth Bullock, Wild Bill, Kit Carson, and Sam Bass as well as others. There was also a separate Deadwood Dick Library of at least 129 issues. The *Buffalo Bill Weekly,* published in the early part of the twentieth century, apparently topped out at 550 issues and then started over as the *New Buffalo Bill Weekly,* at five cents per copy, and reached at least number 168 on the "new" stories. The Dime and Half-Dime series included more than 130 stories whose locale was South Dakota, the Black Hills, or Deadwood, and almost eighty titles featuring Calamity Jane, Wild Bill, Texas Jack, California Joe, Capt. Jack Crawford, Custer, and Sitting Bull. (Oddly, no titles are listed for Crazy Horse.) The famous Dime Novel is difficult to pin down, although Ned Buntline had a great deal to do with its success in the late nineteenth century. There were hundreds of them, just as there have been thousands of longer and more recent novels called "Westerns" emanating in part from Owen Wister's *Virginian*. The Cody show and the dime novels no doubt played an important part in the establishment of "the Western." To professors of American literature, Ned Buntline is at best a curiosity and at worst an outright "literary" villain. It must be remembered, however, that the dime novel and the later "Western" were written primarily to satisfy certain psychological needs of a rather complex and varied eastern society, people who were troubled by the problems of their own lives and wanted to share vicariously in the adventures of the western hero, the individual in a free land, the explorer, the giant killer. People who had actually experienced the frontier put little stock in the books. It is interesting, too, that what is still called the Wild West existed for only thirty years and almost entirely on the Great Plains. The mountain man of an earlier period is not nearly as popular a fictional subject as are scout, soldier, Indian, hunter, guide, and railroad builder of the last half of the nineteenth century. Whatever his particular vocation, the hero is a gunfighter. He may have served in the army, he may have herded cows, he may have gambled, or mined for gold, but in the popular image he was above all a gunfighter. There were town marshals and U.S. marshals and horse thieves and train robbers, but essentially they were all gunfighters. Psychologists have made much of the phallic symbolism of the pointed gun, of the sense of power a man feels when on horseback, and of various Freudian complexes which often seem to motivate the "Western," whether in book, film, or on television. These psychologists see the avid reader of "Westerns" as an adolescent with unfulfilled needs.

It is probably more to the point to say that for a nation which was built upon successive frontiers over a period of two centuries the final frontier was a thing to cherish, to grow nostalgic over, to romanticize about, to try to hang on to. Whether the stories from the last frontier were real or were myth did not matter, because in the establishment of traditions and values, and in memories of the past, myth is often better than fact. It nourishes the aspirations and needs of the culture from which it arises. If Americans should be characterized as expedient, practical, individualistic, sentimental, violent, fighters against evil, on the side of the underdog against impossible odds, and so on, then the western hero, or the gunfighter, is their man. In periods of national difficulty or crisis there is always an escapist literature to relieve the mind of its otherwise inescapable problems. The western story served this purpose after the Civil War. Edgar Rice Burroughs, who had already written several western novels, introduced the Tarzan books around World War I. Detective stories and science fiction became popular during the depression and World War II.

The image of the Romantic West lingers on. Modern writers are more concerned about historical facts than were Ned Buntline, J. W. Buel, Prentice Ingraham, Edward L. Wheeler, and other late nineteenth-century exploiters of the western hero and villain, but they recognize the value of myth. Deadwood is rarely mentioned in contemporary literature, and yet it was, in one sense, the last frontier, a symbol of what is to be remembered as the "free" and colorful American past. And so South Dakota is still sometimes considered a frontier state, perhaps more so than Colorado or Kansas or Texas because it has no large cities or industrial areas to link it firmly to modern technological society.

Whether Deadwood in the 1870s can serve as the material for a composite picture of the American character, or a symbol of its hopes and fears, is debatable but not impossible. Calamity Jane, a ne'er-do-well, a drunk, a whore, was also at least briefly a humanitarian. Wild Bill was skilled in violence, left his wife to look for gold, was restless, but also he was manly and law-abiding, apparently a nice man—killed from behind. Preacher Smith was clearly a good man but was careless about himself and was killed because of his carelessness. Boone May was a lawman who began to enjoy killing. Captain Jack was a fighter, but he also wrote poetry and plays. Buffalo Bill, on the fringe of Deadwood, was heroic, brave, and perhaps even noble, but he was also an exploiter, a showman, and a cold-hearted business man. Everyone in Deadwood was greedy; the town was filled with opportunists. But they were hard workers, rebuilding the town with amazing speed after fire destroyed it. Most of the people there were wanderers, always looking for a new life, a fresh stake, further adventure, and constantly concerned about money. Or does one say "livelihood"? There was a combination of cruelty and sentiment, of the hard and the soft. It is said that the famous author, Ambrose Bierce, did the one good thing in his life while he was in Deadwood. Thirty-eight years old at the time, he was already notorious for his cynicism, his satiric and irreverent writing (in poems, stories, and newspaper work), and his inability to settle down. His fiction was strange, but not as much as his life and death. From his birthplace in Ohio he went through the Civil War right on to California and, later drawn to the Black Hills by gold, he became (no one knows quite how) the general agent of the Black Hills Placer Mining Company at Rockerville. During his year with the company, 1880, it was beset with disorganization, intrigue, dishonesty, and the pressures of politics, as several factions vied for control, lawsuits were brought against the company, and the newspapers attacked it. Through all this, Bierce worked hard, remained loyal to the best interests of the company and its employees, was completely honest, and was just as completely defeated. Precisely why he changed character for that one year is anyone's guess (over thirty years later he disappeared in Mexico), but the frontier could bring out both the worst and the best in people. It was a testing ground. Deadwood was not the only one, but it remains in the memory because it began to flourish in that eventful year, 1876, when George Armstrong Custer and Wild Bill Hickok, among others, were killed, and the nation was realizing that it was one hundred years old.

3

The Big Road to and from Dakota

T may seem preposterous to say that one-fifth of the Missouri River is in South Dakota, because this mighty river is always on the move even though its flow has been controlled somewhat by modern dams. Throughout its known history it has always excited the imagination of the explorer, or the trader and fur trapper, or the steamboat traveler. It has been called a "thoroughly masculine" river, a monster, a gateway to the West, a highway to the Shining Mountains. The Indians called it the Smoky Water, and the white man later gave it the name of Big Muddy. It has been of immense importance to the seven states it touches—Missouri, Kansas, Nebraska, Iowa, South Dakota, North Dakota, and Montana—as well as to the nation as a whole. It has been called an epic poem; but Father Marquette, who with Jolliet is given credit for discovering the Missouri River in June 1673, at the point where it flows into the Mississippi, said later, "I never saw anything more frightful." He had, of course, come upon the river at its most turbulent place and in floodtime. Nevertheless, the big river continued to hold many surprises for those who boated on it in later years.

Figures are often unimportant, but in this case they are at least impressive. The Missouri River from its headwaters in the Rocky Mountains to where it meets the Mississippi near Saint Louis is approximately 2,700 miles long, making it the eighth longest river in the world. If it, rather than the Mississippi, were to be considered the main river instead of a tributary, it would be more than 3,700 miles in length and the third longest river in the world. In either case, the Missouri is more important historically than statistically.

Pierre de La Vérendrye and his sons were almost certainly the first white men to see the river where it flows through the Dakotas. They came from eastern Canada and entered the Dakota region from the north on a long and dangerous mission to find what so many other expeditions sought, water passage to the Pacific Ocean. They did not succeed, but they found a Mandan village late in 1738, in the middle of winter, and a day later one of the sons came upon the frozen river. Although Pierre de La Vérendrye was soon forced to return to Montreal because of illness, his sons continued to explore. Whether, during the next several years, they went as far west as the Black Hills is debatable, but on March 30, 1743, they buried a lead plaque on the bluff above the Missouri River near the present location of Pierre, South Dakota, with names and the date. The plaque was discovered by school children in 1913, and the Vérendryes were honored as the first white men in the state.

The main entrance to South Dakota, however, was to be from the south. And the early travel into the region was to be closely related to national and international interests and wars. Prior to the American colonists' move toward independence from England, the struggle for dominance in North America involved three European countries—Britain, France, and Spain. In general, the British operated from the northeast portion of what is now the United States, and from Canada. The Spanish came in from the southwest. France competed with Britain in Canada and the Great Lakes area and with Spain at the mouth of the Mississippi—New Orleans. The gradual thrust of all three nations was toward the center of the continent, partly because of the hopes that the big rivers there would provide, or lead to, a passageway to the Pacific Ocean and to the Orient. Commercially, the land was important because of furs. How many independent explorers and trappers reached the Missouri River in the Dakotas before 1800 is uncertain, but it is likely that the number was small. A series of wars, partially related and overlapping, provided the stimulus for the first regular traffic on the Missouri River leading into South Dakota: the French and Indian War, 1755–1763, between Britain and France; the Revolutionary War, 1775–1783, between the American Colonies and Britain; and the Napoleonic Wars, 1796–1815, between France and several countries, including Britain, Austria, Russia, and Prussia. Oddly, Spain was not directly involved in any of these wars but was to feel the effects of them in the wilderness of middle and western America.

Much of the Spanish expansion from Florida to Mexico was accomplished in the sixteenth century, shortly before the colonists from England landed farther north on the Atlantic coast. By the eighteenth century, Spain had laid claim to all land west of the Mississippi River, even though much of it had not yet been explored. By this time the British were looking to the western lands. At the conclusion of their war with France—the Treaty of Paris in 1763—the British were given all land which had been claimed by France east of the Mississippi and north of the Gulf of Mexico. After an Indian war, Britain occupied this territory in 1765 and sent traders up and down the rivers, many of them crossing the Mississippi—which was the international boundary line—and penetrating Spanish territory. Both British and Spanish traders complained to their governments of unlawful competition.

The Revolutionary War had little immediate effect on the Missouri Valley but it left the British with a monopoly on trade in the upper Mississippi Valley and therefore a threat to the Spanish through possible expansion to the southwest. Another threat was posed to Spain when the Russians came south along the Pacific Coast at the same time as both English and Americans were entering that region. Spain gave up her land above the forty-second parallel and decided to push exploration on the upper Missouri River in order to establish a line of forts and to find a passage to the Pacific Ocean. In this way the Spanish hoped to protect themselves from the British and the Russians.

And so the stage was set for the "opening" of South Dakota, although it would be a lengthy process and would be limited largely to the river for several decades. In the last quarter of the eighteenth century the geography of the upper Missouri and the vast lands through which it passed was still unknown. The land was a mystery. Even so, it is thought that Pierre Dorion of Saint Louis, a French-Canadian, arrived at a Yankton Sioux village in 1775, married into the tribe, and "settled" in what is now South Dakota. (The certainty of the year is unimportant to those who recognize the fine coincidence between the "beginning" of South Dakota and the Battles of Lexington and Concord in the East, the ride of Paul Revere, and the beginning of the revolution which was to achieve independence for the American colonies.) Not much is known about Pierre Dorion; he was hired as an interpreter by Lewis and Clark in 1804, wandered around for a few years, and returned to the Yankton (near the present site of the town) in 1811 to find his sons grown into men with bad dispositions.

The first traders to represent Spain on the upper Missouri were also French-Canadians with bad dispositions. Jacques d'Eglise, who said he was from Saint Louis, received a license to hunt on the Missouri in 1790. Joseph Garreau was outfitted by Don Andres Fagot la Garciniere of Saint Louis at about the same time. D'Eglise was considered a simple man who spoke a provincial French that no one could understand; he was praised for his business methods but condemned for his morals. Little is known of Garreau, but it appears that many of the Indians distrusted him. Yet, he was forced to live with them because a return to Saint Louis would have meant facing angry creditors. The first trip of d'Eglise, in 1790 or 1791, did not result in much. On his second trip, in 1793, he was accompanied by Garreau. Although d'Eglise obtained enough furs to satisfy his own creditors, he was harassed by the Arikara and Sioux and also annoyed by Garreau's "turbulent and libertine spirit." Upon his return to Saint Louis, he reported that he had been the first Spaniard to trade with the Mandans, which, if true, would mean that he had traversed the entire present-day state of South Dakota, from south to north and back again. In spite of his achievement he was not in good favor with the Spanish when they organized the Company of Explorers of the Upper Missouri (the Missouri Company) and sent out their first expedition in

1794 under the leadership of Jean Baptiste Truteau. A $3,000 prize was offered to the first man to reach the Pacific, but, more to the point, Truteau was ordered to stop d'Eglise and Garreau from trading on the upper Missouri and was to report any difficulties he encountered with the Indians as a result of the earlier misbehavior of those two men.

Truteau had been a school teacher in Saint Louis; he took employment with the Missouri Company in order to supplement his income. The Indians along the Missouri were not yet fully hostile in the eighteenth century, and it was possible for a man of books to proceed in relative safety past the Mahas (Omahas), the Poncas, the Arikaras, and the Sioux on the way upriver toward the Mandans. Truteau built winter quarters near the subsequent site of Fort Randall in South Dakota (frequently considered the first house to be erected in the "state"), remained there until the spring of 1795, and then spent about a year with the Arikara until they were attacked by the Sioux in May 1796. The Sioux, having been pushed out of Minnesota, were at this time moving into South Dakota and driving the Arikaras out of the plains area which was to become home for the Sioux; and so the Indians were more concerned with each other at this time than with the white men who, as yet, posed no major threat to the Indians. Truteau's expedition was successful enough so that his journal was sent by Thomas Jefferson to Meriwether Lewis to study. Truteau went back to teaching school in Saint Louis, but d'Eglise continued to operate along the Missouri, reportedly without success, until 1804. Eventually he went south where he was murdered in New Mexico in 1806.

As George Washington served his terms as first president of the United States, and Spanish expeditions continued to ply the upper Missouri, Americans began to look farther westward. A 1789 geography textbook stated that "The Mississippi was never designed as the western boundary of the American Empire." Our ministers to England and France suggested that the vast western lands called Louisiana be taken by force. The whole question suddenly became academic to Spain when Napoleon, engaged in war in Europe, demanded Louisiana. In spite of the 1800 Treaty of San Ildefonso, which promised

Spain some acquisitions in Tuscany in return for Louisiana, Napoleon abandoned that part of his campaign and was given the trans-Mississippi lands for nothing. The entire venture had been too expensive for Spain anyway, with little return. The exchange of property, however, alarmed the Americans because they felt that France was more of a threat than Spain had been. When the warehouses at New Orleans were closed to Americans, in effect closing the Mississippi, the alarm increased to warlike proportions. President Jefferson then made overtures to France, suggesting that the United States would be willing to pay up to ten million dollars for the purchase of New Orleans and the Floridas. The end result is well known as one of the best real estate deals in world history. Napoleon needed money for his European campaigns, and so he broke his promise to Spain (that he would not transfer Louisiana to any other power) and sold more than 909,000 square miles for about fifteen million dollars. (It cost the United States another eight million dollars in finance charges.) The Louisiana Purchase of 1803 doubled the size of the United States overnight and led immediately to the first thorough examination of the entire Missouri River.

Beginning on May 14, 1804, near Saint Louis, the Lewis and Clark expedition covered almost 7,000 miles before returning to Saint Louis on September 23, 1806. The party comprised about fifty men at the start, although the number varied from time to time during the two-year journey. Some were frontiersmen, some were soldiers, a hardy and disciplined group that lost only one member in twenty-eight months of difficult travel, and he from sickness (probably appendicitis) near today's Sioux City, Iowa, where the monument to Sergeant Charles Floyd stands high on a bluff. They traveled in two pirogues (long wooden canoes) and a keelboat fifty-five feet long and outfitted with oars, pushing poles, and a sail. Besides the men, these boats carried twenty-one bales of presents for the Indians, plus tools and supplies.

The instructions given by President Jefferson to Captains Lewis and Clark were almost as lengthy as the trip itself. Their primary task, of course, was to find a water route to the Pacific Ocean, but they were also to note a few things as they went along: latitude and longitude observations at every remarkable point on the river; commerce which might be carried on with the people inhabiting each region they passed through; possessions, relations with other tribes, language, traditions, monuments, occupations, arts, implements, food, clothing, housing, diseases and remedies, moral and physical circumstances, peculiarities in laws and customs for each of these peoples; the soil and its growth and vegetable productions; the animals of the country, especially those not known in the eastern half of the country; the mineral productions of every kind, particularly metals, limestone, pit coal, saltpeter, salines, and mineral waters; volcanic appearances; climate, as characterized by temperature, the proportion of rainy, cloudy, and clear days, and by lightning, snow, hail, and ice, and by the time of frost, by prevailing winds in different seasons, the dates at which plants bud and lose flower or leaf, and the times of appearance of birds, insects, or reptiles. There was much more. Two sets of records were to be kept, guaranteeing the safety of all the information collected, one set to be on birch bark, which was impervious to water.

The drama and excitement, as well as the occasional tedium, of the journey is best found in the journals themselves—the Biddle edition which was published first, or the Thwaites edition which is most faithful to the original notes, or the condensed DeVoto edition, or the slightly modernized Bakeless edition—and also in the novels written more than a century later based on the expedition, notably Vardis Fisher's *Tale of Valor*. For South Dakota we are concerned only with what happened on a stretch of river approximately 545 miles in length, from what is now Sioux City west and then north to what is now the state line between South and North Dakota. Modern reference points will be useful, although the river channel has changed in a few places since 1804.

On August 23, between Sioux City and Vermillion, hunting parties killed a buffalo and two deer, while another deer was killed from the boats. Elk and wolves were also sighted, but the excitement of the day seems to have been huge clouds of sand blown off the sandbars by high winds. Rain solved that problem on the next day, and as the expedition reached Vermillion the talk was mostly of Spirit Mound, said to be the residence of devils. On the 26th Lewis and Clark took nine men with them and walked the six miles from river to mound. Their dog was tired and hot and was sent back to a creek to cool off. The six-mile walk had taken four hours. Before long, Captain Lewis was also made sick by the heat and the party had to find water after examining the hill. Their first inclination was to believe that the mound was made by man because of its regular form, but they later concluded it was a natural hill. One explanation of the Indians' belief that spirits inhabited the mound was the unusually large number of birds on its summit. Lewis and Clark, in their role of scientists, or objective observers, concluded that the birds were driven there by the wind sweeping with force across the unprotected plains and that they sought shelter on the leeward side of the hill. From the top of the mound the captains looked out at what they considered a beautiful landscape in spite of the lack of trees. Buffalo were seen in herds, feeding, in all directions. (In the 1970s a cattle feedlot has cut into Spirit Mound and almost no one is concerned about the possibility of spirits or devils.)

It took three days from Vermillion to reach Yankton, during which time Sioux Indians and their interpreter, Pierre Dorion, met them near the James River, the wind blew, one pirogue ran into a snag and was badly damaged, and Lewis and Clark were "much indisposed" for some reason they could not identify (perhaps allergies, the most common ailment in this part of South Dakota). At the site of the present-day Gavins Point Dam which has formed a large lake called, appropriately, Lewis and Clark Lake, and which serves as a recreational area, the expedition met for several days with more than seventy Sioux. A fat dog was cooked and eaten. Presents were exchanged. Dorion was upset because the captains did not invite him to their private dinner at the end of the first day. Clark described the Sioux as bold, handsome, and well made, but concluded that they did not shoot as well with their bows and arrows as did other Indians he had seen. Nevertheless, he respected them, took down as much of their language as he could in a few days, asked questions through his interpreter about certain customs, and seemed fairly satisfied with the meetings. Late on the last evening, Dorion was given a bottle of whiskey, the Indians crossed to the other side of the river, and a violent wind brought rain from the northwest.

On a fairly good day the travelers made fifteen to twenty miles, but they were continually stopping to examine the bluffs, to hunt, to collect berries, and to estimate measurements of the river (about 500 yards wide near Bon Homme Island), of the bluffs (both height and length), and even the acreage of areas which appeared to be fortifications of an earlier people. In their descriptions in general, the plains beyond the river were always beautiful, the wind almost always blew hard, and the river—full of sandbars—constantly washed away large portions of its banks. Often, because of the rapid current and the stiff headwinds, the men were obliged to use tow ropes to pull the boats along. But they stopped occasionally, too, out of the same curiosity small boys still have, as when they saw their first prairie dog village south of Fort Randall and after attempting to dig to the bottom of one of the holes, and failing, proceeded to pour five barrels of water into another hole without filling it.

On September 9, five days after they passed the mouth of the Niobrara River and had made the turn to the north, Clark went looking for goats and prairie dogs with the intention of killing one of each. He failed in that venture, but found a herd of at least 500 buffalo near the river and killed one, as did R. Fields. Clark's black servant, York, always the subject of curiosity among the Indians, killed two buffalo. The next day Clark reported the finding of a petrified fish backbone forty-five feet long. On September 11 he finally succeeded in killing four prairie dogs (which he called barking squirrels), intending to have their skins stuffed. The river here was wide and shallow and crowded with sandbars. Clark said there were so many sandbars that they were not worth mentioning, but he continued to mention them. Here, too, the party caught up with George Shannon who had set out with the horse herd sixteen days earlier, mistakenly thought he was behind the expedition and hurried to catch up with it, all the time getting farther ahead. Finally he had run out of ammunition and was unable to kill game, except one rabbit which he shot with a hard stick rather than a ball. When the party found him he was close to starvation, in a land of plenty. On this day the men killed an elk, two deer, and one pelican.

The mouth of the White River, just south of Chamberlain, was passed on September 15, and the following day was spent resting and letting the baggage dry out after three days of heavy rain. Lewis commented on this day about the small size of the oak trees in the vicinity and on the poor quality of the buffalo they shot, so that only the tongues, marrow bones, and skins were taken. He spent September 17 walking, having felt confined in the boat. The short rich grass of the plains reminded him of a beautiful bowling green, on which he saw wolves and polecats, and above which flew hawks. Altogether he found the scenery pleasing and was further impressed by the number of buffalo (which he estimated at 3,000), deer, elk, and antelope. One can only speculate on what the balance of nature would have produced in this area if it had not been subjected to the settler's plow in later years. Certainly Lewis's description no longer applies. The river itself has had something to do with the changes; even while Lewis and Clark were camped on September 21 near the Grand Detour (the Big Bend of the Missouri, north of Chamberlain), so much sand was falling from the river bank into the water that camp had to be broken quickly and the boats moved before they were sunk. In this same area the Sioux reservations of Crow Creek and Lower Brulé were later established, and more recently the valley filled with water backing up above the Big Bend Dam, eliminating that portion of the reservation on which the twentieth-century Sioux artist, Oscar Howe, was born. Much of the land viewed by Lewis and Clark in South Dakota is under water at the present time, and it is likely that considerable evidence of an earlier culture is lost to us; yet, it is difficult to criticize modern attempts to stabilize the active and fickle Missouri River through dams and flood control.

Shortly after the expedition had left Saint Louis back in late May, it had met Regis Loisel, a trader who had encountered difficulties with the Teton Sioux at the mouth of the Bad River and had been forced to abandon his enterprise. Although the Mahas, Poncas, and Yanktons were reasonably friendly, it was known through Loisel and others that the Tetons were stopping traders and ''buying'' their goods at a rate considered no better than robbery. Therefore, when Lewis and Clark passed the house and small fort built by Loisel on Cedar Island, September 22, they began to think about the Tetons waiting ahead. Some years earlier these Indians had forced the Arikaras farther up the river as they began to take over the entire western half of South Dakota. They had been able to frighten the French and Spanish traders, and Lewis and Clark knew that the only way to deal with them was through preparation and control. The Sioux did not take long to realize that these white men would fight if necessary, and that they were not afraid. The white men were outnumbered, and yet they would be able to inflict more damage than the Tetons cared to think about. And so the negotiations in late September, at the Bad River, proceeded through bluster, diplomacy, and guile, with tension hanging constantly in the air like the smoke around the campfires.

The morning of the 25th was fair. Two-thirds of the men of the expedition remained on the boats anchored seventy yards from the sandbar on which the other men raised a flagstaff and prepared to meet the Indians. The first chiefs arrived late in the morning and the council began at noon. Captain Lewis began a speech but the interpreter was not expert enough to get his meaning across and Lewis had to quit. The chiefs were taken out to the boat and were given whiskey, after which several of the young Tetons on shore began to act rowdily and one chief—perhaps under the influence of the whiskey—became insolent. Clark drew his sword and Lewis ordered the men on the boat to draw their arms. The Tetons began to take arrows from their quivers. Clark, whose temper was quicker than Lewis's, grew irritated, but at last he was able to return to the boat and to proceed with the pirogues to a small island for the night. In honor of the recent events, Clark named the island Bad Humored Island.

Next day the expedition was persuaded to stop a few miles

upstream so that the Teton women and children could see the boat. Clark, perhaps still feeling the anger of the previous day, thought the men were ill-looking and not well made, but he conceded that the women were fine-looking, though not handsome. The captains took turns going ashore and visiting among the Indians until it appeared as though intentions were of a friendly nature; then both sat down to eat—after several speeches—a meal of dogmeat, pemmican, and ground potato. Following the meal everyone smoked for an hour, after which a fire was built and women danced to a music of stretched-skin tambourines and jingling animal hoofs tied to sticks. Four of the chiefs spent the night on the boat. Clark did not sleep well, nor did the next day improve his disposition as he began to think the Indians intended to make trouble. That night the chiefs again insisted that they stay on the boat and Clark did not sleep at all. On the morning of September 28 the chiefs were removed from the boat with some difficulty; the entire day was a confusing combination of testiness on the part of some Indians, the giving of gifts to others, and frequent landings by the boat in order to take on a few Indians for a while and put others off. Seen objectively, the events must have seemed like a comedy of errors, but Clark's comment at the end of the day was only, "I am very unwell for want of sleep. Determined to sleep tonight if possible." For the next two days, as the expedition moved upstream again, bands of Indians and sometimes individuals appeared along the bank of the river at frequent intervals, some of them wanting presents (they were given tobacco) and some wanting a ride (they were refused). Perhaps Clark got some sleep, and perhaps he began to see the constant nagging of the Indians as routine; in any case, on the last day of September he once again noted that the sandbars were so numerous that it was unnecessary to mention them.

From subsequent events it appears that the Tetons were impressed by the show of arms and steady nerves and that they passed the message upstream to other tribes that this expedition was not to be trifled with. Some historians have been tempted toward a kind of patriotic zeal in pointing out that the French and Spanish had been intimidated by the Indians on the upper

Missouri but the Americans could not be bullied or frightened. It should be remembered that the traders were opportunists, upriver to make their fortunes, and were not motivated beyond that. The Lewis and Clark expedition, on the other hand, desired information, peace, and safe passage on a long journey under the orders of the president of the United States, and was prepared to achieve these purposes in military fashion. There was a difference. The difference was noticed by the Sioux, and the expedition had no further difficulties with Indians on the rest of the journey.

For two more weeks Lewis and Clark were within South Dakota. On October 1 they met a Frenchman at the mouth of the Cheyenne River, upstream from Pierre where the meeting with the Tetons had taken place. Jean Valle had probably been associated with Loisel; he told of having been to the Black Mountains, far to the west, where great pines grew, where summits retained snow through much of the summer, and a great and strange noise was heard frequently. The captains dutifully recorded his story but kept most of their attention on rising winds and dropping temperatures. By October 7 they were at the Moreau River, just south of Mobridge, and soon they arrived at the villages of the Arikaras, known to the mountain men as Rees. These people grew corn, tobacco, and beans, did not show any fondness for liquor, and were astonished at seeing a black man. Lewis and Clark enjoyed eating cornbread, beans, and squash—Clark, in particular, never able to like the dogmeat of the Sioux. Past the Grand River and on to the north during the second week in October, the party passed and several times visited a number of Arikara villages and one Sioux camp. As is the fashion in this part of the country, the weather changed every other day, fine mornings alternating with wind and cold rain. As they left South Dakota, Clark counted fifty-eight wild goats killed by the Indians, Lewis took out a hunter who killed three, the Indians sang and danced on the shore, and the weather began to turn cold. It was the middle of October.

It cannot be denied that the scenery became more spectacular as the expedition pursued its dream to the west, or that winter in North Dakota was more of a hardship than summer in South

Dakota, or that real dangers from wild creatures, the landscape itself, and the weather increased after the party left South Dakota. The main accomplishment in this early part of the journey was the "taming of the Sioux"—an unfair phrase, but an event of incalculable importance in that it largely cleared the way for Lewis and Clark to proceed relatively untroubled through other Indian lands. Although it is neither totally accurate nor acceptably punning to say that Lewis and Clark opened the floodgates of the Missouri and let people pour in, their safe passage to the western ocean and back did reassure the public and, in particular, the new American fur companies. Word traveled rather quickly and as the expedition neared home again in 1806 it was met by parties of traders beginning their own journeys into the wilderness.

Three major fur companies operating from Saint Louis sponsored the major upper Missouri expeditions for the next twenty years: the Missouri Fur Company, the Rocky Mountain Fur Company, and the American Fur Company. The first of these was largely the work of one man, Manuel Lisa, a Spaniard who had apparently traded for some years in the Osage country. Lisa listened with great interest to the reports from Lewis and Clark and set out in 1807 for the upper Missouri with merchandise to be used for bartering with the Indians. With him was George Drouillard, who had been with Lewis and Clark as interpreter and hunter and who wanted now to take part in a trading expedition, presumably to turn his knowledge into profit for the first time. Near the mouth of the Platte the party met John Colter descending the river alone in a boat and persuaded him to turn around and accompany the party upriver. Colter had not been in "civilization" for over three years but, like most of the mountain men, seemed to be more interested in the wilderness. Lisa ascended the Missouri as far as the mouth of the Yellowstone and then followed that river instead, building his trading post— perhaps on Colter's advice—in the heart of Crow country. He returned to Saint Louis in 1808 quite satisfied with his progress.

Before his death in 1820, Lisa made many trips up the big river. He discovered what other trading expeditions were soon to discover also, that while the Sioux posed no real threat the

Arikaras were beginning to cause trouble. While Lisa had avoided any serious encounter with this tribe in 1807, another party, with a different purpose, was turned back. Lewis and Clark had brought a Mandan chief (known as Big White) back to Saint Louis with them. He was to visit President Jefferson and then be escorted safely back to his village. Ensign Pryor, who had been a sergeant with Lewis and Clark, headed the escort and was accompanied by two trading parties, one wishing to do business with the Mandan and the other with the Sioux. At the lower Arikara village in northern South Dakota, Pryor and his men were fired upon and soon learned that the Arikaras were at war with the Mandans, that they also had vague allegations to make against Manuel Lisa (who had just recently passed the village), and that they wanted the Mandan chief and all the goods carried by the traders with Pryor. A fight ensued in which three traders were killed and seven wounded, and three of Ensign Pryor's men were wounded. The party then returned to Saint Louis.

The War of 1812 did not affect upper Missouri trading in any serious way, although the British reached down from the north and encouraged some Indian tribes as far down as South Dakota to stop Americans from going upriver. For this reason, perhaps, Manuel Lisa was appointed subagent for the upper Missouri Indians in 1814 by William Clark, then superintendent of Indian Affairs in Saint Louis. Apparently Lisa was able to keep a good deal of trading going, in spite of the British, but he was accused of using his position to further his own trading business. Whether that charge had any truth to it cannot be proved. At any rate, Lisa was certainly more successful than most other traders. His letter of resignation to Clark in 1817 is politely defensive and argumentative. After defending his work as subagent, Lisa writes:

> But I have had some success as a trader; and this gives rise to many reports.
> "Manuel must cheat the government, and Manuel must cheat the Indians, otherwise Manuel could not bring down every summer so many boats loaded with rich furs."
> Good. My accounts with the government will show whether I

receive anything out of which to cheat it. A poor five hundred dollars, as sub-agent salary, does not buy the tobacco which I annually give to those who call me father. . . .

"But Manuel gets so much rich fur!"

Well, I will explain how I get it. First, I put into my operations great activity; I go a great distance, while some are considering whether they will start today or tomorrow. I impose upon myself great privations; ten months in a year I am buried in the forest, at a vast distance from my own house. . . .[1]

And so on. Lisa was probably not the last person in South Dakota to fret under the notion that if a man is unusually successful he has probably cheated. The distinction has not hurt his reputation; he remains known as one of the diligent and courageous mountain men of the early nineteenth-century trapping era.

So many well-remembered men roamed the American West during the years of exploration and trapping, say from 1810 to 1850, that historians—professionals and amateurs alike—continue to argue over their relative greatness or importance. Certainly many of those who were to achieve fame took part in the Ashley-Henry expeditions which were a part of the Hugh Glass story. The Rocky Mountain Fur Company organized parties in 1822 and 1823 by advertising in the Saint Louis newspapers. The first party was led by Major Henry and reached the Yellowstone successfully. (Shortly after that, General Ashley took some men upriver but lost his cargo when the boat upset before he reached South Dakota. He then returned to Saint Louis, tried again, joined Henry briefly at the Yellowstone, and again returned to Saint Louis, leaving Henry at the company fort to trade and trap.) The second party, recruited in 1823, was repulsed by the Arikaras, although later in the summer the Indian villages were attacked by the combined parties of Leavenworth, Ashley, Henry, Pilcher, and a large group of Sioux. After some fighting and some negotiations (with the military and the fur company in disagreement), the Arikaras were allowed to abandon their villages at night and escape. It was an unsatisfactory

1. Hiram M. Chittenden, *The American Fur Trade of the Far West,* 2 vols. (Stanford: Academic Reprints, 1954), 2: 901.

conclusion. However, the nucleus of the Rocky Mountain Fur Company of that time and place might well provide the most famous group of men ever to assemble in South Dakota: James Clyman, Jedediah Smith, William Sublette, David Jackson, Thomas Fitzpatrick, Jim Bridger, Hugh Glass, and Edward Rose. Eventually, these men, in addition to a few others such as James Beckwourth (who passed through Dakota once) and Kit Carson, literally opened the American West. They discovered South Pass, Yellowstone, Jackson Hole, Salt Lake; they made most of the paths into and beyond the Rocky Mountains; they roamed widely, individually and in groups, continually running into each other by accident or at rendezvous points.

Hiram Chittenden, the noted historian of the fur trade, points to the return of Lewis and Clark and to the founding of Fort Bridger as the two landmarks which determine beginning and end of a distinct and important period in the history of the American West. The first, as we have seen, offered assurance of passage into the Far West. The second, Jim Bridger's fort, was the first trading post built beyond the Mississippi especially for the convenience of emigrants. Located in what is now the southwestern corner of Wyoming, Bridger's Fort was an oasis in the wilderness, a way station on the trail to Salt Lake and California.

South Dakota was part of the highway to the West, with the Missouri River offering the best route into fur country and the Rocky Mountains. Thousands of people passed through the region during the fur era; few stayed. One who did, more or less, has considered a rascal, if he is remembered at all. Edward Rose, son of a white trader and a half-breed woman (Cherokee and Negro), came into the region in 1807. Major Henry found him living with the Arikaras in 1809. For several years after 1820 he was again living on the Missouri River with these Indians. In between these residencies, however, Rose also lived with the Omahas and the Crows, guided expeditions (including that of Wilson Price Hunt of the Astorians, for whom Rose probably mapped the passage through the Big Horn Range), did as much to map the West as anyone, but was accused of pilfering from the expeditions he guided, was called "a very bad fellow and daring,'' engaged in brawls, and spent time in jail for drunkenness. It may be that the unsavory side of his character somehow kept him from getting the recognition he deserved. An important explorer and guide, he was soon forgotten while his contemporaries' names lived on, attached to rivers, passes, mountains, and forts. Edward Rose was a maverick among mavericks. His death was doubly ironic in that he was with Hugh Glass at the time and both were killed by the Arikaras with whom Rose had lived.

Almost at the same time, another little-known trader was killed near the Black Hills (1832). Thomas Sarpy worked as a clerk out of the company headquarters at Fort Pierre, ascending the Cheyenne into Oglala country and manning a post at the mouth of Rapid Creek. Not particularly successful, he was nevertheless an example of the trading being done away from the Missouri River, particularly on its western tributaries. In the winter of 1829–1830 almost 6,000 buffalo were killed in the Black Hills region and their hides (usually referred to euphemistically as ''robes'') sent to Fort Pierre and then south to Saint Louis. Thomas Sarpy did not distinguish himself, and was in western Dakota for only a few years before being blown up in a gunpowder accident, but his blood line was carried on.

It is impossible to calculate how many of South Dakota's people are descended from the traders, trappers, and mountain men of the early nineteenth century, but the French names, in particular, are noticeable among both whites and Indians. Although the fur company men were visitors in most cases, they left evidence of their passing.

As the first mountain men left the Dakota-Missouri River region and penetrated wildernesses farther west, the river traffic changed over from keelboat to steamboat. Even though the river continued to provide obstacles such as sandbars and snags, the steamboat made traveling faster and easier, and the first trip of the *Yellowstone* to Fort Union in 1832 is often called somewhat facetiously the beginning of the tourist trade in South Dakota. That is, the territory began to get visitors, men who were not engaged in trading and were not in the military service but who came to look, to write, to paint, to record the birds, animals, Indians, and landscape. Two such visitors preceded the steamboat—Henry Marie Brackenridge and Duke Friedrich Paul Wilhelm.

Henry Brackenridge, although the son of Hugh, author of the well-known novel, *Modern Chivalry,* had no intentions of becoming a writer when he went west from Pittsburgh to consider practicing law in Saint Louis. He wanted to see the wilderness, and so he signed on as a passenger (with no duties to perform and no responsibilities) with Manuel Lisa's expedition of 1811. He soon learned to like and respect Lisa and, having heard of the less complimentary things said by some of the men, wrote in his journal a passage of glowing praise which at least partially substantiates what Lisa himself said in his letter of resignation to General Clark a few years later:

> A person better qualified for this arduous undertaking, could not have been chosen. Mr. Lisa is not surpassed by any one, in the requisite experience in Indian trade and manners, and has few equals in perseverance and indefatigable industry. Ardent, bold and enterprising, when any undertaking is begun, no dangers, or sufferings are sufficient to overcome his mind. I believe there are few men so completely master of that secret of doing much in a short space of time. . . .[2]

Brackenridge, of course, wanted a man to rely upon. Two days before the party passed the mouth of the Kansas River, with the last settlement of whites already behind, Brackenridge reflected on his being out in the wilderness and wondered if he had made a mistake in undertaking the voyage without some object of suitable importance in view. About his country, now so far removed, he said:

> I heaved a sigh, when I reflected that I might never see it, or my friends again; that my bones might be deposited on some dreary spot, far from my home, and the haunts of civilized man. . . .[3]

But then he contemplates the inevitable expansion of his country westward:

2. Henry Marie Brackenridge, *Views of Louisiana* (1814; reprint ed., Chicago: Quadrangle Books, Inc., 1962), pp. 199–200.

3. Brackenridge, pp. 219–220.

. . . there is no spot however distant, where I may be buried, but will in time, be surrounded by the habitations of Americans, the place will be marked, and approached with respect, as containing the remains of one of the first who ventured into these distant and solitary regions! [4]

A tone of self-pity coupled with 'pride, perhaps, typical of a young man far from home, and yet there is an element of vision in the remarks, a knowledge that the West would indeed be a part of the civilized United States.

Brackenridge went as far as Mandan country that summer, and his journal of the voyage (*Views of Louisiana, Together with a Journal of a Voyage up the Missouri River, in 1811*) is a captivating document. It records the many times when a "tremendous storm of thunder and lightning" was followed the next day by a "fine serene morning." Brackenridge was sensitive to numerous kinds of extremes, from the "striking and terrific" buffalo which eyed him with the "ferocity of the lion," to the beautiful flowers and the "most enchanting blue" sky on a clear day; from the "filthy and disgusting" Poncas to the Sioux— "they are the best looking people I have seen"; and from the kind of loneliness which fosters introspection to the other kind which was monotonous and dreary. His descriptions contrast the islands of beautiful prairie with the bleak and barren adjacent country. For the historian Brackenridge provides much useful information about the Arikaras, but for himself he makes an enlightening discovery with psychological overtones (at the mouth of the James River):

The beauty of the scenery, this evening, exceeds any thing I ever beheld—The sky as clear as in a Chinese painting, the country delightful. Convert the most beautiful parts of England, or France, into one meadow, leaving a trifling proportion of woods, and some idea may be formed of this. But there appears to be a painful void—something wanting—it can be nothing else than a population of animated beings. It were vain to describe the melancholy silence which reigns over these vast plains. Yet they seem to give a spring

4. Brackenridge, p. 220.

to the intellectual faculties. One never feels his understanding so
vigorous, or thinks so clearly.[5]

Allowing Brackenridge the literary exercise of "Chinese painting," and his nostalgic comparisons of the lower James River
area with England and France, we can appreciate in the rest of
his thought a characterization of place and its effects on people
which continues to make sense in modern South Dakota.

Duke Paul Wilhelm reinforces Brackenridge's feeling of
being alone. Taking a ride out onto the plains from Fort Kiowa,
he becomes momentarily interested in a hill far in the distance
said to be held in awe by the Indians, but laments later that on
the entire ride he saw no living creature except a few prairie
birds. And he adds that the region around the post (near Chamberlain) had nothing worth seeing, and therefore he could think
of no reason to stay there any longer. The reason he was there at
all was simply that in 1823 Europe was relatively peaceful—
following the Napoleonic Wars—and a number of royal families
felt that the young people could add to their already considerable education by taking a trip to the New World. The Duke
traveled partway across the new state of Missouri and up toward
present-day South Dakota by boat, but went overland from Fort
Atkinson to Fort Kiowa. For this reason, he may be somewhat
harsher in his descriptions of the area than Brackenridge was,
the storms being more violent, the objects of beauty less con-
spicuous. He is often confounded by the lack of water and, on
one occasion, by the presence of birds in a place without water
to drink. However, his greatest disappointment was in having
his journey end at Fort Kiowa. Upriver, during this summer,
Leavenworth and Ashley were fighting the Arikaras, and the
Duke was forced to return to Saint Louis without having seen
the Mandan Indians, those strange people with the light hair and
blue eyes, sometimes said to be descended of the Welsh (or at
least mixed with them), and the prime objects of curiosity
whenever Europeans came into the upper Missouri region.

The steamboat was presumably an easier method of transpor-

5. Brackenridge, p. 234.

tation for visitors because, at the least, they could be passengers, able to use their time as they wished. George Catlin, the noted though not first-rate artist who was aboard the *Yellowstone* on its first trip to Fort Union, was able to spend his days viewing the countryside from the boat, making notes and drawings without interruption. Catlin's published work, *North American Indians* (1841), was extremely popular because of the novelty of the subject matter. During his several years among the Indians, he produced hundreds of drawings and paintings and collected many artifacts. He tended to see the strange and the picturesque, the pastoral, and in Indians the romantic, for which he was chided by John Audubon a decade later. Nevertheless, Catlin must be considered one of the distinguished visitors to South Dakota, and he could not have accomplished his work without the conveniences of the steamboat.

The steamboat brought a great variety of visitors to the upper Missouri. Maximilian, prince of Wied, was another royal personage who was able to leave Europe for travel in the new land after the end of the Napoleonic Wars. He had been a general in the Prussian army and was fifty-one years old when he ascended the Missouri River in 1833 as a natural scientist. One of his assistants was Karl Bodmer, a Swiss artist still known in this country for his paintings of Indians. His drawings and paintings were used to illustrate Maximilian's book, *Travels in the Interior of North America,* called by at least one historian of the West "the most complete and elaborate work ever prepared upon this region." As is the case (in varying degrees) with several "traveler's books" from the 1830s to the 1850s in the South Dakota area, and in the 1870s from the Rockies to the Sierra Nevadas, Maximilian's work was a combination of narrative, description, anecdote, history, geology, ethnology, and natural history. Not only was such information of interest to the Americans and Europeans of the time, but it is still indispensable to those who want to know "how things were" near the beginning of our history.

Not everyone agreed on the character of the land of the Dakotas. John James Audubon, whose name has almost become a household word, spent as much time looking for birds (and killing and mounting them) as George Catlin did in observing Indians and landscape. Catlin was impressed by the Indians, seeing them with a painter's eye and a slightly romantic disposition. Audubon, early in his 1843 journey up the Missouri River, was repelled by the sight of dead, swollen, putrid buffalo floating down the river and shocked to see Indians retrieving these carcasses and eating them.

> In some instances this has been done when the whole of the hair had fallen off, from the rottenness of the Buffalo. Ah! Mr. Catlin, I am now sorry to see and to read your accounts of the Indians *you* saw—how very different they must have been from any that I have seen! [6]

And between Vermillion and Yankton, where Brackenridge had found the mouth of the James River almost like a park, Audubon says, "We saw here no 'carpeted prairies,' no 'velvety distant landscape'; and if these things are to be seen, why, the sooner we reach them the better." After which he immediately turned his attention to an old bird's nest filled with dried mud.

Audubon was past the age of sixty—he claimed that he did not know how old he was—and had traveled extensively in Europe, becoming a well-known ornithologist and painter of birds long before he ventured into the upper Missouri country. His ear for bird song was so keen that he identified the western meadowlark as being different from the eastern species even before he had a chance to examine it. His object was to collect, and to this end he brought both a taxidermist and another artist with him on the trip (John G. Bell and Isaac Sprague, respectively). Animals and plants were under the same scrutiny as birds. On May 30, for example, Audubon was called up early in the morning to receive a buffalo calf, and the head of another. Sprague was put to work drawing one of the heads, life size, and the other entire calf was skinned and was to be "in strong pickle" before the end of the day. In four months Audubon and his crew shot so many birds and animals that the steamer *Omega* might have seemed like a slaughterhouse to a conserva-

---

6. Maria R. Audubon, *Audubon and His Journals,* 2 vols. (1897; reprint ed., New York: Dover Publications, Inc., 1960), 1: 497.

tionist in another time. Yet, his studies of life along the Missouri identified many new species, provided information that established a certain uniqueness for the West, and preserved in writing and in drawings some wild life which became scarce or nearly extinct as settlers moved into the area during the next forty years. As for the weather, which all visitors have commented upon, Audubon's journal entries are brief but telling: "Hard rain . . . and uncomfortably hot," "Fine but windy," "Beautiful, calm, and cold," "Wind rose early, but a fine morning," "Wind blowing harder," "Cloudy and remarkably cold," "Rain all night," "Cloudy and threatening"—these comments from early in September on the way back, in southern South Dakota. Fine morning, windy, hot, and cold—these, with rain, are the common terms for the weather on the entire trip. Audubon was in a land of extremes and of quick changes, but he only recorded this fact briefly and turned his attention each day to his tasks as a naturalist. Generally, he was dismayed by the prairie, which he compared to a desert, and was astonished by the abundance of animal and bird life.

Uncounted visitors, some of them leaving a lasting legacy, came into South Dakota by way of the Missouri River, and many left by the same route. Relative safety for these "passers-through" was provided by the many trading posts along the river and by the increasing number of military forts established as the Indians were forced westward across the river and settlers began to appear in spite of the reports constantly suggesting that Dakota was a desert. Hiram Chittenden provides a list of early posts and forts, all along the river, in South Dakota: Big Sioux Post, in the southeastern tip of the state; Vermillion Post and Dickson's Post, one downriver and the other upriver from Vermillion; two posts at the mouth of the James River, one for the Columbia Fur Company, the other for the American Fur Company; Ponca Post, near the mouth of the Niobrara; Fort Mitchell; Handy's Post, across the river from where Fort Randall was later built; Truteau's House, just upriver from Handy's; Fort Recovery, on Cedar Island, a mile below Chamberlain; Fort Brasseaux, Fort Lookout, and Fort Kiowa, all upstream from Chamberlain about ten miles; Fort Defiance, a few miles above the Big Bend; Loisell's Post, thirty-five miles below Pierre, and Fort George, twenty miles below Pierre; Fort Tecumseh, the main establishment of the Columbia Fur Company, rebuilt as Fort Pierre, on the present site of that town—and a host of smaller trading "houses" in that same area; Fort George, near the mouth of the Cheyenne; and the Arikara Post, somewhere near the present-day border between the two Dakotas. There were undoubtedly more, some of them short-lived, so that at the height of the fur trade there were perhaps thirty such waystations on the Missouri River within the modern limits of South Dakota, averaging one per twenty miles.

In what passes for a short time on the prairie, the trading posts disappeared or were turned over to the army. George Catlin witnessed the opening of the American Fur Company's largest post on the river, Fort Pierre, in 1832 and in the company of Pierre Chouteau, Jr., after whom the fort was named. Its sale to the army in 1855 belatedly marked the end of the fur trade, and introduced soldiers to an area about which they reportedly sang around the campfires:

Oh, we don't mind the marching, nor the fighting do we fear,
But we'll never forgive old Harney for bringing us to Pierre.
They say old Shotto built it, but we know it is not so;
For the man who built this bloody ranche is reigning down below.

A year later the army built Fort Randall, near Pickstown, almost at the Nebraska border, even though there were few indications of the "coming flood of emigrants." Besides, at that time, as General Hancock said, the river itself formed a barrier between the "safe" eastern lands and the "dangerous" western territory where the Indians were. Nevertheless, Fort Sully was built near Pierre in 1863 and a new fort with the same name just three years later, in the same area. And two years after the Laramie Treaty Fort Benton was added to the cluster. Estimates at this time indicated that during the travel season each year ten thousand persons used the Missouri River. For a while the river forts were regarded as the front line of defense for Minnesota, southern Dakota Territory, and northwestern Iowa as the Sioux began to resent in earnest the intrusion of the white man. In the 1870s, as the lure of gold pulled people across the river, heading for the Black Hills, the forts guarded the routes to the West. Settlement then proceeded so rapidly that General Sheridan wrote in 1872 that it seemed to him only a year or two since Dakota had been in the possession of the Indians. By 1894 the forts were abandoned and, since most of them had been erected hastily for a temporary purpose, they soon disappeared altogether, with the exception of a few relics. The steamboats remained on the Missouri for a short time into the twentieth century, and then they too were gone. A series of dams closed the Big Road to interstate travel; the river was put to new uses.

Flood control was the most obvious reason for the series of dams built between Yankton and the Fort Peck Dam constructed earlier in Montana. Although flood damage was always greater on the lower Missouri where the larger cities are located, the control had to be established on the upper Missouri; it fell to South Dakota's lot to have four of the six dams in the system. Two decades, from 1946 to 1966, were devoted to the construction of the dams, the southernmost one being Gavins Point Dam at Yankton, the next one upriver at Pickstown (Fort Randall Dam), the smallest at the Big Bend, and the largest at Pierre (Oahe Dam). Three of the dams back up the water into large lakes which are used for fishing, boating, swimming, and other recreational activities. The Big Bend Dam backup flooded a portion of the Crow Creek and Lower Brulé reservations, with archaeologists trying desperately to salvage what they could from "digs" before the ancient land disappeared under water. Electricity is supplied by the Gavins Point Dam; but the irrigation of the James Valley destined to come from Oahe is still argued about twenty-five years later, the system has not been built, Congress still talks about funding it, and many of the farmers are no longer sure they want it. Altogether it is a strange situation, considering that memories of the Dust Bowl of the 1930s are still strong and sharp.

The only "free" water, or wild water, remaining on the upper Missouri in South Dakota is a fifty-mile stretch between Yankton and Sioux City, Iowa. Here the current continues to wash away the banks of the river, angering farmers who watch pieces of their land dropping off into the river, and causing grave concern to the officials of Sacred Heart Hospital in Yankton, which perches on a high bluff above the river, a bluff in danger of eroding away at the bottom. Again, however, arguments continue between those who want this stretch of river controlled and the conservationists who plead for the natural state of the valley, realizing that it is the last on the river. Civilization and the wilderness continue to confront each other as they have done since the first frontier east of the Alleghenies more than two centuries ago. And we are continually tempted to look for symbols, no matter how subtle, to remind ourselves of these major juxtapositions and the changes that can occur within them. The town of Pickstown, at the site of the Fort Randall Dam, was erected as a construction camp. It remains a town, long after the reason for its existence has ceased to exist. During the project, two young boys were schoolmates there, one Indian and one white, their fathers being employed in the building of the dam. Almost thirty years later they met again, on national television, the Blackfeet "boy" having just published his first novel—*Winter in the Blood*—and his friend having become a well-known news commentator: James Welch and Tom Brokaw.

Whatever the inadequacy of symbols, the Missouri River keeps flowing but it is no longer a Big Road into and through the state of South Dakota. More contained now, it tends to serve as a dividing line between two parts of the state, East River and West River, a line of no little consequence for the people who did not pass through but remained.

4

To Become a State

 LTHOUGH South Dakotans think of themselves as independent people, fighting their own battles and making their own decisions, they are certainly aware of their relationship to the federal government and, perhaps to a lesser degree, to the region's financial center in Minnesota—Minneapolis–Saint Paul. In recent years, educational programs and an entire new emphasis on the arts have been provided by federal funds and by grants from out-of-state foundations. Back at the beginning, when the territory was seeking statehood, the colonial system brought money and political jobs into the area, and some of the major forces in the two fights (first for territorial status, and then for statehood) came from Minnesota and Iowa, from selfish and opportunistic interests.

The importance of territorial status was established in the Northwest Ordinance of 1787, a famous document which provided that western land areas not states but politically subordinate to the federal government (i.e., territories) could become states after certain conditions of settlement had been met. Thus the trick was to become a territory, because the ordinance guaranteed that colonial or territorial status would be temporary. Statehood itself was probably as much a matter of pride and identity as it was of anticipation of benefits, but there is no doubt that the benefits of employment (for politicians, merchants, builders, suppliers, freight haulers, blacksmiths, and so

SOUTHERN DAKOTA TERRITORY · 1876

MINNESOTA

IOWA

NORTHERN DAKOTA TERRITORY

SOUTHERN DAKOTA TERRITORY

MONTANA TERR.

WYOMING TERRITORY

NEBRASKA

Bois de Sioux R. (to Red R.)

Lake Traverse

Big Stone Lake

SISSETON AND WAHPETON INDIAN RESERVATION

Big Sioux R.

Medary

Flandreau

Sioux Falls

James R.

Sand Lake

James R.

Yankton

Bon Homme

Bon Homme Island

Dakota Southern Railroad

Vermillion

Elk Point

Harold Faye

YANKTON INDIAN RES.

Fort Randall

Yankton Agency

PONCA INDIAN RESERVATION

Missouri R.

Keya Paha R.

Niobrara R.

SIOUX INDIAN RESERVATION

Fort Thompson (Crow Creek Agency)

Lower Brule (White River Agency)

Cedar Island

Bad Humored Island

Grand River Agency

Fort Sully

Cheyenne Agency

Old Fort Pierre

Teton (Bad) R.

White R.

THE BADLANDS

Standing Rock Agency

Grand R.

Moreau R.

Missouri R.

Cheyenne R.

Belle Fourche R.

Father de Smet Gold Mine

Carbonate Silver Mine

Sturgis

Galena Silver Mine

Deadwood

Homestake Gold Mine

Rapid City

Rockerville

Black Hills Placer Mining Co.

Hayward

Shendan

Hill City

Harney Pk.

Custer

French Ck.

BLACK HILLS

0   25   50   75   100

Miles

on), protection, and representation were the ultimate concern in the first stages of becoming a territory. In what is now South Dakota, this was especially true in the southeastern section, closest to already established territories and states, most vulnerable to outside influences, and, because of farm land, the Missouri River, and the westward move of the Indians, the most logical place for early permanent white settlement. In this area, then, government became a vital part of the economy rather than a code of laws. In contrast, the people drawn to the Black Hills area before statehood had a distrust of government and a stronger feeling about self-sufficiency. Both views were frontier creations, and both still exist, by and large, in South Dakota, and in the same parts of the state as in the earlier territory. The western half of the state is conservative, and the eastern half— the more populated half, still influenced by its neighboring states—is more liberal and government-minded.

A territory went through three stages in becoming a state. First, a governor, a secretary, and three judges were appointed by Congress to have governing powers over the territory, subject only to congressional veto. These men could borrow from the laws of existing states in setting up a code for the new territory. Next, as soon as the territory, or a district within it, had 5,000 people, an assembly could be elected, make laws, and send a nonvoting delegate to Congress. And finally, when the population reached 60,000, the citizens could write a constitution, form a state government, and apply for statehood. During this process, of course, speculators swarmed into the territory, some to acquire land against the day when a demand for it would bring a high price, some to seek government jobs, and some to establish as much political and economic control as they could. To what extent the speculators themselves increased the population, bringing it closer to the figures established by the Northwest Ordinance, is difficult to determine, but it must have been considerable. The speculators therefore served two purposes, one good and the other destructive.

It is useless to argue the question of territorial status and statehood because the American belief in Manifest Destiny would not have allowed any alternatives. Yet, some people recognized the dangers of the prevailing direction. On May 11, 1860, when bills for the organization of Nevada and Colorado territories had been tabled, but the bill for Dakota was still on the floor, Eli Thayer, congressional representative from Massachusetts, spoke to Congress:

> These people of Dakota are as well off today as they would be if they had our territorial officials over them. They have known no Indian wars. The Yanctons and the Sioux are all quiet. But organize the Territory, and send out your executive officials; and then, sir, these speculators will greatly desire an influx of Government gold. There is no method so sure and so convenient to produce that result as to stir up an Indian war. It will be done, sir, to raise the price of town lots. The Yanctons and the Sioux will come down on the white settlements and we shall hear of the terrible inroads of the savages. Then, sir, a heart-rending appeal for protection. Then, sir, a regiment of soldiers and a million dollars. Then, sir, damages and pensions and war claims to the end of time. They are better off today than they can be with these Government speculators turned loose upon them.[1]

Mr. Thayer was far from Dakota and had perhaps forgotten the cost of statehood for his own Massachusetts and the other states east of the Mississippi River, but his speech proved to be prophetic, even as it succeeded in postponing for a year the creation of Dakota Territory. What he predicted came true, even the "war claims to the end of time." (At least, claims are still being made and argued over a century later.)

At the time of Thayer's speech there were approximately 2,000 people in that portion of South Dakota east of the Missouri River, which was temporarily free of Indian problems and considered safe for settlement. According to the 1860 census, the birthplaces of these people represented at least twenty-five states and territories and nine foreign countries in addition to Dakota itself. The Dakota figure is the largest, but partly because of the inclusion of children born shortly after their parents arrived from somewhere else. The other places of birth, in

1. Quoted in Howard Lamar, *Dakota Territory 1861–1889: A Study of Frontier Politics* (New Haven: Yale University Press, 1956), pp. 57–58.

descending order of numbers, were Norway, Canada, New York, Wisconsin, Iowa, Ohio, Ireland, Washington Territory, Michigan, Pennsylvania, Illinois, Vermont, Connecticut, England, Nebraska, Scotland, Virginia, Arkansas, Maryland, Kentucky, Switzerland, Russia, District of Columbia, Rhode Island, North Carolina, and California. The figures are high for Iowa, Wisconsin, Illinois, and Minnesota because many of the families from Norway, Ireland, and the eastern United States had children in those places on their way west. Some hunters and trappers were listed in the census, most of them French-Canadian or from Washington Territory. Otherwise, the most commonly listed occupations were farmer, laborer, or Indian agency employee. Mixed marriages were neither frequent nor rare but always involved white men (either French-Canadians or New Englanders) and Indian women—never the other way around. There were almost no military men from pre-1860 service in South Dakota, and almost everyone was below the age of fifty-five.

Do we call these people a motley crew, or a typically American melting pot? Although the French-Canadians and the New Englanders left their mark upon the state, the largest influx of immigrants in the next three decades was to be from the Scandinavian countries and Germany, so that variety among the people of South Dakota lessened until the period of relative mobility following World War II. Whether that intermediate condition should be described in terms of "stability" or mere "sameness" is open to question. One thing is certain: during the so-called middle period the chief attraction in South Dakota was agriculture, so that the people who came to the state (and especially the Scandinavians and Germans) did so for the common purpose of farming. Therein lies the stability, altered only by those acts of God or nature which occasionally bring disaster to a farm economy. Mining in the Black Hills during the territorial period brought an assortment of nationalities, including a colony of Chinese, but that pocket of South Dakota history wore through quickly with the first accumulation of gold.

Nevertheless, it is proper to say that this was the last agricultural and mining frontier in the continental United States, and that its settlement was made possible only by federal policies and by propaganda which minimized Maj. Stephen Long's earlier report of the Great American Desert. Many of the first pioneers were from woods country, and when they came to the Great Plains they could see nothing which seemed to be of value to them, so they pushed on to the West Coast or the Southwest. President James Polk's expansionist policy then made the plains safer, and talk of railroads to be built through the West appealed to those who had worried about transportation and marketing. In order to be prepared, land speculators from Saint Paul began to acquire land in eastern Dakota, to sell to settlers, and gradually the preliminaries to settlement went into motion during the 1850s. The first speculators, in addition to those in Saint Paul, were from Iowa. The infiltration occurred, then, at two points, Sioux Falls (only fifteen miles from the Minnesota border) and along the Missouri River from Sioux City, Iowa, to Yankton in the southeast corner. Each group had the same general aim, to make money from land speculation or rise in land values caused by settlement; and also to profit from the army units sent out to give federal protection, as well as from transportation, railroad grants, and political patronage—all offshoots of provisions made by the federal government in relation to the establishment of a territory. But there was a difference, too, between the main groups. At Sioux Falls the methods of the large-scale speculator led into corporate business methods and wholesale exploitation of an entire region. At Yankton the speculators were merchants organizing on a smaller scale to benefit from the wealth associated with the settlement of one new community.

In 1856 Dr. J. M. Staples of Dubuque, Iowa, having been impressed by Nicollet's report on the area of the Big Sioux River, organized a group of businessmen from his town into the Western Town Company, its purpose being to secure choice locations in eastern Dakota. Their first foray into the area of the falls was turned back by Indians, but in 1857 the company took possession of 320 acres there and named the location Sioux Falls. Almost simultaneously a group of land speculators in Saint Paul organized the Dakota Land Company with the intent of obtaining a number of townsites in eastern Dakota and having one of these sites chosen eventually for the territorial capital, thus enabling the company to provide political offices and public contracts for its members and friends. One site so established immediately adjoined the acreage of the Western Town Company. (Named, not very originally, Sioux Falls City.) Two other sites located at the same time were named Flandreau and Medary. By consent of the members of the Dakota Land Company, Sioux Falls City was to be the capital. (Eventually, what Sioux Falls got in the dividing-up of public institutions was not the state capital but the state penitentiary.) The company persuaded the Minnesota territorial legislature to create three counties with Sioux Falls City, Flandreau, and Medary as their county seats. Shortly thereafter a band of Yanktonnais Indians drove many of the settlers away and burned the buildings at Medary. Sioux Falls City entrenched but the Indians withdrew, having accomplished, at least, a slowing-down of settlement. And the Dakota Land Company failed in its plan to set up a provisional government.

Coincidentally with these events, Capt. J. B. S. Todd, a cousin of Mary Todd Lincoln, and recently resigned from the army, helped organize the Upper Missouri Land Company at Sioux City for the purpose of establishing townsites along the river between Sioux City and Fort Pierre. By 1860 this company had presumably built posts or cabins near Sioux City, near Elk Point, halfway between Elk Point and Vermillion, at Vermillion, at the James River, at Yankton, and just upriver from Yankton at a place soon known as Smutty Bear's Bottom. In one sense this was still Indian country, but the speculators gambled on the fact that settlers would begin coming up the Missouri River anyway and that perhaps a railroad would be built in the near future. They wished to be ready. Captain Todd envisioned Yankton as the territorial capital (which it was, a few years later), and took part in the negotiation of a treaty with the Yankton Sioux which, in 1858, culminated in the sale of 14,000,000 acres of land between the Big Sioux River and the Missouri for twelve cents an acre. As Minnesota became a state that same year, Captain Todd and his partner, Col. Daniel Frost, began working for territorial status for Dakota. Just as "squatter assemblies" had met at Sioux Falls before the Indian threat (with Henry Masters, a Swedenborgian and poet, elected provisional governor, and W. W. Brookings of the rival Iowa company made president of the council), so did they at Yankton, while residents of Yankton and Vermillion met and decided that they would not support "squatter" officers.

These problems were soon resolved (leading to others) when President James Buchanan signed the bill which created the territory of Dakota on March 2, 1861, just two days before his term ended and Abraham Lincoln became president. Lincoln then chose as first territorial governor of Dakota his neighbor and family physician in Springfield, Illinois, Dr. William Jayne, whose administration proceeded rather smoothly. There was the normal frontier rough behavior and humor in the legislature, and, when Jayne resigned to run for delegate to Congress against Captain Todd, the voting procedures were not exactly legal, with ballot-box stuffing and a questionable bloc of votes from the French-Canadian settlements up north along the Red River (later North Dakota), votes which ultimately gave the election to Todd. But the real fights were to come a few years later.

As Governor Jayne arrived in Yankton (chosen as territorial capital over the protests of the residents of Vermillion), the town was primitive, so much so that Jayne sent his wife back to Sioux City to live. The buildings were sod huts and log cabins, housing fewer than 300 people. Broadway, the main street, boasted a ragged hotel, a few cabins, and the law office of Captain Todd. The people of the town were mostly men, single, in their twenties or thirties. There were half-breeds, full-blooded Indians, and a variety of whites—fur trappers, squaw men (in the language of that time), army couriers, Indian agents, and speculators of various kinds. And there was James E. Witherspoon, as colorful as any of them. According to early descriptions, Witherspoon was the tallest man in town and had a peculiar disability, "a constant wriggling motion of his body and limbs, which affected his vocal organs." He was, nevertheless, an energetic laborer with more than the normal amount of schooling. Rejecting the authority of Captain Todd and Colonel

Frost and their land company, he "jumped" a claim west of Broadway, held onto it, and eventually brought it into Yankton as Witherspoon's Addition. In the course of the jurisdictional dispute concerning his claim, he is said to have walked from Yankton to Washington in order to present his case. Whether he walked a great deal to ease his wriggling, or whether—as some suggested—he was too frugal to travel any other way, "Limber Jim" is said to have walked to Montana and back, as well as to the Black Hills and back two or three times.

The entire Dakota Territory, from Nebraska to Canada, had only a few thousand people at this time, not counting the Indians. In the immediate area of the capital, rich soil along the river gave way to barren prairie, flat and almost treeless. The buffalo were gone, many of them killed before 1850 and the others having migrated west. Cottonwood and willow trees along the river were plentiful enough for a sawmill to be opened by Jacob Deuel, who was married to an Indian woman. Some Norwegians from Minnesota and Wisconsin had settled along the river bottoms. Vermillion had a general store in addition to the sawmill, and Norwegians were settling nearby. But most of the people in the area were skeptical of farming and were instead trying to make money from the sale of land, from trading, and from government offices. They were perhaps wise, though unscrupled, because after a brief period of optimism the Indian war of 1862 in southern Minnesota carried over into Dakota, causing panic among the farmers, many of whom promptly went back East. Those farmers who stayed lost most of their crops in a drought the following year. Until 1866, when the military began to contain the Sioux somewhat, the new territory had few citizens, little income, and a doubtful future.

Political factions manage to endure under any conditions. The business of turning a territory into a state continued, although not without its squabbles and chicanery. For a while there were two Republican parties, competing with each other as well as with the Democrats. Generally, however, the early Democratic party was mixed-blood, French-Catholic, frontier-American, and nonagricultural; the Republican party was Protestant, Scandinavian-American, and pro-agricultural. Considering these differences (which have altered somewhat in the twentieth century), there may be at least a little significance in the fact that of the eleven men commissioned as governor of Dakota Territory between 1861 and 1889, one declined the appointment, two were removed after holding the office for two years, four resigned (one of them being requested to do so), and only two served out their full terms. (Of the remaining two, one died in office and the final man, Arthur C. Mellette, became the first governor of the new state.)

During the twenty-eight-year territorial period many major events occurred, along with some minor ones which were equally important to Dakotans, to affect the settlement of the territory. The Civil War took some Dakotans into battle, but, more than that, the war negated for several years the potential impact of the Homestead Act of 1862, which "gave" to every man or woman 160 acres of public domain for the price of the filing fee—$18.00 in parts of Dakota Territory—and after five years continuous residence. "Free land" was the call of the West, and eventually the impact on Dakota was as great as it was anywhere in the nation. The Treaty of Laramie in 1868 made eastern Dakota more attractive than it had been, with the Sioux now apparently under control. Railroads, a major political item as we shall see, reached Yankton in 1872 (the Dakota Southern) and Bismarck in 1873 (the Northern Pacific). Gold in the Black Hills attracted thousands of people in the mid-1870s while grasshopper plagues wiped out crops in eastern Dakota during those same years. The death of Custer in Montana at the hands of the Sioux in 1876 brought a new scare to the territory. Factions were at work to divide the territory into two states, North and South Dakota, while other factions strove for a single state. In 1877 "North" Dakota had only seven of the thirty-six territorial assembly seats. Gov. Nehemiah Ordway, a single-state man, changed the territorial capital from Yankton to Bismarck in 1883, but a number of the government offices refused to move, and although southern Dakotans failed in their attempt to change the capital from Bismarck to Pierre in 1885, from then until statehood they controlled the office of delegate to Congress as well as the assembly itself. When, in 1889, two states were created, with capitals at Bismarck and Pierre (two of the loneliest landscapes on the continent), the battle of the Dakotas was finished. And one year later the battle with the Dakota Indians was also finished.

Before that came to pass, some of the territorial officers whose names were to grace counties and towns in the states of South and North Dakota and Nebraska (Burbank, Burleigh, McCook, Brookings, Moody, Spink, Barnes) engaged in a railroad-related election campaign in 1872 that has been called bitter and dirty in understatement. Gov. John Burbank owned most of the town of Springfield, upriver from Yankton, and persuaded Congress to put the terminal point of the new Dakota Southern railway in his town. Partly toward that end he had been instrumental in forming a Burbank-Grand Trunk incorporation which had in mind a railroad-townsite monopoly. The election of 1872 (for delegate and assembly) came while Burbank and other Grant-appointed officials were under fire for their railroad schemes. One Republican faction, with W. W. Brookings and Walter Burleigh, stood by the governor in hopes that they might profit by mutual support; the second Republican group, led by Gideon Moody, opposed the governor. The incumbent delegate, Moses Armstrong, had been a Grand Trunk incorporator but had not allied himself politically with Burbank, so that his nomination for re-election by the Democrats was popular. (Armstrong was probably the best man of the lot, but no county or town was named after him. Such is the fate of a prophet in his country.) The vote for Armstrong was seen as a vote against President U. S. Grant's administration, which Dakotans deemed corrupt and inept, and Armstrong was re-elected.

During the campaign, Moody was accused for a second time of embezzling, Brookings was denounced for his part in the railroad scheme, and newspapers called Moody a trickster and the Brookings group snakes. After the election, assembly seats were contested and a newspaper campaign led to Judge Brookings's removal from the Yankton federal district court early in 1873. That year, however, Grant reappointed Governor Burbank and, in spite of protests, refused to remove Secretary

Edwin McCook. In June, the Yankton County commissioners
brought one aspect of Burbank's Grand Trunk Line stock deal-
ings to court and obtained a ruling in their favor. The governor
had approved a plan to water the stock and in his anger at the
interference of the court he tried to have Judge Barnes removed
from office. Investigations turned up further "oversights" in
connection with the stock. Sides formed as the court's ruling
was argued. Brookings and Burleigh joined the governor;
Moody and S. L. Spink sided with the people of Yankton—as
they put it. To settle the issue, a public meeting was held in
Yankton on September 11 in the evening. It was to be a memorable evening.

A local banker, P. P. Wintermute, started things off with a
formal motion to express a lack of confidence in the Dakota
Southern railroad organization. He then left the hall to get a
drink at the Saint Charles Hotel. Either the meeting was making
him nervous, or he did not want to be around during the discussion and voting. In any case, he should have stayed, because at
the hotel saloon he bumped into E. S. McCook, the territorial
secretary, a Burbank man in favor of the railroad faction. For
some reason, Wintermute asked McCook to lend him ten cents,
and, when McCook refused, a violent argument broke out between the two men. This in itself was foolish on Wintermute's
part (suggesting that he may have been drinking already) because he weighed only 135 pounds while McCook was over-
sized and very strong. As the story goes, the secretary picked up
the banker and threw him into a glass mirror, which shattered,
and then pushed the little man's face into a spittoon. While
Wintermute threatened to kill McCook, the secretary simply
walked out of the saloon as though the matter were finished.

Back at the meeting arguments were becoming loud also,
with Brookings, Moody, Spink, and Burleigh defying the formal authority of the chairman and seeming to be ready to do
more than exchange words with each other. What might have
happened will never be known, because suddenly the bloody
little banker, Wintermute, came into the room with a gun, looking for McCook. By coincidence, McCook entered the hall just
a moment later. Wintermute, without hesitation, shot him four

times. The crowd panicked, but McCook had enough strength left to throw himself at Wintermute, knock him to the floor, kick out a window, and attempt to toss him out of it. Several men finally got McCook under control while Dr. Burleigh began to tend his wounds. But McCook would not remain still. He was furious. He got up again and again, ranting and cursing and stumbling around the room while blood poured from his chest. He died the next day.

The Burbank-railroad faction sought vengeance, partly by arranging that McCook's father-in-law, Oscar Whitney, be appointed as the new territorial secretary. Whitney then spent most of his time in trying to convict Wintermute of murder and have him executed, going so far as to tamper with the judicial process in order to get revenge for his son-in-law's death. Ultimately, after three years of trials and retrials, Wintermute was acquitted but ruined. Meanwhile, the shooting had accomplished something. The railroad case was settled out of court, the two Republican groups finally got together after six years of wrangling, and Burbank resigned as territorial governor—all this in 1873. Burbank, as might be supposed, did not get a county named after him—only a tiny settlement near Vermillion.

The importance of railroads in transporting settlers to within one hundred miles of their free land is obvious. But in a territory which emphasized individualism in so many ways it is equally important to point out the tangled relations of railroad promoters, territorial officials, and the federal government which existed in the 1870s and foreshadowed nonindependent policies of South Dakota in later years. Moses Armstrong identified the territory's relationship to the federal government in a letter to the *Dakota Herald* in 1872:

> The Western Territories are prone to think that they are not liberally treated by the eastern States in Congress. But we in Dakota forget that the people of these same eastern States are usually taxed to pay sixty thousand dollars to sustain our courts in the Territory, $70,000 to survey our lands, $20,000 to run our Legislature, $15,000 to pay our federal officers, many thousand dollars to supply us with mail, several thousand dollars for rent of public buildings, besides stationing troops upon our frontier to protect our

settlements, and feeding and clothing 30,000 Indians to keep the peace in our Territory.

Along with this outside support there was, of course, the usual exploitation, this being at its worst in Dakota Territory during the administration of President Grant. The exploiters were often called "carpetbaggers," the same as in the South following the Civil War. Of the territorial people, one group took part in the exploitation and its accompanying politics, and another group opposed it, sometimes to its own detriment. Those who actually ran the territory were the townsmen, the public officials, the merchants—all in favor of the railroads. The homesteader, on the other hand, although needing the railroad to ship his products to market, opposed it in order to oppose the people who were in power. The homesteaders were largely German and Scandinavian and could feel a political kinship through cultural and national-background ties. The townspeople were a mixed group, but they lived alike and therefore tended to vote alike.

The conditions of leadership remained rather constant to the time of statehood. In spite of new political ideas and programs of social reform which were being talked about and considered in other parts of the country around 1890, and even though some Dakota farmers were aware of these movements, the political leaders in Dakota for the most part concentrated on their own positions and whatever power might accrue to them. As the territory began seeking statehood in earnest during the 1880s, just a few men, and their followers, got the job done. In the late 1870s and well into the 1880s Dakota Territory experienced what historians have called "the Great Dakota Boom." Almost all the land east of the Missouri River was taken during a ten-year period; land was more of an attraction than the gold in the Black Hills; the building of railroads coincided nicely with good rainfall. Settlers poured in from the more populous states to the east, especially Iowa, Wisconsin, Illinois, and Minnesota. But not all of these people were especially interested in the politics of statehood; indeed, many of them came only because of the good free soil, and when hard times followed the boom they left just as easily as they had come. Even so, the permanent popula-

tion of the Dakotas rose rapidly, beyond the necessary require-
ments for statehood. In 1890, one year after the admission of
North and South Dakota into the Union, there were more than
500,000 people in Dakota, 328,808 of them in South Dakota
and 182,719 in North Dakota. (Just preceding statehood, these
proportions were part of a fear in the northern half of the territory that only the southern half would be admitted as a state,
and some of the officials sought a single-state admission rather
than a division into north and south.) Of this total population,
one-third were foreign born, the largest number being Norwegian, then German, Russian, Irish, and Swedish, in that
order.

As Governor Ordway (a one-state man) came to the end of
his term, Grover Cleveland's election to the presidency of the
United States brought the Democratic party into control of
Congress for the first time in over two decades. This Congress
knew that statehood for South Dakota would mean two more
Republican senators in Washington. And if two Dakota states
were admitted—which southern Dakotans wanted just as much
as they wanted statehood itself—there was a possibility of four
new Republican senators. It was apparent, then, that this
Congress would not look kindly on statehood for the Dakotas, a
fact which angered many of the Democratic leaders in Dakota
and caused a party split. Gov. Gilbert Pierce approved a second
constitutional assembly, the first in 1883 having failed. The
1885 convention did little to rework the document from two
years earlier but raised new questions about Prohibition and
woman suffrage. Setting the tone for future South Dakota governments, Colonel Moody strongly suggested that the assembly
be prudent and conservative and refrain from trying new experi-
ments (leaving open the possibility of referring them to the
people later on). Liberal Hugh Campbell of Yankton pointed up
the major issue of the convention: should South Dakota become
a state on the terms of the federal government or on its own
terms? In spite of all the financial aid the territory had received
for almost twenty-five years, some of its citizens now began to
assert their rights as individuals and to demand these same
rights for the state. In the southern Dakota election to approve

the constitution (which remained conservative), a light turnout of voters elected a state government, a governor (Arthur Mellette of Watertown), approved the constitution, and barely supported Prohibition. The legislature met then in Huron, the "new state capital," with the "governor" urging the members to make distinctions between their ideas of state sovereignty and those of the Civil War. The legislators felt they were not rebels and elected Moody and Alonzo J. Edgerton (the latter a moderate from Yankton) to the U.S. Senate.

Congress met that same week to consider the admission of Dakota. Benjamin Harrison introduced the bill for admission, but it was contested on the grounds that Hugh Campbell and his radical associates were promoting state sovereignty. The debate lasted into 1886, when Harrison's bill was passed. Moderates Edgerton, Moody, and Mellette went to Washington to plead their cause before the House took up the matter and returned with reassurances. Then, in succession, the House Committee on Territories rejected the Harrison bill, northern Dakota politicians endorsed the one-state bill of Sen. Mathew C. Butler, and President Cleveland appointed Louis Church, a one-state proponent, as territorial governor. In the face of these disappointments, the constitutional convention for southern Dakota met again and agreed to continue with the provisional state government. Meanwhile, the Northern Pacific Railroad was seen as a major force in favor of the one-state plan, and factions divided according to professions, political parties, newspapers, and geographical locations to push for one kind or another of statehood.

National sentiment entered the discussion also, favoring the admission of not only two Dakota states but Montana and Washington as well. The election of Harrison to the presidency may have helped too, although it was President Cleveland who signed the bill into effect, just before he left office, creating the four new states in 1889. Moody and Richard Pettigrew were the first elected senators from the state of South Dakota, and Mellette became the first governor. Campbell, who had worked as hard as anyone for statehood, but who had sounded too much like a rebel to some people, got no political reward for his efforts. The history books have differed on the importance of those who actively sought statehood. Locally, men like Gen. William H. H. Beadle and Joseph Ward, with their school lands and Prohibition causes, have become heroes. The struggle for statehood has been seen as a people's movement for reform. At least one "outside" view has it that a relatively small group of men (notably Campbell, Moody, Edgerton, Pettigrew, and Mellette) found the technique of controlling local government for itself, and that an altruistic desire to democratize the last of the settlement frontiers was—simply—missing.

Americans have been told over and over, and have "developed" the point themselves, that they are a pragmatic people, highly independent, and extremely leery of government. South Dakotans are as conservative and independent as anyone, and yet when the first settlers arrived in a big, open, different land from what they had been accustomed to east of the Mississippi, they wondered whether they could survive without help from the federal government. Consequently, in spite of their independence, they have been in the forefront in calling for agricultural subsidies and certain aspects of welfare over the years. They point to the uncontrollable villain—weather—and ask for help. But perhaps there is little difference, finally, between federal aid to rural areas and the kind of aid given to large stricken metropolitan areas. Do not all Americans accept federal monies even while fighting against the regulation of it? The development of South Dakota, first as a territory and then as a state, seems to symbolize national attitudes toward politics, government, independence, and subsidies in a kind of paradox which is no longer viewed as such.

5

"This Couldn't Be It"

$\mathcal{M}$OST of the people who settled in South Dakota between 1860 and 1910 came from east of the Mississippi River, from the woodlands, or from Europe (mostly northern). They were accustomed to trees, or water, or both. If they were farmers, their experience was on small-scale plots, especially in Europe. Coming out West to the immense open spaces of the Great Plains was a shock; the soil was often rich, but there was nothing else—or so it seemed. Only along the rivers could they see a few trees. When they arrived out in the middle of nowhere, the location of most claims, the only consolation was the prairie grass rippling and waving in the wind like the swells of the sea, a dubiously comforting thought to the Scandinavians, at least, who had lived near the sea. The best of the widely scattered houses were built of logs hauled out from the nearest river bottoms; more typical was the sod hut with dirt floor. For a long time it was impossible even to see the soddy of the closest neighbor; the sky was unbelievably big; and there were no relieving landmarks to break the flatness of the land. Until the small towns sprang up and the railroads came into the land, life on the open prairie was lonely. And even with the towns and railroads, distances remained great and the alleviation of the isolated life was often negligible or deceiving. It took courage to live in Dakota. Each family was at the mercy of the weather, as were their crops, unlike the relative security of the hills and forests of the eastern farm lands, with their abundant rainfall. Survival of the people in Dakota was as important as survival of their crops.

Why did they come to Dakota? The pursuit of the American Dream had already taken the restless and the adventurous and the believers in the new Garden of Eden far beyond South Dakota to California and Oregon. Everyone knew—or should have known—from the published journals of explorers and the descriptive narratives of early travelers that the middle part of the continent was almost a desert, that the weather was foul (too cold in the winter and too hot in the summer), that Indians roamed the plains, and that uncivilized dangers lay at every . . . . Every what? There were no corners, no bends in the roads, no roads, no hills—not even a landmark to finish the phrase.

They came mostly for the last free land on the continent. Americans have always been attracted by what is free. To make it sound better, and to include the Europeans, it is true that the lands to the east, where rainfall and humidity helped the crops grow in relative ease, were getting crowded. Not crowded as we think of it well through the twentieth century, but too crowded for the people of a hundred years ago. And so the overflow wandered west. After enough of them settled down in the new land, and railroad builders saw the feasibility and the opportunity of transportation, advertising lured Europeans and easterners to a "land of plenty," a "garden," a world of rich soil that grew more and taller wheat and oats and corn than any other part of the nation. As the Indians were forced across the Missouri River, and then still farther west, and as several periods of better-than-normal rainfall actually did result in heavy crop yields, the region seemed more and more attractive. But, mostly, it was free land. It was opportunity.

The phenomenon was not entirely new. The history of the United States is, in a real sense, the history of the frontier. For two-and-a-half centuries that sometimes elusive line between "civilization" and the wilderness moved westward across the continent. At the six locations identified by Frederick Jackson Turner the line was pronounced in varying degrees. In the seventeenth century the natural barrier was the "fall line," the highest point of navigation on the eastern coastal rivers. A century later it was the Allegheny Mountains. Settlement then progressed rather steadily through the forest lands which now constitute the Midwest until reaching the Mississippi River early in the nineteenth century. (Meanwhile, of course, another kind of settlement, largely Spanish, had cut across the Southwest and moved up the West Coast.) By the middle of the nineteenth century the noticeable frontier line was at the Missouri River where its direction is approximately north and south. The fifth line, some twenty-five years later, is the one which most directly affected South Dakota. This line could not be seen as easily as the others, but it came close to paralleling the upper Missouri. Its importance lay in its definition: the line of arid lands. That line, if drawn on a map today, would descend through Jamestown, North Dakota; Aberdeen, South Dakota; Grand Island, Nebraska; and the middle of Kansas. West of this line the rainfall was, and still is, markedly lower than to the east of the line. From here to the Rocky Mountains (the sixth and final frontier line late in the nineteenth century) lay that Great American Desert mentioned in early reports such as the one by Maj. Stephen Long, what today we call the Great Plains. This was long considered the least desirable of all the western lands and was, in truth, the last frontier. Frederick Jackson Turner considered the frontier closed in 1890, a date which coincides with the Battle of Wounded Knee in South Dakota.

To label South Dakota one of the last of the frontier states is to point up its relative youthfulness. Just over one hundred years ago, the only portion of the state considered "settled" was a short strip along the Missouri River from Sioux City, Iowa, to Yankton, in the southeastern tip. By 1870 the settled area had increased only slightly, to the north to Sioux Falls (about seventy-five miles) and to the west to Bon Homme, just beyond Yankton. In 1880 the area covered the eastern one-fifth of the state, plus an island in the western Black Hills. And as late as 1890 the Missouri River still blocked the western half of the state except for an enlarged area around the Black Hills. Land claims under the homesteading act continued well into the twentieth century, two or three decades after South Dakota became a state.

"Settlement" is a curious term because it implies permanence and yet allows for abandonment of land claims, something which happened several times *en masse* because of Indian raids or unsuitable weather. Consider, too, the word "settler." Many terms have been applied in different parts of the nation to denote the first people to enter a new area, or the first to stop there and make homes, or the kind of person who moved around, usually west, and may or may not have stopped long enough to establish a farm or business or family. Consider: settler, newcomer, tenderfoot, foreigner, outsider, immigrant, colonist, homesteader, squatter, nester, plainsman, mountain man, pioneer, sodbuster, maverick, shorthorn, sooner, sourdough, backsetter, backwoodsman, mountaineer, hillbilly, desert rat, frontiersman, villager, townsman, dry farmer, and honyocker. There are more. And there is a problem of distinctions—the first to come into a new area, the first to break sod, the first to stay for a while, and those who stayed longest from near the beginning. Terminology differs somewhat during the stages of the frontier and in different regions. "Colonist" applies to the eastern seaboard prior to the Revolution; "immigrant" and "foreigner" identify Europeans; "backwoodsman" and "frontiersman" are usually reserved for the Daniel Boone type who moved into Ohio and Kentucky and the Old Northwest; "sooner" labels the Oklahoma "settler"; "sourdough" is associated with mountains and mining, just as "desert rat" is obviously the term for the desert prospector. And so on. The most subtle, or troublesome, differentiation may be that of "settler" and "pioneer." Willa Cather dignified the latter term, and no novel comes to mind with the title *O Settlers!* In spite of Cather's use of "pioneer," that word seems broader in usage than "settler." It has been used outside the experience of farming or ranching to include forerunners in business, in town development, in education, in science, in transportation and many other areas of accomplishment. Sometimes pioneering is thought of as the period immediately preceding that of settling; and, on the other hand, it is used constantly on the Great Plains, at least, to describe the period just following, i.e., the period of building a new society *after* the initial settlement of the region.

Be that as it may, it was the settler who claimed the free land of South Dakota, who upon arriving at the site of his claim often thought to himself, or said aloud, "But this couldn't be it." His was the difficult life of the open plains, frequently made more difficult (if he were at all sensitive to it) by the disdain shown him by other classes of people (once they arrived) who called him by names less respectable than settler—sodbuster, dry farmer, nester, squatter, honyocker.

Dakota Territory was not the only recipient of the Homestead Act of 1862. Neighboring territories wanted their share of the settlers, and competition began as early as 1864 when a Dakota politician accused Iowa of trying to hold on to the people who passed through on their way to South Dakota: "All the little hungry newspapers along the line of the Fort Dodge and Marshalltown road are continually howling in the ears of immigrants the most pitiful lies concerning the 'barren, desolate, Godforsaken lands of Dakota.' The aim is to hold travelers in Iowa." It took an adventurous spirit to continue on to Dakota where, indeed, the climate was more variable and extreme, the quality of land generally good but less consistent, and the distances from civilization greater, but thousands did go on. Early town agencies, with their own interests at heart, provided some of the exaggerated advertising about Dakota, and territorial officials sent speakers to more heavily populated areas to extol the opportunities of Dakota and to praise the land in the face of counterpropaganda which made good use of the cold winters, hot summers, grasshoppers, and wild Indians. Pamphlets printed in German and Norwegian, as well as in English, were distributed in eastern cities, particularly in New York where the immigrants landed. And the people came: Germans, Norwegians, Russian-Germans, Swiss-Germans, Yankees from New England, Swedes, Danes, some to establish colonies and some to settle independently. Wherever the settler was from, his basic problems were the same as those of his neighbors—the neighbors often being out of sight of his homestead, anywhere from five to fifty miles away.

On arriving at his claim, the settler's first task was to build a house—or, more properly, a shelter of any kind—which took various forms depending upon the location, the materials available for building, and the time of year. Although many sodbusters were unmarried (mostly men, but a few women too), the typical settler had a family—a wife who was not at all sure that she had done the right thing in agreeing to move West, and perhaps two children who ran and played in the spirit of unexpected adventure, at least for a while. One of the children may have been born in Illinois or Wisconsin or Minnesota as the family traveled slowly westward. As the family approached their claim, they remembered some of the railroad advertising: "The traveler sees with delight the flowering meadow of unimagined fertility stretching out to the faraway horizon, grasses watered by numerous streams near whose banks grow abundant stands of trees." Or something like that. What our man saw (let us call him Henry, with wife Anna and children Lucy and Fred) was bleakness, emptiness, darkness falling like a shroud on frightening infinity. There was only time for a campfire supper before the family bedded down in their wagon and slept fitfully to the yipping and whining of coyotes. In the morning a sense of freedom and the smell of fresh grass overcame the fears of the night. The sun was warm and bright; there was little except the people themselves to cast shadows. Henry started from the surveyor's mound and paced off his 160 acres, liking the feel of virgin soil beneath his boots. One of the lucky ones with a creek not too far away, he began plowing after breakfast, both for planting and for building. The day before they had stopped to visit at a bachelor's dugout in the side of a swell in the land. It was the easiest kind of shelter to build, but his wife would not hear of it. And so Henry cut sod for a house, at the same time exposing the earth for tilling and planting.

With his oxen he cut long strips of three-inch-deep sod, the prairie grasses holding it together as he stripped and furrowed. Then, with a spade, he cut the strips into three-foot lengths. The entire family worked together in stacking the pieces of sod like bricks into four walls with openings for a door and a window which would be put in later. Several miles up the creek Henry found enough willow branches to make poles to support the roof. By criss-crossing enough poles, he got the support needed for the roof sod with only a slight sag in the middle. The completed sod house was windproof, fireproof, and sturdy, but it would not keep out the water during the rainy season, and this was one of the paradoxes of sodbusting—Henry had to pray for rain for his crops while his wife felt like praying for a dry house. They could not have both.

The first crop was difficult to plant because the rooted grasses kept the earth firm and the plow could not soften it. As Henry chopped at the earth with an ax, his son dropped seed into the crevices. The first crop would not be as good as later ones, but for the present the family was optimistic. They explored the prairie where each small object—flower, stone, prairie dog, buffalo bone—was an event, where they had to look down rather than out to see anything other than sky and unending prairie grass. They stumbled upon an entire pile of bones, left by the buffalo hunters, and loaded them into the wagon and took them on the long journey to the nearest town, where they were traded for a door and a window. And then they waited in their crude but snug soddy for the grain to grow.

If Henry and his family are to be considered typical homesteaders, their story must stop here, after a bare beginning. Even though it is possible to talk about such a thing as *the settler's experience,* as though it were a genre, the experience varied, sometimes substantially, according to time and place. The family whose claim did not border a creek or river often had to haul drinking water from a considerable distance, or collect it in barrels when it rained, or melt snow to get it in the winter. If a town were established nearby, the settler could soon build a tarpaper shack or even a frame house. If his first crop were spared by drought, hail, grasshoppers, and fire, he could by the end of the summer have enough money for seed to plant the additional acres he had plowed during the summer. With luck, the size of his grain field would grow each year. With luck, his wife would maintain a vegetable garden. With luck, he could buy a milk cow and the children would stay healthy and go to school. With luck, he would stay on his land, improve it, and eventually bequeath a successful farm to his children. With luck.

Inventiveness and resourcefulness and endless work could keep the meagre equipment in shape and could add bit by bit to the worth and the comfort of the homestead. But only luck could bring in the good crops necessary to survive at all. Thus, each settler's discomfort, or fear, or delight, or success depended on the weather and on his own psychological attitude toward solitude and mixed fortune. And on luck.

If Henry, Anna, Lucy, and Fred lived in southeastern Dakota during the year 1869–1870, they had to beware of consumption, freezing, fever, and pneumonia, the most common causes of death that year. The next most frequent causes were croup, dropsy, acute diarrhea, cancer, diphtheria, gunshot wounds, cholera, lung fever, bronchitis, and fits. Single cases were reported of suicide by drowning, suicide by poisoning, drowning in a well, dysentery, congestion of the brain, spasms, erysipelas, bilious colic, apoplexy, inflammation of the liver, and knife wounds. Ten years later, in the entire area which was to become South Dakota, the frontrunners were diphtheria and consumption. The latter term was often used for tuberculosis, but the census of 1880 specifically showed one death from tuberculosis (a Chinese man in the Black Hills) while listing many cases of consumption. The largest number of deaths that year occurred in the Black Hills area, newly opened to gold mining, and so a number of the causes of death (such as from mine cave-ins) were not available to the settlers. The list of causes in 1880 is more varied than for a decade earlier: struck by lightning, Saint Vitus's dance, teething, kicked by horse, gravel, worms, inanition, alcoholism (with one case being listed as intemperance), struck by a falling body, calculus, scalding, asthma, gored, sunstroke, hanging, heart disease, menses, murder, suicide by hanging, endocesditis, killed by Indians, and "shot sparking another man's wife." Civilization was getting closer to Dakota.

In spite of these various dangers of disease and violence, the settler who survived and stuck it out became a toughened and healthy individual, acquiring a quality which has remained through his descendents into modern times. There has been very little of the "life of leisure" in South Dakota, and vigor and long life have often been attributed to hard work. Any large-scale failure on the part of the settlers was the result of climatic conditions rather than a reluctance to toil from dawn to dark. Because natural disasters are dramatic, they have been emphasized in the farm novel of the Great Plains, a genre which flourished in the Middle West from the late nineteenth century (as in works by Hamlin Garland) well into the 1940s, and whose western edge was represented most frequently by South Dakota and Nebraska. These disasters affected the people and the land in different ways, and whenever they cut down crop production drastically they affected the nation as well.

To plot the "bad years" is to ignore the drama and to disregard local or short-lived catastrophes which did not greatly influence the economy of state or region. Nevertheless, a brief recitation may be useful. Major blizzards occurred in 1873, 1880–1881, 1888, and 1975. Old-timers who were children during 1888 argued the severity of that blizzard against the force of the recent one and decided that they were about equal, with more human deaths in 1888 and more cattle casualties in 1975. Plagues of grasshoppers were most damaging in 1864–1865, 1873–1874, 1876, and 1936. Drought, which appears in somewhat uneven cycles, was most severe in 1889, 1894, 1910–1911, and during the dust storms of 1933 and 1934.

The blizzard is a special Northern Plains phenomenon which can strike as early as October and as late as April, although November, January, and March seem to be the most common times. A rapid dropping of temperature is especially characteristic in November and March, so that the storm may begin as rain, which then turns to sleet, icing the ground, and finally heavy snow. What keeps these developments from being a mere storm is the high wind, usually blowing in swirls so that it seems to be coming from all directions at once. One of the distinctions of the East River 1975 blizzard, according to the old-timers, was that the wind blew straight. In either case, the world turns into a white nightmare, cold and dense. It does not harm crops, of course, unless it strikes before harvest in the fall (which is unlikely) or after the spring growth has begun (which is rare). The damage is to people and livestock. During the years of settlement the animals were usually protected in their own dugouts or soddies, but it was extremely hazardous for the farmer to leave his house and go out to check on the animals or feed them. Common practice was to use a rope strung between buildings. Even so, many people froze to death in those years, some of them school children caught by the storm on their way home (blizzards strike suddenly and deceptively), others simply caught out in the open for one reason or another. The lack of natural shelter on the open plains made it difficult to hole up for the duration of the storm. In the 1880s, at the height of the open-range cattle industry, the effects of a big blizzard were devastating. Ironically, the 1975 storm was equally destructive because shelters for the animals in feeder lots and fenced pasture were inadequate. To be out in a blizzard is to know fear. The wind takes the breath away, its velocity creating a vacuum in which there seems to be no air. Directions are confusing because of lack of visibility. No sensible person on the plains leaves his house or car during a blizzard.

Prairie fires destroyed crops but were usually restricted to limited areas, unlike winter storms, and did not generally cause widespread destruction. For the individual settler whose house and life were threatened, however, the experience was terrifying. A high wind could move the fire at a rapid rate, making it difficult to dig breaks in time. Even without wind, the fire created its own through the vacuums and suctions caused by intense heat. In contrast to the whiteness of the blizzard, the prairie fire blackened the sky and turned day into a night of ashes.

Hail, too, always a threat, tended to be spotty, skipping one area, hitting another, with the same caprice shown by tornadoes. For these sporadic but frequently destructive acts of God, the modern farmer carries insurance and is to that extent better off than his predecessors.

The young territory was beset by both grasshoppers and

drought in those crucial years when the attempts to attract more settlers were turned instead into adverse publicity. Sometimes called locusts, or Rocky Mountain locusts (in what seems like a method of blaming them on another region), the grasshoppers occasionally appeared in huge clouds, like dust, that blotted out the sun and, for no apparent reason other than the prevailing winds, blew into some areas and out of others. When they did alight, usually in late July and for about a week, they completely stripped fields of grain just ripening. In 1876, following grasshopper destruction of corn, garden vegetables, potatoes, and some wheat, the governors of Missouri, Iowa, Nebraska, and Dakota Territory met in Omaha to discuss possible methods for controlling the insects. All they could come up with was a planned day of prayer for the following spring as crops were planted. It worked; but the settlers gradually introduced rye and flax—resistant to the grasshoppers—and diversified their crops, proving that the plains environment was suitable for grains other than wheat.

Perhaps the worst infestation of locusts was that of 1936, following the dust storms of a few years earlier, and adding to the general disaster of the depression. Although the notable drought years were by that time in the past, South Dakota has never been entirely free of the fear of dry years. There were some in the 1950s and more in the 1970s, although not affecting the entire state each time. Because South Dakota is a marginal state in terms of rainfall—the eastern half wetter than the trans-Missouri half—questions surrounding dry spells become complicated. For a while in the 1890s artesian wells were promoted as a means of irrigation, the system being backed by land-speculators and mortgage-holders, but the publicity bothered those people who were intent on boosting the young state and wanted to keep ideas related to drought away from prospective settlers. The lack of success of the project in the James River valley (probably the very thing in the minds of the modern farmers who oppose irrigation in the same valley from the Oahe Reservoir) and several years of good rainfall toward the end of the century lessened interest in the project.

The problems of the 1930s were not confined to South Dakota. The entire Great Plains—north, central, and south—suffered from lack of water, from storms of dust as the wind removed the topsoil, and from widespread deprivation. That story is well known from such notable novels as John Steinbeck's *Grapes of Wrath* and, in South Dakota, Frederick Manfred's *Golden Bowl*. Lessons were learned in contour plowing and crop rotation, and yet even today a high wind during a dry winter will blow the topsoil from those fields which were tilled in the fall and left bare. Generally, however, the climate has moderated in the past forty years, the farmers have hail insurance and drought subsidies, and with the use of pesticides and chemical fertilizers they usually get a good crop even under adverse conditions. If everything goes well, there are record crops. A different kind of problem has replaced those which plagued the early settlers: environmentalists denounce the use of chemical fertilizers which are often washed off the fields and into the rivers and streams, polluting them, endangering wildlife, and contaminating sources of drinking water.

In literary treatments of the settler, defeat is more dramatic than success, and many of the farm novels are therefore gloomy in tone and pessimistic in outlook. Perhaps Per Hansa's death in a South Dakota blizzard (Rölvaag's *Giants in the Earth*) is the classic example of man pitted against an alien land and the forces of nature and losing his life in the struggle. There is, however, a variety of conflicts and psychological reactions and degrees of success or failure in the multitude of stories coming under the general heading of the "farm novel." Some of the drama has disappeared from the life of the farmer, and contemporary versions are rare. With a few from the 1960s, the 136 novels listed in Roy Meyer's book, *The Middle Western Farm Novel in the Twentieth Century* (1965), range over a period of more than half a century and twelve states, with South Dakota being near the top of the list. Thirty-one are set in Iowa, nineteen in Minnesota, fifteen in South Dakota, twelve in Nebraska, and so on down the line.

One of the most popular writers of settling and pioneering (perhaps because her stories are not entirely grim) is Laura Ingalls Wilder, whose *Little House on the Prairie* books have become a successful television series forty years after the publication of the first of the eight books. Although the books were written for children, they follow closely the author's own experiences during the period of settlement and offer many insights into family relationships, the land, the weather, the building of railroads and towns, and they provide an accurate portrait of a time and a place to which modern readers look back not only with the pleasures of escape but with a desire to learn about—or remember—the trials and joys of a newly born society. Laura Ingalls was born in Wisconsin in 1867, spent her childhood in Minnesota (after a brief stay in Oklahoma), and then grew up in Dakota Territory (DeSmet) before marrying Almanzo Wilder and moving to Missouri in 1894. She was over sixty when she began writing, almost forty years after leaving drought-stricken South Dakota, crossing Nebraska (which reminded her of Lydia Locket's pocket, "nothing in it, nothing on it, only the binding round it"), being told that there was nothing in Kansas, and looking forward to a new beginning and a new farm in the Ozarks.

It often seems strange that more books have been written about the "South Dakota Experience" by people who eventually left the state than by those who stayed. Perhaps the only relevant theory is that the people who remained were too busy to write books, too busy with survival. In any case, Laura Ingalls Wilder, and her daughter Rose Wilder Lane, could look back at several environments and see the differences from the objectivity of distance. In the Wisconsin forests the family was closely knit, the landscape was dark but comforting, the deer often provided food, the bears could be frightening, and although it was difficult to clear the land for plowing, at least the plowing itself was not hindered by the tough sod of the plains. The open spaces of South Dakota introduced the elements of a new psychology which embodied a fear of infinity never suspected in the woods but also a new freedom of movement and of vision, the latter unobstructed by anything except distance. With hunting severely limited, with only prairie dogs and jackrabbits and prairie chickens scattered about in miniature, food had to come from gardens or be purchased in the nearest town. Pa Ingalls worked for the railroad, as many farmers did, until he could establish a claim and develop a successful farm. In many respects life proceeded at a slower pace on the plains because of the distances. Schools were farther away, the mail was slower, a trip to town for supplies or equipment took an entire day or more, and it was not possible at first simply to run over to the neighbors for a quick afternoon visit. Everything took time and a great deal of patience.

Paradoxically, the new freedom suffered with the encroachment of civilization as well as from the economic setbacks caused by slim hunting prospects and by poor crops. Independence gave way to a reliance upon the railroad, first for wages and then for the food brought in by the trains from other regions. The inefficiency of the standard plow used in Wisconsin called for a modified design, a "breaking plow," which was shortly developed by an urban manufacturer whose only motive was to profit from the settler's problem. Because the prairie could not be conquered by the relatively simple equipment of the woodsman, the settlers, stouthearted and independent in spirit as they were, had to reach out for help, and so their destinies became linked to those of the nation. (It cannot be forgotten that the settlers were in Dakota in the first place as a result of, among other things, Indian treaties made by the federal government, the Homestead Act through which the federal government, in effect, gave free land, and the "overcrowding"—as seen then—of eastern agricultural lands which "forced" a portion of the population to move West.) The settlers were individuals—and South Dakotans still are—but they were pressured not only by the immediate environment but also by the economic and political changes that were felt all over the nation following the Civil War.

From a literary point of view, all this is to say that the regional novel is not divorced from the geographical or political entity which encompasses the regions. Nevertheless, it has its special appeal of place, and when its material is from the past it can do a better job of bringing life to that past than the best of history books. In the case of novels such as Mrs. Wilder's, an even more important function is that of reminding man of his place in the natural world. In spite of his technology in a later time, he must still come to terms with drought, blizzards, floods, and all the capriciousness of nature. The "Dakota Experience" can be a valuable teacher.

In July of 1894 Laura Ingalls Wilder left South Dakota with mixed feelings, a common reaction among the early visitors to the territory and contemporary visitors to the state. In her diary she commented on the worst crops she had seen yet, on the dust and the hot wind, on children that could hardly be distinguished from the pigs, on her craving for water, and on a Russian settlement where she saw a full grown idiot, "an awful sight." Her husband killed a snake one evening, and when they arrived at Yankton she had her revolver fixed. But at the James River, just as they were preparing to leave South Dakota, Mrs. Wilder stopped, looked back, and wished that she were talented enough at painting or writing to record the beauty of the scene. The river wound through the valley picturesquely, with trees growing on the banks, and, although the bluffs beyond the valley were brown the contrast with the green trees and the shining water touched her emotions. Her parting thought was that if she had been Indian she would have scalped more white folks before leaving this land.

Whether a homesteader left South Dakota with reluctance or with relief, he was part of a mobility which characterized the land rush even while the "permanent" population increased, spectacularly in the 1880s. A few hundred Negroes who came north after the Civil War found acceptance not easy to achieve and gradually left. Hutterites were suspect because of their strange ways and drifted north, many to Canada. Other short-time settlers were easily discouraged by hardship and moved on to greener pastures, not always easy to find. But the population kept going up, with one temporary slip backwards during a bad period of drought. From 1870 to 1880 the population increased from 12,000 to 80,000. Ten years later it had quadrupled to 328,000 (plus 20,000 Indians who were counted in the 1890 census). A drop of almost 40,000 in the next five years merely slowed settlement for a few years, and by 1900 there were 380,000 whites in the state. The people came for different reasons, although free (or cheap) land was the basic attraction. And they left for different reasons.

Edith Ammons and her sister, Ida Mary, left Saint Louis in the summer of 1907 to claim Section 18, Range 77W, west of the Missouri River, thirty miles southeast of Pierre in the relatively barren center of the state. Their grandparents had come up to Illinois from Tennessee, and the family moved into the vicinity of Saint Louis, some of them working the land and others entering professions. Left motherless at an early age, Edith and Ida Mary became independent before most women did and, when their father remarried and later suffered financial losses, the girls decided to give in to the lure of the frontier. At that time the era of straggling settlers was giving way to a steady stream, almost a tidal wave for a while after Indian lands on the west side of the Missouri River were opened to settlement. Even so, the newly opened area was desolate when the Ammons sisters arrived, prompting Edith to think, "This couldn't be it." She almost turned back, but she had heard so much talk about West River, South Dakota (along with Wyoming, Montana, and Colorado) being the new frontier, the place midwesterners were going to for cheap land, that she assumed more people would arrive soon and relieve the emptiness. She also argued that land would always be worth something, and that the experience, even though brief, would be fruitful. Finally, she made arrangements to be taken back to Pierre, and having made the arrangements felt less trapped out on the prairie and stayed.

Her first chore was to clean up the tarpaper shack which stood on her claim, the relic of a former homesteader who had not remained long enough to prove his claim. The nearest neighbor agreed to haul in water for her. As her distance-vision improved and she was able to see objects near the horizon, she realized that other shacks were set here and there, although some of them turned out to be empty. In her area, at least, it seemed to be the practice to build a shack, stay the required eight months, and then leave as quickly as possible. It was like the pause of migratory birds.

The Ammons sisters met more women than men in their first

months on the prairie. They were encouraged by Widow Fergus who lived ten miles away with her young son, said there was not time to be homesick, and was brown and calloused but had no time for self-pity. Three women in their thirties rode in from eighteen miles away to say hello. One of them, Wilomene White, was from Chicago, an artist from a wealthy family which had sent her to South Dakota for her health. She had been on the prairie with her two friends for almost two years, returning to Chicago during the worst winter months. The visitors seemed self-assured, but Edith and Ida Mary were confused by directions and distances and did not venture far from their shack for several months. They had been told that it was easy to find their claim—"three miles from the buffalo waller"—but when they wandered too far they could not find the buffalo waller.

In spite of misgivings they discovered that over a period of time, and perhaps even against their wills, they absorbed a peacefulness from the open spaces and the bigness of the land. They admitted to the isolation, the hardships, and the crudeness of the life, but responded to "air that was like old wine" and to the brightness of the moon and stars. The heat of midday was a small problem in the context of cool, invigorating mornings and evenings. Thus the sisters made adjustments while offering themselves small congratulations on being among the gamblers without whom the West would not have been settled. When they ran out of bacon they learned to make gravy from the grease; when they ran out of coal they pulled dried prairie grass to burn in the little laundry stove; when they wanted to keep water from becoming warm they dug a hole and set a can in it. They learned to adjust cooking procedures to the higher altitude. But, with only a small plot of corn on their land, they soon realized the necessity of finding wage-earning work. Ida Mary agreed to teach school, and neighbors moved the Ammons shack to the other side of the claim, nearer the school. Edith got a job by accident one day when she went to McClure to check for mail. No longer on the map, McClure was then a one-building "town"—general store, post office, and small restaurant—at the halfway point on the stage line between Pierre and Presho. But a shack had been moved in, close to this building, and inside it Edith found a small handpress used to publish the proof notices of the homesteaders, as required by law. Myrtle Combs, a homesteader who had once worked on a Minneapolis newspaper, told Edith that she was proving up and going home, and that the McClure Press needed new management. It was owned by E. L. Senn, who had a string of these "final-proof" newspapers in South Dakota.

Not only did Edith Ammons get the job, but she quickly turned the paper into something more than a publication of claims proofs, and as more settlers poured into the area and a drawing was held for 350 homesteads on part of the Lower Brulé Reservation nearby, Edith decided to enter a claim of her own, the first one having been in her sister's name. The shack was moved again, and a second building erected next to it to house the printing press. It was early spring, 1908, and rain had brought green grass, bluebells, lavender and white hyacinths, and other flowers to the prairie. The beauty took the edge from the new sense of loneliness; on this new piece of land there was no sign of any living thing except, one day, an antelope far in the distance. Optimistically, Edith petitioned for a post office, was granted her request, and the "town" of Ammons was in business, waiting for customers. In less than a month they came in swarms, like grasshoppers. Each day the prairie changed in appearance. The first woman ever to establish a newspaper on an Indian reservation, Edith Ammons named her paper the *Reservation Wand* and began to print information designed to help the new settlers learn plowing and cultivation methods. As the paper became the center of the new community, people clamored for a store as well, and Edith and Ida Mary had one built. The Ammons empire was under way.

Not for long. Just as many western towns disappeared as survived. The location of railroads, shifting population, changes of various kinds could alter the destinies of the small communities on the prairie. In the case of Ammons, South Dakota, 1909, there were two reasons. The Ammons buildings were destroyed by fire, and Edith, hearing of new land openings in Wyoming, got the itch to move. She was as restless as some of the people she had criticized; the news of another frontier, and the psychological demand of the very open spaces she had once disliked, pulled her on into the West. She married in Wyoming and spent the rest of her life in Denver, and it has been said about her that she never forgot South Dakota and the peculiar combination of fear and love on the plains.

The so-called "surplus" lands on the Indian reservations west of the Missouri River were not free to settlers. The government established price ranges up to approximately $1,000 for a 160-acre tract, and latecomers (following the main drawings) often paid more. In the first sale of Indian lands in 1904, more than 2,000 claims were made available but 106,000 persons registered for them at Yankton, Chamberlain, Bonesteel, and Fairfax. At Bonesteel rioting had to be quelled by armed citizens. Among those disappointed in the drawing was Oscar Micheaux, from Kentucky, the grandson of a slave. As a Pullman porter working out of Chicago he saw parts of the West and liked what he saw. Unable to draw a claim, he purchased a relinquishment four miles southeast of Gregory and arrived there in the spring of 1905, the only colored man, he said, engaged in agriculture from Gregory to Omaha, a distance of 300 miles.

Micheaux immediately became involved in a number of controversies, large and small. The smallest was racial prejudice, soon overcome, said Micheaux, when he broke out 120 acres while many other "real farmers" had not managed one-third as much with better equipment. His success brought him into a different light, and he was no longer called "a free-go-easy coon," but was considered a booster for the area. A larger problem was the lack of black women. Micheaux was attracted to a young white neighbor girl, but his own condemnation of interracial marriage kept him from wooing her, although he admitted being in love. Instead, he went to Chicago several times until he located a black girl who was willing to try life on the prairie. Her father, a minister, objected to the marriage, disliking Micheaux, but finally gave in. At this point a third problem entered, affecting both the marriage and Oscar's reputation in the community. The railroad was moving west through the Rosebud country and as it neared Tripp County and townsites were being considered for a western terminus, Micheaux arranged for his wife to file a claim in Tripp County. His own farm was in Gregory County, and because residence was necessary for the establishment of a claim, the couple had to live apart much of the time. Mildred Micheaux was dissatisfied and wrote complaining letters to her father in Chicago, until a year or so after the marriage her father went to South Dakota and took her back home. Because Micheaux had filed on a particular piece of land near Gregory, where the railroad might pass, and because he had his wife file in the next county where the railroad might terminate, his neighbors wondered whether he intended to farm or had purchased his land for speculation. More than half a century later the pioneers who knew Micheaux insisted that his game was to outfox the railroad and that farming was merely a front. If so, he failed. The railroad played its own game and missed the Micheaux claim by several miles.

Perhaps Oscar Micheaux had the last laugh. He was an ambitious man, believing that most Negroes did not put forth enough effort to better themselves. Living alone on his homestead for several years, he not only farmed with some success but began to write his fictional autobiography. Then, suddenly, he disappeared. Rumor had it that he owed money to "a lot of people" and that he skipped out to avoid payment. When South Dakotans next heard of him, in 1940, he was producing motion pictures, living in New York, and making trips to Chicago in a 16-cylinder car with a white chauffeur, and his weight of 300 pounds indicated that his life as a homesteader was far behind him. In 1970 an issue of the *New Yorker* mentioned the showing of a Micheaux film, "God's Step Children," made for black audiences. He had also written at least five books before he died in 1951.

The prairie frontier accepted and rejected many kinds of people. Enough of them survived loneliness, blizzards, drought, and hunger to populate the state comfortably, though sparsely by eastern standards. Some did not survive. Many simply left, often to go on to useful and satisfying lives elsewhere. Were the settlers the real heroes of the prairie states? They had to adjust to a new and often hostile environment, to suffer privation during bad years, to cling to a vision of success and freedom, and yet the modern militant Indian will insist that there was nothing heroic in forcing the "first people there" off the land or coercing them into selling it. Given the argument that the homesteaders did not do this, that they came later, after the Indians had left as a result of wars and treaties, the "first people" might still insist that for them the land was friendly, life-giving, not hostile, and only naturally harsh, or fickle. The white man should not be considered heroic for simply getting along on this land.

Perhaps the settlers were indeed heroes. Or perhaps, already in their time, the day of the hero was long past, not only in South Dakota but throughout the nation, and, except in myth, it was time to learn to believe in and cling to the common things.

6

Beyond the 99th: Short
Grass and Gold

$\mathcal{A}$ SIMPLIFIED geographical image of the westward movement during the nineteenth century would consist of three areas, east to west, each with its own occupation: farming which extended from the moist middle of the nation as far west as the ninety-ninth meridian; cattle-grazing on the immense plains to the foot of the Rocky Mountains; and mining, especially for gold and silver, in the Rockies and the coastal mountains. To the homesteaders, cowboys, and miners add one more ingredient, the Indians, and we have an overall view of the broad frontier West as the nation expanded toward the Pacific Ocean. Because of its unusual location, South Dakota is a replica of the entire "frontier" in reduced size. Its eastern third (east of the ninety-ninth meridian) is lower in elevation and higher in rainfall than the rest of the state. Here the prairie grass once grew as tall as a man, and the soil is rich and black. It is an area of rolling farmlands and, in the north, of lakes created by the glaciers which swept over neighboring Minnesota. Agriculture is intensified; farmers are no longer the patchwork homesteaders of more than half a century ago but are as economically comfortable as any other businessmen. The term for their occupation is "agribusiness."

Across the magic meridian the elevation begins to rise and the annual rainfall is lower. The tallgrass prairie gives way to the mixed-grass plain and eventually to the shortgrass high plain. This country is more suited to cattle and wheat than to corn, flax, and soybeans. The grasses here are blue grama, little bluestem, buffalo grass, and side oats grama, and the wild creatures are prairie dogs, coyotes, cottontails, golden eagles, hawks, and sharp-tailed grouse. Although the plain covers two-thirds of the state, its population is only one-third, including the majority of the Sioux Indians. And at the western end, where the plain is at a 3,000-foot elevation (three times as high as the eastern prairie), it suddenly confronts the Black Hills where Harney Peak is the highest point in the United States east of the Rockies—7,242 feet. Here more gold is produced than anywhere in the nation.

Because South Dakota stretches across three different kinds of land, it serves as a transition from the Middle West farms to the Far West mountains. As such, its identity is sometimes muddled, its labels confusing. The most certain fact is that it is a rural state. One city stands at each end, Sioux Falls a kind of gateway to Minneapolis and Rapid City a gateway to Denver, each of the South Dakota cities somewhat resembling in attitude and atmosphere the larger city it "faces." Although only six states do not have any cities as large as Sioux Falls, the combined population of Rapid City and Sioux Falls is over one-sixth of the total for the entire state. Between these two sentinels there are many open spaces.

It is space that most Dakotans think of as typical of the state. And the western space is associated with a feeling of freedom and independence, although these qualities have both flourished and diminished over the past 200 years. For a time, tremendous herds of buffalo ("bison" to the purists) roamed freely up and down the Great Plains. They had, in fact, inhabited the East also, providing trails for the first explorers into Kentucky and other regions; but by 1810 the buffalo no longer ranged east of the Mississippi. In the Dakotas, Wyoming, and Montana they found an excellent grazing ground of prairies and river valleys, broken up by buttes and pine-covered ridges, with an abundance of buffalo grass, bunchgrass, and, along the rivers, buffalo berries and water. Although most nineteenth-century travelers described the buffalo as clumsy and stupid, the animal was almost revered by the Indians who depended upon it for food, clothing and shelter, and tools. As the buffalo disappeared, so did the comfort and freedom of the Plains Indians.

Constrictions upon the free movement of both buffalo and Indian began with the covered wagon traffic on the Overland Trail across Nebraska and Wyoming during the 1840s and 1850s, when in a single year as many as a hundred thousand "westerers" passed along the trail. These travelers killed the buffalo for food, grazed their own cattle on grass needed by the buffalo, and eventually created a wide, dusty, grassless, treeless strip which prevented the animals from wandering freely between the Dakotas and Kansas. As the buffalo became more scarce a chain of events was set off that determined the immediate future of South Dakota. The Sioux were relatively peaceful as long as they could move freely with the herds and could hunt. Once their source of food and shelter and clothing was endangered, they grew restless, then annoyed, and finally became angry enough to attack wagon trains and small settlements. Their actions brought troops into the territory, accompanied by hunters who killed more buffalo in order to feed the army units. And, as military protection increased, the railroads extended farther west and provided transportation for those products which sought an eastern market—buffalo hides being one of these products. With the popularity of the buffalo robe beginning as early as 1860, more than a hundred thousand hides were sent to market annually. The army encouraged the hunting of buffalo, assuming that the demise of this animal would break the spirit of the Sioux and bring peace. For ten years or more, leading up to the eventful battles of 1876, the process escalated until at last the Sioux had to choose between surrender and starvation.

The buffalo, then, played a key role in the settlement of South Dakota. Even as the Sioux were making their last stand, homesteaders were crowding into the other end of the state. When crops were poor, in a year of drought or hail or grasshoppers, the homesteader could at first survive by hunting buffalo. By the mid-1870s the range was empty. Even then the homesteader could collect the bones of previously slaughtered animals and sell them for up to $12 a ton at the nearest railroad shipping point. In the eastern cities the bones were used to refine sugar, to make fertilizer, and sometimes (as an additive) to make bone-china dishes. Since the dry air of the plains preserved the bones for ten, twenty or more years, and because the railroads were later in crossing the Northern Plains than they were farther south, Dakotans continued to pick bones until almost 1890, ten years later than the practice ended in Kansas. The year coincides with the final surrender of the Sioux at Wounded Knee and with Frederick Jackson Turner's date for the termination of the American frontier.

The land determines its own use. While the cast changed, the play went on. Western South Dakota was obviously good range country, and the cowboy replaced the Indian and the cow replaced the buffalo—a major change in terms of the people who were involved but a continuation in the use of the land.

Cattle had been brought into the territory by settlers and by the army in the 1860s, but in small numbers. When the army ran out of beef and was forced to buy it, some settlers in the eastern section served as suppliers. Perhaps the first cattleman as far west as the Missouri River was Paul Narcelle, a French-Canadian and former employee of the American Fur Company, who established a herd of cows near Fort Sully in order to supply that military post. He and Basil Claymore, an interpreter at the fort, became informal partners when they married the daughters of Thomas L. Sarpy. Narcelle had two sons, Ed and Narcisse, both of whom became ranchers west of the river, and Claymore's seven sons married mixed-bloods and went into the cattle business on the Cheyenne Reservation. But the big influx of cattle into South Dakota came from those in the Texas industry, who started large-scale ranching with Spanish longhorn cattle and quickly looked for markets. With beef scarce in the North and in the East, Texas cattlemen began their famous long drives as soon as the railroads reached into Kansas and the Dakotas after the Civil War. The construction of the Kansas Pacific Railroad was of the first importance because it provided access to the eastern markets and was the halfway point between

Texas and the North. It was during the building of this railroad that William Cody became the famous hunter, Buffalo Bill, and Dodge City, first a center for the buffalo trade, joined the list of "wicked" cow towns in Kansas—Abilene, Wichita, Ellsworth, and others less notorious. The thousands of cowboy and town marshal novels, the longrunning television program, "Gunsmoke," and the mythology of the western town all rose from the dust of the Kansas cow towns.

There were no similar towns in South Dakota, nor any Bat Mastersons or Matt Dillons. The cattle that came north as far as Montana, Dakota, and Wyoming in the 1860s were intended only in part for sale to beef-starved mining camps; the main herds were put out to graze on the northern grasslands because Texas had more cows than could be fed. Because of the Indian wars in the 1870s, South Dakota was the last plains state to develop large herds, but by 1878 there were a hundred thousand head of cattle in the Black Hills region alone, many of them from Texas. Very quickly, with ready-made markets—the government (to supply the reservations), the railroads, and the eastern cities by way of stockyards in Chicago, Saint Paul, and Sioux City—the open range became the scene of a beef bonanza. Both territorial and eastern newspapers hailed the opportunity in this fenceless and limitless new land where the expenses were small (a few cowhands and corrals) and the profits large. Free grass would turn a five-dollar calf into a fifty-dollar cow; such an attractive business could not fail to appeal to rich and poor alike, and to foreign as well as American investors. The northern ranges, with their plentiful grass, soon were stocked with cattle from the Midwest as well as from Texas, and even so, during the 1880s, the demand for beef was often greater than the supply. Fortunes were made by outside investors and a number of ranching empires were begun that lasted well into the twentieth century and provided men for the state legislature, for governor, for Congress, for a variety of positions of influence, in addition to their product, the beef which helped feed a nation.

There was a difference, of course, between the cattle baron and the cowboy. In modern times the terms "rancher," "cattleman," "stockman," "stockgrower," and "cowman" mean essentially the same thing—one whose business is the raising and selling of cattle for beef. Within the structure of the business operation are the owner, the foreman, and the hired hands. All are considered respectable people. But in the earlier days of the cowboy, when the range was wide open and the men herding the cattle ate dust and tasted loneliness and made their occasional trips to town momentous affairs, it was possible for the cowhand to recognize a line of distinction between ranching and respectability, a line which he did not set for himself but which was drawn by the more "polite society" of the towns. As for himself, the South Dakota cowboy retained a sense of pride in the work he was doing and often felt antagonistic toward the country lawyers and "windy farmers" who made up the state legislature and whose most important work was adopting a state flower and setting a wolf bounty, after which they would spend the rest of their time in "chasing chippies" and getting drunk.

Everyone has seen the benevolent baron, the tenderfoot Englishman, the crusty foreman, and the cowboy—both the "good guys" and the "bad guys"—on television or in motion pictures. Exaggerated human relationships—between individuals and between rival groups—have usually received more attention than the cows, probably stemming from Owen Wister's novel, *The Virginian,* which established many of the features of the popular western image, including the showdown on a dusty street, but which singularly lacked the object behind it all, the cow. What the range cattlemen did was to use the semiarid plains and the native grasses to construct a business, a large and very profitable business which, in spite of changes, continues in force because of the never-ending demand for beef in the diets of Americans. Methods have changed; the demand for beef has not. The cattle barons, many of them British, are gone, and perhaps the glamour associated with that cattle empire stretching from Texas to Canada from the Civil War to about 1900 is gone also, but the realistic business of marketing cattle is still one of the major sources of income for several states, including South Dakota.

What brought about the changes was that old nemesis, the

weather, coupled with a few coincidental events. Drought in the mid-1880s necessitated the removal of huge herds of cattle from Texas to the grasslands of the Northern Plains, and these ranges were overstocked. Cattlemen using the Indian Territory lands for grazing had been ordered off the Cheyenne-Arapahoe Reservation, and many of these herds had been sent north. Just as the northern ranges were teeming with cows, severe cold and unusually widespread blizzards hit the entire Great Plains from November 1886 to March 1887. The most drastic losses were suffered by the major "cow capitalists," both American and British, and by southern owners who had sent to the north cattle ill-prepared to face a long, hard winter. Casualties reached as high as 90 percent in some areas and the cattle boom was suddenly over. South Dakota had lighter losses than did the surrounding areas, partly because its cattle had already spent winters on the range and were somewhat used to cold weather, and partly because in the Black Hills region there was shelter in the foothills. Nevertheless, South Dakota was affected by the industry's overall losses and set about learning the lesson of commercial beef-raising. It was a mistake to rely entirely upon the grass of the open range. (Besides, homesteaders and sheepmen were encroaching upon the range and the day of the fence was at hand.) The solution was to grow hay for feeding the cattle throughout the winter. Later, corn became the popular feed, to give the meat a higher quality for increasingly fussy consumers. And so, although a disastrous winter wiped out a large number of South Dakota's one million cattle, and left many of the survivors emaciated and unable to bear calves in the spring, two new important industries were born—the raising of feed corn and the growing of hay as a substitute for open-range grass during the winter. The result has been to make beef more expensive but also more palatable, and the need for corn and hay has strengthened the economy not only in South Dakota but in the surrounding states as well.

Not all of the cattle empires disappeared in the blizzards of 1886–1887. In 1904, one year prior to the establishment of a livestock commission in South Dakota, Murdo MacKenzie (who had just finished a term as president of the Texas and Southwestern Cattle Association) brought the famous Scottish-owned Matador into South Dakota. With the Diamond A, it was the last of the massive organizations to operate in the state. Eventually the Matador was sold for $19 million, but an even more memorable result of its activities in South Dakota is the narrative told by one of its cowboys, Ike Blasingame (*Dakota Cowboy,* 1958). Ike is an example of the "temporary Dakotan," born elsewhere, employed in the state for a time, leaving his impact on the historical totality, and then moving on to die in still another place. When he came north from Texas in 1904 he was twenty years old and had already worked as a cowhand for six years. While with the Matador Company on its large leased range on the Cheyenne River Reservation, he "repped" with the surrounding outfits, spent three summers in Canada, returned to find settlers moving into western South Dakota (he predicted that the big outfits would not last much longer), and when the Matador closed its reservation lease, started a small ranch of his own on the Little Moreau River. Here he remained, with wife and three children, until the 1934 drought sent him farther west, eventually to California. Loyal to his calling, he managed ranches on the West Coast until shortly before his death in 1962, watching over Herefords rather than longhorns, working behind wire fences rather than on open range, and riding gentle broncs.

During his years on the Cheyenne River Reservation, Blasingame was, presumably, a typical Dakota cowboy. He liked the range, which he described as a wild scattering of little parks, draws which often provided taller grasses, and thickets of buffalo berries, chokecherries, wild plums, and Juneberries. Water was plentiful in this land of rivers and creeks. Daily work began at dawn and ended at sunset, except when one's turn came up for night guard. The big events—although they occurred in a constantly repeated pattern and were not all that special—were the roundups, the cattle drives, bronc riding, sitting in on Indian festivities, and occasional hell-raising in one or more of the tiny towns in the area. Blasingame also emphasizes the rigors of winter and the joys of spring, the latter spoiled only by the gray wolves that attacked isolated cows. There were other things which menaced the cows—cold, snow, wind, heat, flies, mosquitoes, and drought—but the cowboy accepted them as part of the job. What he really got excited about was his string of horses. For the variety of tasks he was called upon to perform, he needed a roping horse, a cutting horse, a night horse (with special awareness in the dark), and a circle horse (to amble patiently around the perimeter of the grazing herd with little or no attention from its rider). In addition to these, there were outlaw horses, some good and some bad, and the all-round horse with a general competence but no special talents. It was rare for a cowboy to own each of these types, but he was always on the lookout for a good horse and knew the names of most of the horses in his outfit as well as in some of the neighboring outfits. Blasingame dwells at length on his favorites, some of which he never owned but was permitted to use, and for which he was nostalgic and almost sad when their owners left.

The area grazed by Matador cattle, along with other brands, covered almost three million acres and bordered the Standing Rock Reservation on which white cattlemen had also taken leases. The eastern end of the range bordered the Missouri River, to which the Milwaukee Railroad built a line terminating at Evarts, just south of Mobridge. The railroad also established a strip six miles wide and eighty miles long through the center of the reservations, to the west, a corridor through which cattle could be driven to the railroad, with watering places twelve miles apart—a day's drive for a herd. The strip was used by the reservation outfits but also by large cattle companies west of the reservation, so that thousands of cows were funneled into the strip, so many that Blasingame refers to an empire of unbelievable size, including the famous Turkey Track brand, the Sword & Dagger, and the Narcelles and Claymores, now referred to as Indians because of the many mixed marriages in the two families. Everything converged on Evarts, one of the great shipping points in the north, now buried beneath the Missouri River to exist only in the mind.

Toward the end of the big Matador operation in South Dakota, Murdo MacKenzie put together a herd and took it to Brazil to start what was intended to be a giant concern in South

America. He asked Ike Blasingame to go along, but Ike had heard of the big snakes in Brazil and decided, anyway, that he liked South Dakota. His only regret at not going was that two of his favorite horses, Tignor and A Bar, went with Murdo. However, his decision was a wise one; during World War I the Brazilian enterprise failed and the Matador men returned home. By that time settlers and fences were blocking off much of the open range, and with the drought of the 1930s, Ike Blasingame left the smothering dust and "drifted on west, like the old gray wolf, following the cattle trail."

Traveling west from the Cheyenne River Reservation and the old grazing lands of the Matador and other big outfits, the trail passes rivers with such names as Redwater, Red Earth, Worthless, Thunder, Rabbit, Antelope, Grand (in Hugh Glass country), and Bull, small towns named Glad Valley, Meadow, Bison, Prairie City, and Buffalo, and arrives in the northwest corner of the state, north of Sheep Buttes, Deers Ear Buttes, Haystack Buttes, Crow Buttes, and Slim Buttes. Here, where signs have warned motorists, "No gas next 50 miles," Claude Olson has for half a century been an example of the native-born rancher who weathered the droughts and the blizzards and adjusted some of his methods to contemporary circumstances. Born to a Swedish immigrant and a Yankee mother near the mountain that has since been named Rushmore, Olson leased the ranch he and his wife were working on in 1927 and established his own K-slash-O Ranches, stocking both cattle and sheep. Later he got rid of the sheep and acquired 600 acres of irrigated hay land along the river. In 1974 Olson's cattle were grazing on 23,000 acres, including school land leases and Forest Service permits. With the available hay, and with winter protection for his cows in the Slim Buttes, Olson felt that he had an ideal situation for cattle raising. Not an educated man, he has ranched by instinct and experience, changing operations according to the markets and the weather. He refuses to "go by the book," to follow the crowd, or to accept government subsidies, relying instead on tax-cutting methods such as spending as much as he can on deductible items and conservation practices instead of participating in cost-sharing programs. He has also carried fewer cattle than other people thought his range could handle and, for this reason, has always had enough grass, even during dry periods.

A rancher like Claude Olson is tough and is critical of the softness of the newer people in the state. He is also critical of the Homestead Act, which lured easterners into a country they could not cope with, and which their horses and cattle could not adjust to. He worries about contemporary Americans who no longer "buck the crowd" and who have lost the frontier spirit, have lost their pride, and have too easily accepted welfare. Such Americans would not have survived on the plains fifty or seventy-five years ago.

The land not only determines its own use but it also demands certain characteristics in the men who work on it. By the circumstances of their jobs, the rancher and the sheepherder must lead somewhat isolated lives, and the isolation literally forces them into independence and courage if they are to succeed in their business. It may be oversimplifying matters to insist that South Dakota has, by its very nature, attracted people who want a measure of isolation, a measure of individual choice, and who want to stand apart from the crowd. These qualities need not deprive such people of sociability or humor or even sophistication.

As a sheepherder in Harding County before and after Claude Olson's arrival there, Archer Gilfillan turned from an honors degree at the University of Pennsylvania to a life of solitude in the far reaches of South Dakota. Born on an Indian reservation in Minnesota, and part of a family that produced twenty-five books, Archer herded sheep for twenty-three years before illness forced him to retire. He then began to write a weekly column for a newspaper, and these humorous pieces together with his book called, simply, *Sheep,* made him the state's Mark Twain. But first he was a sheepherder.

Having worked on farms in the East, and liking the work but not the pay, Gilfillan took his Latin, his Greek, and his Phi Beta Kappa key to the cattle country of northwest South Dakota, decided after a few months that he did not like cows, contracted "land fever," and took up a homestead, investing all the money

SOUTH DAKOTA

A photographer's essay by David Plowden

his father would give him in sheep. Within three years he discovered that he was not suited to management. In another three years, after studying theology, he discovered that he was not suited to the ministry, so he returned to Harding County and took the first job offered to him—sheepherding. He defended the profession by pointing to Abel, second son of Adam, but felt that if Cain had been a cattleman rather than a farmer he would not only have killed Abel but would have skinned him and nailed his hide to the barn to warn all other herders. More soberly, Gilfillan admitted that the hatred between cowmen and sheepmen which existed farther west was not a problem in South Dakota. He lived comfortably in his sheep wagon and watched the animals, the sunlight and cloud-shadows, a car crawling along a distant road, and felt the calm of the land, and the interior peace which came with it.

Yet he did not find the job monotonous. The sheep did not usually act the same from one day to the next. One day they would run; the next day they were quiet. Their behavior was different in a high wind from what it was in a gentle breeze—a characteristic also noted in Northern Plains people. They traveled ahead of a cold wind and into the face of a warm one. Where grass was plentiful, the sheep stayed contentedly in one place; if food was scarce, they strung out and began to run. Change of season altered their actions and habits, so the sheepherder and his dog were annoyingly busy on some days, just as they quietly enjoyed each other's companionship on other days, the herder smiling at the thought of the "civilized" chaos beyond the boundaries of his world of grass.

Curiously, the sheepherder like Gilfillan and the cattleman like Olson, who speak sharply against a man's following the crowd, make their living off creatures which have a strong herd instinct. What bothers these men the most are times when environmental conditions prompt the animals to "throw off their inhibitions" and act individually. Perhaps psychological reasons do not apply to this apparent anomaly, and the practical matters of herding are all that count. In any case, Gilfillan's worst season of the year (and that of all sheepherders, according to his account) was "the verdant springtime." The sheep, having been fed on dry hay or grass all winter, were wont to go wild when the first tender shoots of green grass appeared in the spring. They smelled the green almost before it showed above the ground and ran frantically looking for it. In the normal feeding pattern, a ewe would graze first on one side of her, then on the other, and then take a step ahead and repeat the process. In the spring, possessed by a hunger for green grass, she took perhaps five steps between each bite, and the herd moved forward too quickly. Stories have been told of sheep outrunning antelope and trampling to death jackrabbits which got in their way. Since a sheepherder and his dog handled two or three thousand sheep, and control was possible only because of the strong herd instinct, the spring running, splitting, and spreading was too much for man and dog and they had to enlist the aid of horse in rounding up the sheep.

In spite of the problems of spring, the danger of fire in late summer, the excessive snow or wind in the winter, summer storms, and of sickness in an area so isolated that a herder could die and not be found for weeks, Gilfillan insisted that the sheepherder's life was a good one. "Sheepherding is what you make of it," he was told when he began; and although he knew from his classical education that the modern sheepherder did not have the status of the shepherd of pastoral romance, he nevertheless enjoyed and defended his profession. Admittedly, the man who needed constant human companionship could not think of herding, nor could the man who had no resources within himself, nor the man who looked down on sheep and herders. But while Gilfillan recognized the physical limitations of the job—he was not able to go farther than he could walk, and was confined to the location of the herd—he felt that his mind was free to roam and learn. Cut off from some of the benefits of civilization, he was also free from some of its restrictions and distractions. He had time to think. He found the West freer than the East, and its people more honest in speaking to each other, more hospitable, more open, and even more unconventional than easterners. All of this he liked; most of it was the result of open land, uncrowded.

When Archer Gilfillan's sister, Emily, urged him, in 1926, to

write a book about his experiences, he began it caustically—
"To reassure those who think that a herder is necessarily so ignorant that whatever he may write is negligible, let me hasten to
add that this book is my *magnum opus,* the *apologia provita
mea,* and my *terminus ad quem"* —and concluded on a note of
naked exuberance:

> Such is the land of the sheep and the herder. A great land! a free
> land! and, in its own way, a beautiful land. Pure, clean air; a frank,
> open, and friendly people; a healthful and interesting job—what
> more could anyone ask? Above all, the opportunity to live his own
> life in his own way—that is the herder's privilege and his very great
> reward.[1]

When Gilfillan retired from sheepherding in 1933 because of illness, he moved into a log cabin in Spearfish, in the Black Hills.
Unable to settle down completely because of his years on the
open range, he began to write for the *Queen City Mail* of Spearfish, the *Sturgis Tribune,* the *Aberdeen American,* the *Belle
Fourche Bee,* and other papers. These columns were informative
and became the nucleus of two books (*A Shepherd's Holiday,*
1936, and *A Goat's Eye View of the Black Hills,* 1953), but they
were also humorous and irreverent, quite different from anything else written in South Dakota in those days. While at the
state capitol one day, Archer was struck by the variety of beards
in the portraits of early legislators. One had such an enormous
mustache that his entire lower face was covered.

> Over it his eyes twinkled roguishly, as if to say: "Don't you wish
> you knew who I am?" Frankly, I was curious, but I knew his secret
> was safe as long as he let his razor alone. He might have been
> anyone from Socrates to Jesse James. Probably no one knew who he
> was but his wife, and he had doubtlessly sworn her to secrecy.
> Probably in the event of his election [he was running for governor]
> he planned to make a kind of public unveiling of himself, with the
> help of his razor, so that the people could see who it was that they
> had elected.[2]

1. Archer B. Gilfillan, *Sheep* (Boston: Little, Brown, and Co., 1929), p. 272.
2. Gilfillan, "Vanity, Thy Name Is—Man!" *South Dakota Review* 4 (Spring 1966):
97.

Such commentary goes far beyond beards and mustaches and deep into the mechanisms of politics. But Gilfillan could poke fun at himself and his profession also, as in the case of the sheepherder who was admitted to a hospital because he had found that "he didn't need all of his brains in his work, so he had come to the hospital to have part of them removed, for fear he might be taken for a schoolteacher." Again, there was the aristocratic blue-blood sheep who lived in a Chicago penthouse, surrounded by luxury, and whose sole purpose was to donate blood once a week. Undoubtedly a good sheepherder, Archer Gilfillan was also a wise man with a penetrating insight into the foibles of his fellow men, and a Twain-like storytelling ability which can still be appreciated. He is remembered in the annual creative writing awards at the University of South Dakota, provided by his sister, Mrs. Emily Heilman.

Because livestock and livestock products make up three-fourths of the state's billion-dollar-a-year agribusiness, it is not just metaphorical to say that grass is one kind of gold. At the extreme western end of the state, south of the rangeland of Olson and Gilfillan, there is real gold, more than anywhere else in the United States. The Homestake Mining Company at Lead, in the Black Hills, is the leading gold producer in the Western Hemisphere. Its annual production of upwards of $20 million does not put it within reach of agriculture, but its consistency has been vital to the state and the nation for a hundred years. Although the Homestake became an early amalgamation of a number of mines in the same area, the original discovery of the mine has been credited to Moses Manuel, a French Canadian from Minnesota who, in 1876, was looking for a deep-rock lode with his brother Fred, Hank Harney, and Alex Engh. A knowledgeable miner who had prospected in Canada as well as in several locations in the American West, Moses found the exposed quartz in the spring while snow was melting and his brother was urging him to wait until the snow cover was gone. The brothers knew that they had found a "homestake," but they were satisfied to sell it for $70,000 (which was a considerable homestake for any miner) rather than attempt to build the removal operation themselves. The buyers were Sen. George Hearst of California, Lloyd Tevis of the Central Pacific Railroad and the Wells-Fargo Express Company, and James Haggin. These three men already owned two large mines and were to buy more later, including the famed Anaconda in Montana. A stamp mill was transported from San Francisco to Lead, by railroad and bull team, and was ready for operation in July 1878. Hearst also arranged for the incorporation of the Homestake Mining Company in California. At first he owned most of the stock himself, with Haggin next in line and Tevis last, but by 1919, when Mrs. Hearst died, the estate showed ownership of about one-fifth of the total shares, still considerably more than anyone else owned. For this reason, the Homestake has been considered a Hearst operation; however, over the years, in spite of the Hearst influence, the ownership has shifted into the hands of many stockholders.

It is true that Homestake gold formed the basis of the Hearst fortune, expanded by other mining ventures and then by the newspapers of son William Randolph Hearst. Hearst was rich, and he served two terms in the U.S. Senate before he died in 1891. Yet his business acumen was accompanied by a kind of benevolence which his widow nurtured after his death, so that the town of Lead was never a typical company town but was rather a beneficiary of the industry owned by outside interests. As the Homestake grew, purchasing adjoining land and neighboring mines in order to get control of the entire mass of ore in the region, the town and its people prospered. Until the tourism following World War I, the Homestake was the only source of wealth in the entire region of the Black Hills. (It was not until the advent of tourism that Lead lost its population leadership in the Hills to Rapid City.)

The Homestake had the normal problems associated with mining—fires, cave-ins, gas, accidents with machinery, a fear that the gold would run out, and tiffs with labor unions—but it survived them all through good management, a willingness to adapt new methods, and a fairness in labor relations. It also contributed to the town, the region, and the entire state through the panics and depression of the first four decades of the twentieth century. During the brief nationwide money panic in 1907 and 1908, Homestake officers went East and demanded gold coins in exchange for the mine's gold bars. As a result, the Lead bank may have been the only one in the United States at that time to remain on a cash payment system during the period of panic. As the mine became famous, President Taft visited it, guided tours began in 1920, and Calvin Coolidge received a special tour in 1927. That same year a change was made from mass mining to selective mining, allowing more gold to be retrieved from the ore. With the stock market crash of October 1929, the Homestake became an island of prosperity in a financial desert. Gold is always worth more in times of depression. In 1934 the Federal Gold Reserve Act, prohibiting the use of gold coins as legal tender, made the government the sole buyer of Homestake gold, but at higher prices. Everything seemed to go right for the company, but the state government soon realized that the only thing even resembling prosperity in South Dakota during the 1930s was the Homestake; so the legislature passed an ore tax in 1935, with a tonnage exemption that excluded other mines in the Black Hills. Through the new 4 percent tax, the Homestake provided one-third of the entire state budget in 1935.

In that same year the first complaint of water pollution was made against the company. It was dismissed on the grounds that the Homestake controlled the water rights in the area. Two years later the company stock was split eight to one, and the state legislature responded by raising the ore tax to 6 percent. Shortly after the beginning of World War II, the War Production Board stopped all gold mining, and the Homestake turned to minerals such as tungsten and coal which were necessary in the war. The foundry and the maintenance shops were geared to the production of forgings for defense plants, hand grenades, and other metal items for the military. The changeover was accomplished swiftly and, it seems, cheerfully. When the ban on gold mining was lifted in 1945, the state also reduced the ore tax to its original 4 percent. By 1953 the Homestake Mining Company had bought into other mines throughout the West and the big holdings of the three original families had been broken up. The major offices of the corporation were still in San Francisco, but Lead was no longer the only corporation town; while the gold mine there was still of utmost importance, the company had gradually acquired interests all over the world so that stockholders were not entirely reliant on one mine. After all, gold in one place does not last forever.

The state, too, lessened its reliance upon the Homestake, lowering the ore tax to 2½ percent in 1957. The major annoyance to the corporation during the 1950s and early 1960s was the insistence of outside labor unions that they be allowed to organize the miners. Four times the issue was brought to a vote. Each time campaigns were waged by union officials who came in from other states and, in response, by the Homestake officials. Various kinds of propaganda were tried by the labor unions, while the Homestake repeatedly pointed to the benefits given voluntarily over the years to its employees. "Paternalism" could be a derogatory term to the unions, but in practice in Lead it had worked well, and four attempts to unionize were defeated. Resistance held until 1966, when employees finally voted to accept representation by the United Steel Workers of America.

Because gold, cattle, and sheep go out of the state, it is relatively easy to say that they contribute to, and affect, the nation. A more delicate matter is the determination of whether a South Dakota, or Great Plains, characteristic can be located in the practices and policies of the Homestake Mining Company as well as in the attitudes of the miners and, out on the range, the cattlemen. The miners who told the unions that working conditions at the mine were the best in the industry wanted to be left alone. And just as they felt that the unions were trying to interfere, for political reasons more than for welfare, so did the cattlemen in the 1960s attempt to tell the federal government to stay out of the livestock business. The president of the South Dakota Stock Growers Association spoke in favor of free enterprise, accused the U.S. Department of Agriculture of socialism, and proclaimed the livestock industry the last stronghold of the unsubsidized, or free enterprise, system. Since many farmers in the eastern half of the state are willing to accept certain kinds of assistance from the federal government, it seems that the split in opinion first seen in the territory, when one group wanted state sovereignty (the right to change the form of government of the future state) and another group supported the federal point of view, still prevails. The right to individual opinion and belief is sacred in a land where extremes of climate, weather, and topography are reflected in the people.

7

East River, West River

$\mathcal{W}$HILE South Dakota may be considered a transition state, linking the Midwest to the mountains, it is also in some ways a divided state, with the Missouri River serving as a kind of barrier between the two halves. Almost everyone in the state recognizes that East River is different from West River, different enough so that those terms are used as though they were geographical names to be found on the map—which they are not. Yet, no one has come up with a satisfactory vocabulary for describing those differences with precision. The characteristics of the land have something to do with the distinctions, of course, as does the population distribution. South Dakota is one of the three most rural states in the nation, but 70 percent of its people live east of the Missouri River in the smaller half of the state. (The river comes into the state almost exactly halfway between the northeast and northwest corners but then from the center of the state, at Pierre, angles southeastward and leaves the state at the southeast corner.) Only thirteen "cities" in the state have more than 5,000 people, and ten of them are East River. Of the seven state-supported universities and colleges, five are East River. In contrast, approximately two-thirds of the Sioux Indians live west of the river, with the major concentration at the Pine Ridge Reservation.

Because East River is more heavily populated, has the largest city in the state, has most of the educational institutions, and is

121

closer to more heavily populated states (Minnesota and Iowa), its people are generally considered more urban, more sophisticated, and more liberal than the people of West River. On the other hand, because of the degree of isolation, because of a deep-seated conservatism, and through the characteristics of the Sioux, West River people are probably more fiercely independent and distrustful of outside influences. It might be argued that since the west end of the state is the chief attraction for tourists, the constant stream of visitors from all over the nation would bring a certain amount of cosmopolitanism to West River, but that depends, of course, on the quality of the tourists. There can be highly intelligent visitors who have some knowledge of the area and engage in productive conversations with the residents over a period of a week or more. At the other extreme, however, are the quick in-and-outers who contribute nothing and learn nothing. Such a person was the woman who, with her family, stopped briefly at Mount Rushmore and then hurried over to the Badlands where she said to a student guide, "I recognized George and Martha, but who were the other couple?"

Fortunately, neither half of the state feels inferior to the other half, although strong feelings are occasionally passed back and forth. Many West River people are suspicious (at least) of Sioux Falls, the largest city, and of the university, the major educational institution. Both are occasionally considered hotbeds of sin and corruption, the city said to be run by labor unions and the university by liberal thinkers who are out of touch with the land. All this is relative, of course, because unions are not strong in South Dakota and many professors at the university have a deep and understanding attachment to the land. But Sioux Falls has most of the state's industry, and the university is the major center of learning in the nonagricultural professions (medicine, law, the humanities and the arts), and so both are frequent targets of criticism. Sioux Falls is not large, but it ranks high among the nation's cities in its population category, is an attractive place, and likes to think of itself as a little Minneapolis. The university, as well, is one of the smallest state universities in the United States but has consistently maintained an extremely high quality of instruction and has graduated students who became outstanding national figures.

Another point of contention, and a more real one, is the East River-West River ratio in the election of governors, congressmen, and senators in the eight decades of statehood. In each case, approximately seven successful politicians have resided in the eastern half of the state to every one living in the western half. While this figure does not follow the general population distribution, it does reflect the predominance of larger towns in the East River area. Nevertheless, South Dakota politics have been overwhelmingly conservative and Republican over the years, so that East River's statistical "dominance by residence" has not been the important factor in party politics that might be expected. Voters throughout the state have reflected, in their national preferences, a tendency toward isolationism, including a distrust of expanding federal government and a wish to stay somewhat out of foreign affairs, especially in the matter of foreign aid. This is not necessarily a sign of complete disinterest in the rest of the nation or the world but, rather, a belief that one should mind one's own fences. Self-reliance can make some strange sounds in the modern welfare world, and it can often backfire economically in a state like South Dakota, but the philosophy as such cannot be all wrong, at least in the minds of a pioneer people who have worked hard and long on their own to achieve a modicum of success.

The Populists of the 1890s (South Dakota's first decade as a state) have usually been called "progressive" by local historians, but the term is confusing. As in North Dakota, where so-called "radical" politics caught hold and continued to influence that state far beyond the influence on South Dakota, the progressives were attempting to break away from economic domination of other states, notably Minnesota. At the same time they wished to curb the power of government and to give more voice to the people. The Populist party soon filtered into the Republican party and lost its identity, but its effect was felt in the administration of Gov. Peter Norbeck, who has been characterized as a "careful reformer," so that legislation was adopted concerning child labor, hail insurance, workmen's compensation, and a state cement plant which is still in operation. (North Dakota, in contrast, has several state-owned enterprises.) Limitations on campaign spending, and direct primary measures, indicated the people's desire to keep a hand in government.

Just as "progressive" is a slippery term, so is "socialistic." South Dakotans, with the possible exception of a bloc of East River farmers of Scandinavian background, feel that socialism is an invention of the devil. Yet, of the five "big name" politicians emanating from South Dakota (one of them West River), only two were completely and clearly divorced from big government and from anything remotely resembling socialism. Sen. Karl Mundt—who became a kind of hero to old-time Dakotans—made a name for himself by presiding over the 1948 House Un-American Activities Committee, whose hearings led to the conviction of Alger Hiss. Then, in an alliance which made itself felt twenty-four years later in the presidential election in South Dakota, he co-sponsored the Mundt-Nixon bill which required Communist organizations in the United States to register as such. Later he presided over the Army-McCarthy hearings and voted against censuring his good friend Joe. Mundt's talent lay in his oratory against communism, and although he used his Senate committee ranking to bring some pressure to bear in favor of funding for dams and irrigation in South Dakota, he did little that could be called memorable. Yet the voters returned him to the Senate for four terms and spoke of him as a patriot and a nice man (which meant conservative and antisocialistic). The other Republican senator whose name still seems to echo the conservatism of the state seems to have accomplished even less. Francis Case had a stake in the interstate highway system—not an insignificant enterprise—but was characterized in Washington as "deadly dull."

Of the three South Dakotans who became nationally-known and who made solid contributions to the nation's welfare, two left the state before entering politics and represented New Mexico and Minnesota. It does not seem proper, however, to dissociate them from their native state. Clinton Presba Anderson was born in Centerville, South Dakota, and lived also in Parker and Mitchell, all East River towns. Like many Dakotans, he went out of state for part of his education (after attending Dakota Wesleyan), but he returned for a time. The son of Swedish immigrants, Anderson was considered one of the more intellectual members of the Senate, his interests and his energies embracing conservation and environmental protection, the space program, public policy in the sciences, and the care of the elderly. It is difficult to say how much his native state imbued him with these concerns, because New Mexico—which he served as Democratic representative and senator—is much like South Dakota in many ways. Certainly his place of birth gave him some of the knowledge he needed in order to be secretary of agriculture under President Harry Truman. And, ironically, he moved to New Mexico because a doctor advised a drier climate. Contrary to the popular notion that South Dakota is a desert, East River is humid.

The other two senators, Hubert Humphrey of Doland and Huron and George McGovern of Mitchell, have locked horns on some notable occasions and have gone in separate directions to a certain extent, but they have shared a deep concern for people as individuals, regardless of economic class or political leanings. Humphrey, whose political career has been as a Minnesotan, and who was once mayor of Minneapolis, has perhaps courted the labor unions more strongly than McGovern has, and McGovern has understandably championed the farmer through his efforts to support the family farm and to obtain for the farmer liberal credit, electrification, better bargaining powers, and higher price supports. On the practical level of the constituency, both men have had enviable records in their respective states for taking care of the individual problems caused by the complexities of big government and bureaucracy. Both preach a kind of welfare system, Humphrey in the endless but often witty verbiage of the old-fashioned orator, and McGovern in the mixed delivery of the professor-minister. Where they differ was highlighted dramatically in the California primary of 1972 when the two men debated national issues. Humphrey attacked McGovern's welfare proposals, presumably because they were too candid and simple, and chastised his opponent for his views on defense spending. McGovern, adhering to his state's traditional policy of isolation, or, probably closer to the truth, insisting on peace through practice rather than through a military force, advocated a lower defense budget. Right or wrong, Humphrey damaged the McGovern image more than any Republican could, and the South Dakotan never recovered, even though the Minnesotan campaigned for him in the 1972 presidential election.

Humphrey's theories of the role federal government should play in economics came from yet another South Dakotan, Alvin H. Hansen, the first American economist to accept and promote the once-radical argument put forth by the British economist John Maynard Keynes in his 1936 book, *General Theory of Employment, Interest, and Money*. The Keynesian theory, put into practice by the American government in recent years, is that if the people do not spend enough money to maintain high employment, the government should compensate with deficit spending. Hansen, born on a farm near the tiny town of Viborg, South Dakota, the son of Danish immigrants, had to convince his father that he should be allowed to finish high school and had to teach in order to pay his way through Yankton College and the University of Wisconsin. Later he taught in Minnesota and at age fifty was brought to Harvard, where for twenty years he held the Littauer chair in political economy. As a consultant to several Washington agencies during the 1940s, Hansen was influential in turning the Keynes theory into national policy. More than any other politician in modern times, Senator Humphrey has preached this policy of government spending. Conservatives can attack the policy, and the *Wall Street Journal* can call it obsolete, but in one form or another, Republican or Democratic, it prevails in our time.

Perhaps it is an out-and-out paradox that such radical notions have been held by politicians whose roots are in conservative South Dakota. More specifically, observers have wondered how the state of Karl Mundt and Francis Case could elect George McGovern to the U.S. Senate. His initial election in 1962 was a close one—fewer than 600 votes decided it—over a Republican who was virtually unknown. (McGovern had just directed President John F. Kennedy's "Food for Peace" program.) He actually lost in West River, and in East River he had a majority only in the rural areas. However, his margin of votes increased in the next two elections, and in 1970 the usually Republican state also chose a Democrat for governor. In its small way, perhaps, South Dakota was telling the nation that agriculture was getting a bum deal, that Republicans, already rich, were getting richer in office, and that it was time to get out of Viet Nam and tend to the nation's ills. The fact that this message did not win the presidency for McGovern in 1972 does not reflect on the message itself. Quite to the contrary, the issues raised by McGovern were soon found to be valid, and the American public, along with McGovern's fellow South Dakotans, witnessed the resignation of the man who had soundly defeated him at the polls, Richard Nixon. Prairie populism has long been a source for valid issues and for government reform, even though its candidates lose elections through bad advice, reckless idealism, or the distrust of an electorate that does not wish its boat to be rocked.

This is not to say that South Dakota is a feedlot for politicians. It is not. On the state level, government has been described as slow, unoriginal, and drab, much like the location of the capital. One problem is that the capital, although on the east side of the Missouri River, is in neither East River nor West River—it is out in the middle of rangeland, cut off from both ends of the state. A centralized location—which at least partially dictated the choice of Pierre in the first place—is effective only if the surrounding body is nearby. In South Dakota this is not the case, since the population clusters at the ends rather than in the middle. While, for other purposes, it is quite proper to make use of the East River-West River distinction, this device leaves the state capital hanging in the crease of the map. However, it must be said in all fairness that many kinds of inaction express the people's will. The outstanding problem of the legislature, year after year, is that of maintaining a quality school system and at least an adequate highway system without undue taxing in a nonindustrial state. Rather than seeking a combination of possibilities, the lawmakers have each year in recent sessions introduced a state income tax bill, which has failed. The

people would like to find another solution. At worst, conditions
remain as they have been, sometimes preferable to new measures taken in desperation. Two main fears attend the question
of the income tax: the transfer of income from South Dakotans
who are working to those who are not, and the possible expansion of state government among a people who would like less
government. Local political analysts talk about the people's in-
herent fear of change, and there is some truth to the charge. The
state was so discouraged by the depression of the 1930s that it
became cautious to the extent of always maintaining a bank account and refusing to go into debt. To many other states this
sounds un-American. To Dakotans it is common sense.

As self-sufficient as South Dakota would like to be, it is at
the mercy of Washington more often than it would care to
admit. Reliance on agricultural products, and the absence of
jobs and revenues provided by industry, can lead to an
eagerness for federal assistance. Granted, all the states tend to
comply with federal "suggestions" which are accompanied by
cash payments, and it is likely that state and nation are inseparable in such matters as aid to education and the recent imposition
of the fifty-five mile-per-hour highway speed limit. However,
plains states—including South Dakota—may have special problems which call for special solutions, and no voices are raised to
make the call. Distances are unusually great in Dakota and
transportation is limited almost entirely to the family au-
tomobile. Highways are excellent and traffic is relatively light;
yet, in order to get federal highway assistance, the adoption of
the lower speed limit was mandatory. As a result, traveling long
distances takes more time, and a large segment of the population no longer travels as much as it used to. This will, in turn,
result in further isolation. In the schools, federal aid dictates the
length of the academic year, and educators go to great lengths to
formulate outrageous theories of the desirability of a certain
number of school days per year, as though to pretend that there
is indeed valid justification beyond the obvious fact of official
bribery. These bureaucratic measures extend deep into the
schools at all levels, until the entire system seems weakened by
lack of protest, lack of an occasional rebel, lack of serious ques-

tioning about the nature and basic philosophy of the system. Here, as much as in economic matters, a fear of the system leads to unnecessary apathy, contrary to the Dakotan's imbued wariness of outside interference.

If East River seems to bear the brunt of political problems in most areas, West River suffers the most from the continuing difficulty of bringing Indians and whites into some kind of harmony. The word "harmony" is important because it is a traditionally vital part of the Indian's relationship to his natural environment. He believed (as some still do) that the Great Spirit made all the creatures and the natural objects for the Indian to use, not only for food and shelter but, even more importantly, as things to speak through when sending a voice to the Great Spirit for help. Every living thing as well as every inanimate thing has, therefore, a religious use as well as a practical application, and this, in effect, makes all things holy. This belief stands in strong contrast to the attitudes of the European, or white man, who (often in the name of his own religion) freely destroyed many parts of the natural world in order to exploit the other parts in the name of civilization, enlightenment, progress, Manifest Destiny, or whatever term he used to condone what he did and to explain his taking of what he wanted. In the twentieth century some non-Indians have taken the Indian religions seriously and others have pretended to do so in a kind of rebellion against white society. At the same time, many Indians have strayed from the traditions of their ancestors and, often unable to replace the old values with new ones, have drifted without identity through a no-man's land.

However, the physical identity remains. The Sioux, especially, are recognizable almost anywhere. Sparked, perhaps, by the wars of the late nineteenth century, and fanned into flame by the defeat of Custer in 1876 and the Wounded Knee Massacre of 1890, the Sioux have appeared in books, motion pictures, television (as well as Buffalo Bill's Wild West Show at an earlier time) until they are probably the best known and least understood of all the American Indians. In spite of the historical fame, the modern Sioux are among the most poverty-stricken and troubled tribal groups in the United States, and since most of them live in South Dakota it has been only natural for outsiders to link the plight of the Sioux with an indifference (at best) or an intolerance on the part of the state. To a certain extent the relationship is indeed strained, and South Dakota has its share of racial suspicion, but the complexities of the "Indian problem" go far beyond such a simple cause as prejudice. To make the concept of harmony a part of the political or economic environment in the last quarter of the twentieth century is a very different proposition—and exceedingly difficult—from the religious or philosophical harmonies stressed in the traditional pantheism of the Sioux.

Many factors are involved in the relationships between two groups of dissimilar people. For one group to say, "We were here first, therefore the land is ours," does not resolve the problem. Right or wrong, world history is the record of people constantly moving westward; the phenomenon is not limited to western America. Where the Sioux came from originally, even on the North American continent, is guesswork, but they were east of the Great Plains as recently as the first half of the eighteenth century, when their homeland was Minnesota, north of Lake Mille Lacs. They were driven from this region by the Chippewa who were by that time armed with the white man's guns and pushing west from the Great Lakes. To establish themselves on the plains, the Sioux had to come to terms with the tribes already there. In only one case—the Cheyenne—did this mean peaceful alliance and co-operation. With other tribal groups it meant war. The Arikara were driven north, the Kiowa south; the Crow, language cousins to the Sioux, were pursued into Montana and raided periodically by the Sioux for half a century; and the Pawnee in Nebraska were pushed across the Platte River and kept there. The Sioux, a warrior nation, waged its first series of important battles against other Indian tribes to conquer the land which they had to defend later against the armies of the United States.

Who owns the land? The Black Hills, considered the holy land of the Sioux, were presumably the property of the Cheyenne before the Sioux arrived. When gold was discovered in the Hills, the white man moved in. The difference in the conquest was not so much a matter of rightness as of motivation and attitude—greed replacing the religious veneration which the Sioux had developed toward the Hills.

When the Sioux entered what is now South Dakota they were organized—as they still are—into seven tribes or council fires: Mdewakanton, Wakpekute, Wahpeton, Sisseton, Yankton, Yanktonai, and Teton. The first four of these tribal groups remained in the eastern part of the territory, and the Yankton and "Little Yankton" occupied the Missouri River valley from the center of the state to the southeast. The Teton tribe was the one which ranged throughout the West River country and into North Dakota, Montana, Wyoming, and Nebraska. The Tetons have always been the largest of the Sioux tribes and probably the best known in popular history, being divided into seven groups with the names which appear most often in the accounts of western settlement and Indian wars: Oglala, Brulé, Two Kettles, Sans Arc, Blackfeet, Hunkpapa, and Miniconjou. In the wars which preceded the 1868 Treaty of Laramie and which followed the breaking of that treaty by the U.S. Government when gold was discovered in the Black Hills, the famous Sioux names were Spotted Tail (Brulé), Red Cloud and Crazy Horse (Oglala), and Sitting Bull and Gall (Hunkpapa). Today—with exceptions caused by intermarriage and other factors—the Oglalas live on the Pine Ridge Reservation (which includes the site of Wounded Knee), the Brulés live on the Rosebud Reservation, and the Hunkpapas are located at Standing Rock, which is partly in South Dakota and partly in North Dakota.

Whether cause and effect can be applied to reservation problems in terms of the early tribal leaders is difficult to determine. However, of the five major leaders in the Indian wars of the 1870s, it was Crazy Horse who was least willing to stop fighting, and it is his people, the Oglalas, who generate or are subjected to the most violence in our own time, a century later. The Oglalas seem to have been the most warlike of the Sioux, but they are also the largest group and, even if it were only a coincidence, the Wounded Knee Massacre, with its recent symbolic importance to militant Indians, occurred on Oglala land. Spotted Tail was the most anxious of the five leaders to make peace with the white man, and his Brulés on the Rosebud (which touches the Pine Ridge Reservation at one corner) seem more concerned with their own affairs today, and less willing than the Oglalas to renew the old struggle against the whites. The militance of various tribes is all relative, of course, and the Sioux are united through an organization of the various tribal councils, even though their individual concerns may differ somewhat. Curiously, there is even a kind of loyalty to the geographical area of South Dakota, although in Indian terms. When Sitting Bull was killed by Indian police in 1890, he was buried at Fort Yates, on the North Dakota side of the Standing Rock Reservation. Sixty-three years later Clarence Grey Eagle of Bullhead, South Dakota, requested that the medicine man's bones be brought "back home" (Sitting Bull was born on the Grand River), thereby touching off a controversy between the two states which seemed to indicate that the former foe of the U.S. Army had become a hero to Indians and whites alike. When North Dakota refused to allow the transfer, Grey Eagle and some friends, accompanied by a mortician from Mobridge, went to Fort Yates at 5:00 A.M., April 8, 1953, disinterred Sitting Bull's bones, and took them to the Grand River near Mobridge where they were buried under twenty tons of concrete and steel. Ironies abound in this incident. In 1954 Sen. Karl Mundt, the South Dakota conservative, eulogized Sitting Bull in the Senate and said that the famous Indian had made his reputation in South Dakota and North Dakotans could not have him back. A year later North Dakota Sen. William Langer responded in a speech for the *Congressional Record,* insisting that Sitting Bull's bones had been scattered over North Dakota and that the monument at Mobridge was a fraud.

To hear U.S. senators arguing over the ownership of an Indian's bones, while the descendents of that Indian were hungry and looking for jobs, made little sense to anyone on the reservations. Moreover, it is possible that Sitting Bull was first buried in quick lime, in an unknown location, and that the bones later moved to South Dakota belong to someone else. Even that is unimportant; what matters is the symbol. The spirit of the

Hunkpapa Sioux medicine man floats over the entire Northern Plains and the white man's state boundaries can make no difference. Yet, in another curious twist of fate, on the seventy-fifth anniversary of Sitting Bull's death he was called "overrated" by an amateur Indian historian from North Dakota, who argued correctly that Sitting Bull was not a chief (the Sioux did not have hereditary chiefs) and that he did not lead the Sioux in the defeat of Custer, but who said nothing to diminish the stature of the Hunkpapa medicine man.

Facts of the Old West are hard to come by, shrouded as they are in myth. The same is true of facts of the "New West." Although the American Indian Movement takeover of Wounded Knee in March, April, and May 1973, was covered by newspaper reporters, magazine writers, and television cameras, the episode was completely confusing. AIM had its version, militant Indians who came to the scene from other parts of the country had their version, the Oglala leadership had another version, and the FBI and other law enforcement officers called in to keep order had their versions. No one version emerged as creditable.

Yet, the problems of the reservation Indian in South Dakota (as well as in other states) are clear enough. The Great White Fathers in Washington have made promises which they did not or could not keep, and the Sioux have lived in poverty ever since they were assigned to reservations. The unemployment rate is staggering, even though South Dakota as a state has less unemployment than the national average. When the government does appropriate money for the reservations, only a fraction of it seeps through the BIA bureaucracy and the power-hungry Indian officials. There is serious disagreement among the Indians themselves as to directions to take and kinds of solutions to look for. Some advocate termination of the reservation system and an assimilation of the Sioux into the white man's way of life; others feel that the tribes must hold fast to their land, such as it is, and maintain tribal traditions and a degree of sovereignty while developing job opportunities of their own. Still others, such as the members and camp followers of AIM, combine a nostalgia for the past with a desire to dictate the future by any means. Because of language problems (English is still a second language, not the first, to most Sioux), and because of inadequate education, the Indian is usually unable to adjust to life off the reservation. But while he remains ''at home'' he is subject to family squabbles, to drinking, and to all the conditions of poverty. And there are the young ones who go away to school, perhaps to the university, and are faced with the choice of competing with better-prepared students or dropping out and perhaps feeling that they are outside both cultures at that point.

Some of them, of course, survive the obstacles and take their places in a world beyond the reservation. This does not mean an abandonment of their native culture. Ed McGaa, a marine pilot during the Korean War and a law school graduate, went back to the reservation to participate in the sun dance even though he lives and works elsewhere. Vine Deloria, Sr., an Episcopalian minister, has never forgotten nor given up his Hunkpapa heritage during a distinguished career. Oscar Howe, accused by his brothers of ''turning white,'' and no longer welcome on the Crow Creek Reservation where he was born, works hard at preserving his Yanktonnai culture in the symbols, colors, and designs of his paintings.

Father Deloria believes that land allotment and inconsistent and inadequate government economic programs have undermined the well-being of the Sioux. More personally, whites have resented Indianness and have felt insulted that the Sioux did not respond eagerly to white American ways. For several decades the government barred the use of the Sioux language and condemned Indian customs, according to Deloria. Recent innovations in mixed schools have improved the cultural condition somewhat in the 1970s, but one wonders if there will ever be a change in the basic attitude Father Deloria has described:

> America bullies the weak instead of going to bat for them. This is one of the great, great differences between Indian culture and white culture. We remembered the weak, the sick, the stranger long before the diluted, distorted religion was brought here in the name of Jesus who would not recognize this religion preached in his name, if He were here today. When the cry rang out in old Indian life, *Ohunke sni kin wicakiksuyapo!* (Remember the weak!) even the

feeblest, wayward Indian . . . rose to his finest to defend the weak.[1]

East River whites encounter Indians mostly on or near college campuses and mix socially with those who are in teaching, counseling, and administrative positions at the schools. They deny any form of prejudice and say that if there is any racial hatred it is in West River. Bob Lee, editor of the *Sturgis Tribune* in the Black Hills area, a white related by adoption to the Oglala Tribe, has compared the West River attitude toward Indians with the South's attitude toward blacks—in areas heavily populated by the minority groups, friction arises from daily confrontation between the whites and nonwhites. West River whites tend to see the Sioux as lacking in any kind of motivation to improve their own conditions, which in turn leads to charges of laziness, dirtiness, and lawlessness. The fact that the Sioux may have been mistreated or dealt with unfairly in the past does not change the attitude of the non-Sioux. Although the modern Indian may well be the product of the white man's government, in which all whites share some responsibility, West River residents are tired of being blamed for events which occurred before they were born. Lee, and others, can admit shame but not blame for what their ancestors did.

In economic terms, the argument is that Indians make up only 5 percent of the state's population but have received government aid far beyond that proportion and yet have remained poverty stricken. Therefore, West River whites "consider the reservation system as the classic example of the failure of the welfare state," according to Lee. They are inclined to believe, however naively, that the Indian has the same opportunities as everyone else and with a little determination could succeed within the white man's society. To prove the point, they identify men of all colors who have succeeded in spite of cultural handicaps. Often forgotten, according to Lee, is the simple fact that there are too many Indians on the reservations for the land to support adequately (and it is not the best land in the state). Put the same

1. Vine V. Deloria, Sr., "The Standing Rock Reservation: A Personal Reminiscence," *South Dakota Review* 9 (Summer 1971): 193.

number of whites on this land, with their skills and industriousness, and they too would fail to make a decent living.

These arguments, and others, are ultimately subsumed by the overriding reality that the great majority of South Dakota's Indians live west of the Missouri River and that violence is a function of numbers. Therefore, most of the conflicts between Indians and whites, or among the Indians themselves, occur in West River.

There are about 30,000 Indians in South Dakota. Whereas all other counties decreased in population between 1960 and 1970, all counties with a large percentage of Indians increased. Their voices, too, will be heard increasingly in the future. As with any impoverished people, some individuals will do better than others, perhaps through sheer determination, perhaps through pure luck, or perhaps by compromising certain surface functions while holding fast to the soul. Ben Black Elk, South Dakota's most familiar Sioux for many years, and the most photographed Indian of all time and of any tribe, found that he could pose for tourists during the summer at Mount Rushmore and remain Sioux in all the essential matters of the heart and of tradition. Ben was the son of the holy man celebrated in John Neihardt's book, *Black Elk Speaks,* which, although published in 1932, did not fully enter the American consciousness until it was reprinted in 1961 following almost thirty years of popularity in Europe. (Americans often fail to see the riches in their midst until they are pointed out by appreciative "foreigners.") Black Elk was cousin to Crazy Horse and was a prophet, or seer, with such powers that Dr. Neihardt and others became true believers. Ben was the seventh generation in a family which acquired its name from an ancestor who killed a rare black elk. While smiling for the camera-laden tourists at Mount Rushmore, acting in a number of Hollywood movies which demanded Indian characters, or traveling around the world, Ben retained his Sioux beliefs and willingly talked about them to anyone who was seriously interested: the sweat bath, the sun dance, the visions, the importance of the colors of the four corners of the universe (black or dark blue for the West with its thunderbirds, white for the North and its giant and its cleansing power, red for the East and for knowledge, and yellow for the South and the source of life), the medicine pipe, songs, and prayers. Sadly, Ben admitted that his people were more civilized at an earlier time than they are today. For this reason, prayers become essential, a way of trying to bring the Sioux back to a better time.

Too often the term "Great White Father" is used in a hackneyed way by popular writers of Indian books; to Ben Black Elk, as an honored representative of his people, the term was a serious one and the president of the United States was a man to be respected and loved. On the November afternoon in 1963 when John F. Kennedy was murdered in Dallas, Ben Black Elk was in the television studio at the University of South Dakota, recording a program. Someone burst into the studio and said the president was dead. Ben sat for a moment and then got to his feet and began the Sioux death dance. The cameras were turned off. The dance finished, Ben left the studio to mourn in his own way. Two days later he returned and completed the program. It was the Sioux custom, Ben said, to leave the people after a relative or close friend died, to mourn and pray and sing a song to the dead one, and then to return to the people, welcomed back as though from the dead. "Be one of us again!" When Ben's son died, he rode 800 miles on horseback, first in grief, then in search of the son's spirit, and finally in victory as he rejoined his people.

Before Ben Black Elk's own death he was often referred to as the fifth face at Mount Rushmore, joining Washington, Jefferson, Theodore Roosevelt, and Lincoln in a tribute to the spirit of America. Some of his people have jeered at this shrine of democracy, feeling that it represents a way of life contrary to their own. Some tourists view the monument in idle curiosity. Skeptics see only a commercial venture, like any other device used to lure tourists into an area which needs an injection of life-giving money. President Coolidge, speaking at the site on the first day of construction (August 10, 1927), said: "The union of these four presidents on the face of the everlasting hills of South Dakota will constitute a distinctly national monument. It will be decidedly American in its conception, in its magnitude, in its meaning and altogether worthy of our country." A few minutes later, sculptor Gutzon Borglum began to drill into the six-thousand-foot mountain. Fourteen years and $1 million later, the drilling was completed by Lincoln Borglum, seven months after his father's death. Political, economic, and esthetic objections continued throughout the years of blasting, drilling, and carving on the granite mountain in the Black Hills, but the sixty-foot-high faces 500 feet up on the mountain are too impressive to be written off as a foolhardy venture or as the despoiling of a mountain. In their setting of pine, spruce, birch, and aspen high in the clear western air, the faces inspire awe even in those visitors who normally shun patriotic monuments.

And if Ben Black Elk's face is no longer there to give approval to the white man's images, not many miles away an equally gigantic monument is being blasted from another mountain, this one to be the figure of Crazy Horse, Sioux warrior, seated on his Indian pony and gazing over the striking landscape of his former home. The sculptor, Korczak Ziolkowski, has blasted more than two million tons of rock from Thunderhead Mountain, but the projected design of approximately 650 by 550 feet is barely visible. Again there are scoffers and critics, but the project seems to be justified in several ways. When Doane Robinson, state historian, first suggested the appropriateness of granite carvings in the Black Hills he had in mind the Needles as place and a notable Sioux like Red Cloud as subject. The rationale behind the suggestion included recognition of the people who had lived in the area, artistic and cultural value as well as historical, and economic worth to the state. Robinson, like many South Dakotans and many westerners, was both idealistic and practical. His idea was replaced by the concept of a national shrine, with four presidents rather than a group of regional heroes including the Sioux, but artistic integrity was maintained and the economic impact upon the state has been undeniable. Mount Rushmore is the chief tourist attraction in the state, bringing millions of people into the Black Hills and Rapid City and millions of dollars into the otherwise agricultural economy of the state. The Crazy Horse monument will do the same and will also fulfill part of Robinson's dream.

There are those opponents of mountain carving who say that the entire Black Hills region could be turned into a gallery of statues or bas reliefs, thereby destroying the natural scenery. The suggestion is both fascinating and ludicrous. Were such a project to be completed, many centuries in the future, it might well puzzle anthropologists in a still more distant future in the same way that the Easter Island figures baffle us now. However, a deeper concern of the moment is the possibility of extensive mining in the Hills, which would result in a more real disfigurement of the natural scene, and South Dakotans in the tradition of a man like Peter Norbeck must guard their hills. Norbeck, governor and then senator, was a leading conservationist in the first decades of the twentieth century, involved in the establishment of Custer State Park in 1919, the Migratory Bird Act of 1929, and the Mount Rushmore National Memorial. He also helped to plan the scenic roads in the park, at that time the largest state park in the nation. Even some of his political opponents praised him as a leader in the development of a new art form—road building that framed the natural scenery for the public. Not unmindful of economic benefits, South Dakota has nevertheless made its western beauty available to the nation with a minimum of disturbance to the original landscape.

In spite of their size, the man-carved monuments in the Black Hills are miniscule in relation to the total environment of the mountains, and as for sheer artistic effect it is possible to argue that these man-made shapes pale in contrast to the natural shapes of the Badlands. Now a national monument, this unbelievably stark, desolate, and beautiful area lies on the northern edge of the Pine Ridge Reservation, a little east of the Black Hills. Many millions of years ago, when the inland sea receded, this area was a great marshland, tropically hot, inhabited by the huge beasts and reptiles that we have come to call dinosaurs. The reasons for extinction of these creatures remains a mystery; but when they died, they were covered with sediment over thousands of centuries. As the earth cooled and firmed, and grass grew on the new plain, new species evolved—the three-toed horse, the small camel, and the sabertooth tiger. Fossils of remains have provided scientists with a rich store of information on ancient life before the appearance of man, and petrified wood has added to the peculiar beauty of the region.

During another long, almost incomprehensible period of time, streams carved into the soft soil, and western winds chiseled the soft rock into spires and turrets and pinnacles which, when seen in a cluster, often resemble the minarets of a medieval city. Color and shape change according to the position of the sun, and at night a traveler can easily imagine himself on another planet. The beauty is of a special kind—harsh, yet often delicate, and desolate, yet harmonious. Frank Lloyd Wright, the famous architect who designed many desert houses as integral parts of the natural environment, felt that the Badlands offered him both a release from materiality and a confrontation with God. Nevertheless, the land has frightened many of the people who traversed it before highways were built. The Indians called it *mako* (land) *sica* (bad), and the first French explorers described it as *les mauvaises terres à traverser* (bad lands to travel across). Whether Custer was the first person to refer to the Badlands (there is a somewhat similar area in North Dakota) as "a part of Hell with the fires burned out" is debatable, but the description has lingered in South Dakota lore. Contrary to opinion, however, the Badlands are not a desert, just as the eastern third of the state is not a part of the arid or semiarid lands of the West as at least one noted historian has mistakenly said. The Badlands, in their own way, are a part of the prairie, of the grasslands, albeit slashed and carved by wind and water erosion. "Prairie," as a general term, is the common denominator for the state, although variations from east to west result in a variety that at least makes a little sense out of the slogan, "Land of Infinite Variety."

There are other kinds of variety. In the Black Hills northern, western, and eastern trees all grow together, one of the few places where this happens. Because South Dakota is in the center of the continent, it is subjected to prevailing winds from both north and south, receiving plant seeds and pollens from both directions. Southeastern South Dakota would be the logical place for a national research center for allergies. At the other end of the state the air is drier and clearer. This would suggest that characteristics of the people should differ somewhat from one section of the state to another, and in a sense the Missouri River does indeed provide a kind of dividing line. West River people are conservative, proud, independent, healthy, and reasonably contented, except that they are subject to violence in an Old West way, often preferring local or individual justice to legal justice, especially in relationships with the Indians. They drive pickups, outfitted with guns, and are not entirely opposed to illegal hunting as long as it is for food, not sport. They are an open people, like the land, and friendly and hospitable. But they are suspicious of change, of the power of the intellect, of the university, and of the "big city"—Sioux Falls. They want to be left alone to work out their own problems. Ironically, Pennington County, containing their own "big city" (Rapid City), with only 9 percent of the state's population, furnishes 46 percent of the population of the state penitentiary, located in Sioux Falls. In spite of the complexities caused by a sizeable Indian population, thousands of tourists moving in and out daily, and transients from the small towns south and west, Rapid City maintains a feeling of unity, as was displayed dramatically after the serious flood of 1972. In contrast, Sioux Falls, with fewer apparent problems, also seems to have less general agreement on how things should be done. East River people are inclined to be a little more liberal, more varied in opinion, more influenced by neighboring states (Minnesota and Iowa), and more mobile. Their habits are more easily influenced by the weather, they have more sinusitis and allergies and spend more time going to doctors (often out of state), and, because many of them are relatively new to South Dakota, they are perhaps less concerned about being called Dakotans.

The big difference is probably the simple fact that although South Dakota is a rural state the East River half has more towns, more schools, and easier access to Minneapolis, Sioux City, Des Moines, Omaha, and Lincoln, giving the people at least a slightly more cosmopolitan view of life and an easier acceptance of ideas and cultural trends coming from the East. Their language and speech patterns are midwestern, while those of West River are western. It is not quality that distinguishes East River from West River, nor even racial relationships, but rather the degree of isolation and the differences in social structure caused by the differences of the land. "The character of a country is the destiny of its people," said the New Mexican novelist, Harvey Fergusson, speaking of a state not unlike South Dakota. To the extent that South Dakota is two countries, separated by the Missouri River, it has two destinies. But it is just as easy to say that it is one big prairie, and that its people may be characterized as one people: stubborn, but not pushy; generally conservative, but not always; desirous of preserving what they have, rather than risking it in an attempt to get more; religious, but not zealous; quiet and friendly, but also independent and usually quick to object to interference of any kind.

8

The Struggle for Culture

$\mathcal{W}$ITHIN the anthropological definition of "culture"—the patterns of learned behavior which are descriptive of religious, ethnic, and nationality groups—South Dakota contains a variety of cultures which have more or less mixed together and become less definable than they were almost a century ago. East River, in particular, might illustrate the theory of which Americans were once proud—the melting pot. While Norwegians and Germans have dominated, this half of the state has also been home to Swedes, Bohemians, German-Russians, Dutch, Danes, French, Hungarians, Scots, Swiss, Irish, Welsh, Poles, Yankees, and Indians. West River, on the other hand, has been predominantly Yankee and Indian, with some Germans and a few Scandinavians (especially Finns in the Black Hills area). Some Old World customs persisted into the twentieth century but nationality distinctions have been breaking down. Only the Sioux remain a distinct cultural group, set apart from the other merged groups by racial rather than nationality characteristics.

Emigrants from the Old World, as well as Yankees born in the United States, put all of their energies into the settling of the land and had little time for the cultivation of the arts. Their contributions to the general culture were confined to religious values, a morality which may in part explain the relatively low crime rate in South Dakota, and native foods. (Dakotans like to

143

eat, although they generally favor beefsteak over more exotic dishes and are inclined to refer to the noon meal rather than the evening one as dinner.) Some towns remember their origins with annual festivals, such as that of the Czechs at Tabor, but the emphasis is always on food.

The Hutterite Mennonites of the James River valley are a striking example of the process of assimilation. Organized as an Anabaptist church in Moravia in 1526, the Hutterites were dedicated to communal ownership and to pacifism. Their leader, Jacob Hutter, was burned at the stake in 1536. They were driven to Transylvania in 1621, to Rumania in 1767, to central Russia in 1770, and to south Russia in 1840, always seeking asylum from military conscription and from interference by local rulers. These German-Russians finally emigrated to the United States—and largely to South Dakota—during a six-year period beginning in 1873. Under the Homestead Act it was difficult for them to settle in colonies, but they managed to establish three, the rest of the people settling on individual family farms. From the three colonies, however, came the additional 200 that exist now in the Dakotas, Minnesota, Montana, Washington, and Canada. The exodus from South Dakota began during World War I when the Hutterites, as conscientious objectors, were persecuted by their neighbors and in some cases punished by the government. Following World War II, some returned to the United States, although the major population is still in Canada. Today one may find settlements of *prairieleut* (prairie people) Hutterites near Onida, Huron, and Freeman. Good farmers and businessmen, affable and religious, they have entered the mainstream of American smalltown life. The business envelope used by Pine Hill Printery in Freeman has a green map of the United States on the front, with a bold black arrow pointing to the location of the town. Next to the map is a scripted slogan: "One of the Fastest Growing Towns in South Dakota." Scattered over the back of the envelope are the inducements: "Dairy Herds, Livestock Feeding, Poultry Farms, Milk Processing and Egg Processing Plants, Sweepstakes Winner Statewide Community Betterment Contest, Host City, Junior College, 2 High Schools, 2 Elementary Schools, Special

Classroom, Rich Historic Heritage, Outstanding Hospital and Medical Facilities, Many Fine Churches.'' This is typical boosterism. A reminder of who the people are rests at the bottom of the envelope: ''Home of the Famous Schmeckfest.''

On a nonethnic cultural level (politics, economics, types of jobs and their relationships to the behavior of the people) there is some friction between the conservatism of ranchers and small businessmen and the more radical views of the farmers who organize co-operatives and favor government subsidies. Labor, as such, is not a cultural force because there is very little industry in the state. More significant is the pattern of managers and professional people who often pass through on their way to better jobs, better locations, and a more suitable climate for both weather and culture. In this latter use of ''culture''—which has to do with refinement, knowledge, and the arts—it would appear that South Dakota has not changed much since the passage of Lewis and Clark, that the people who stay are those who are directly tied to the land, and that the so-called purveyors of culture pass through the state, using it while they are there (in different ways), but leaving before their contributions or their artistic talents reach fruition or can be called ''native.''

Certainly this was the case for many years. The first literature of the region which was to become South Dakotan was the travel narrative written by explorers or military men or visitors from Europe—usually royalty—who traveled up the Missouri River on steamboats or keelboats, or, engaged in military campaigns or government surveying, struck off on foot and on horseback to the west of the river. These people—Lewis and Clark, Joseph Nicollet, John Evans, G. K. Warren, F. V. Hayden, Duke Paul Wilhelm, Maximilian, George Custer, and others—wrote, or kept notes, as objectively and descriptively as possible, but their accounts were frequently touched by emotions of awe, amazement, irritation, or fear. Although they were not writers in the same way that Washington Irving and Francis Parkman were—men who traveled to Oklahoma and along the Oregon Trail and who polished and refined their narratives once they returned home—they nevertheless made important contributions to the nation's knowledge of the region and often did so in graphic and personal terms which are still of value on at least one artistic level.

Some of the expeditions employed artists to keep pictorial records of the Indians, birds, animals, and scenes which were different from those in the settled East. These paintings, sketches, and drawings constitute the first non-Indian art in South Dakota. Of the two best-known very early painters on the Missouri, George Catlin worked independently but Karl Bodmer (from Switzerland) traveled in the employ of the German prince, Maximilian. Catlin painted the Sioux as they rode on horseback out on the prairie or gathered in encampments of tipis, as well as painting scenes of the river, bluffs, and forts. His work was as realistic as his talent, enthusiasm, and leisure allowed it to be, and while the paintings are not considered first-rate art, they at least brought some authenticity of the visual images of the time and place from the Dakota wilderness to the civilized world, where they were received with curiosity if nothing else. Along with the artist's written notes, the Catlin paintings remain a valuable source of information. Bodmer had the advantage of viewing some of Catlin's work before he left Saint Louis to look at the upper Missouri with Maximilian. Knowledge of Catlin's work enabled him to see the scenery with a somewhat better perspective and a better eye for composition and detail. Even so, these early artists, with George Caleb Bingham and Friederich Kurz (the latter another Swiss painter), continue to be appreciated more for their visual documentation of the wilderness than for artistic achievement—a judgment which applies as well to the written documents of early travelers and explorers.

The two most famous painters of the western landscape, Alfred Jacob Miller and Albert Bierstadt, are sometimes mistakenly associated with South Dakota. They worked farther west, in Wyoming and along the Rockies. But after 1870 a few assorted artists actually settled in South Dakota, their contributions varied and uneven but nonetheless encouraging to the new territory. Isabelle Weeks studied painting in Michigan before moving to Yankton in Dakota Territory in 1872, and her work shows more influence of her studies than it does of her new home. William Fuller, who arrived in the territory as a railroad employee and then became a carpenter at Crow Creek Agency, took a more active interest in local subject matter, spending his vacations on Indian agencies, where he recorded scenes in fine detail and sometimes in an attractive misproportion that seems more modern than it is. It has been suggested that Grace Ann French, who studied in Boston and moved to Rapid City in 1885, introduced still-life painting into South Dakota. Her work was traditional and extremely professional. Her teaching left an impact upon art in the Black Hills.

South Dakota has had more than its share of mavericks who led interesting lives but whose professions contributed little or nothing to the state. Perhaps their work has been appreciated elsewhere. John Banvard left New York to paint portraits and to set up a museum on a raft. During the 1840s he painted a panorama of the Mississippi River, claiming that the painting itself was three miles long. It was unrolled for exhibitions in Louisville, Boston, New York, and Paris, presumably creating considerable excitement and most certainly making Banvard financially successful. He then went to Egypt and painted a similar panorama, this time of the Nile, which was shown in London. With his small fortune he opened a theater-museum on Broadway in New York City and, when it failed, moved to Watertown, Dakota Territory, in 1883. But he did not paint Dakota, which is a pity, because he might well have done a ten-mile-long panorama, to top the others, of the endless prairie. Instead he put together a diorama with sound, motion, and light (a kind of forerunner of the motion picture) called "The Burning of Columbia," whose subject was the ruin of Columbia, South Carolina, by Sherman during the Civil War.

Frances Cranmer Greenman, born in Aberdeen just as South Dakota became a state, more nearly represents the struggle (or change) toward culture in a frontier region. According to Mrs. Greenman, her father, S. H. Cranmer, accompanied the Russian Duke Alexis on his western buffalo hunt, was a friend of Bill Cody and Wild Bill Hickok, once arrested Texas Jack, and courted Calamity Jane. Later he went to college, became both teacher and lawyer, helped write the state constitution in 1888, and was a Democrat, a Populist, a Socialist (entertaining Eugene V. Debs in his home in Aberdeen), and perhaps finally an anarchist. Mrs. Cranmer, meanwhile, was stumping for suffrage. This kind of story borders on the western tall tale, but even if it were to be taken only symbolically it would point up (albeit in a rather special way) the background out of which western culture emerged—with the help, of course, of what had already been accomplished in the older states. Frances, as a teenager, thought of Aberdeen as a good place, seemed to like the fact that there was only one level of citizenry, and did not think it strange when a townsman wondered why her father should waste money by sending her to study art in the East, when anyone could paint a picture. But she went, first to the Corcoran School of Art in Washington, then to Europe, and back to Washington, becoming a portrait painter. When her parents moved to Minneapolis, and she joined them, she was prompted to say that although some people go to heaven to find their happy hunting ground, people from Aberdeen went to Minneapolis. Frances Greenman traveled across the nation for years, painting one thousand portraits, including those of Mary Pickford, Dolores del Rio, Lily Pons, Olga Petrova, and a few governors. For two years, while traveling, she contributed a column to the *Minneapolis Sunday Tribune,* and while she still lives in Minneapolis, she is frequently listed as a South Dakota artist.

The state also likes to claim L. Frank Baum, the creator of *The Wonderful Wizard of Oz,* who lived in Aberdeen for two years, leaving the year Frances Cranmer was born. A native New Yorker, Baum was a writer of children's stories, a successful playwright, and an occasional editor. After a stint of newspaper reporting he opened an opera house in Pennsylvania; when it burned, he wrote plays which were produced in New York City, Syracuse, and Rochester; and then, unaccountably, in 1888, he became the editor of the *Dakota Pioneer* in Aberdeen. Although the first Wizard of Oz story was not published until 1900, while Baum was living in Chicago, it is quite likely that he got the Kansas prairie and tornado for that story from South Dakota. Be that as it may, the history of art and literature in Dakota Territory and the first years of statehood is a succession of writers and painters coming and going, rarely staying.

It is customary to think of South Dakota as a place harboring themes and historical characters of interest to writers outside the state rather than as a place which nourishes its own writers. Significant events—especially those associated with frontier conditions—have been dealt with in a rash of historical or semihistorical novels. The Lewis and Clark expedition has been a popular subject because of its symbolic importance in the experience of westering and because of its ranking as one of the great journeys of all time. In literary form it becomes a quest in the tradition of the search for the Holy Grail, but it usually retains the structure of the travel narrative. Beyond that, the individual treatments of the expedition can be distinguished by their titles: *No Other White Man,* by Julia Davis; *The Conquest,* by Eva Emery Dye; *Westward the Course,* by Hildegarde Hawthorne; *Star of the West,* by Ethel Hueston; *The Magnificent Adventure,* by Emerson Hough; *Hobnailed Boots,* by Jeannette C. Nolan; *Forward the Nation,* by Donald Culross Peattie; *The Shining Mountains,* by Dale Van Every. Several of these novels are quite patriotic in tone and theme, and they vary in the degree to which they follow the actual events of the expedition. Vardis Fisher's *Tale of Valor,* 1958, includes scenes of Lewis and Clark entering information in their journals, thereby giving an air of authenticity to the narrative. Even so, Fisher heightens the drama of the story by setting up a carefully calculated series of dangers which constantly threaten to halt the journey (grizzly bears, Indians, rapids on the rivers, hunger, and cold) and emphasizes an alternation of attitudes to (and among) the Indians along the way. The Sioux, encountered first, in South Dakota, are enemies and troublemakers; the Mandans of North Dakota are less hostile, almost friendly; the Blackfeet, farther west, are said to be deadly but they never appear—are hanging in the wings, so to speak, as a dramatic device for suspense; and in Idaho the Shoshones, the people of Sacajawea, are very friendly.

Thematically, Fisher stresses hunger and fear, problems that in his context are subsocial. That is, they concern man in direct conflict with elemental and natural life, with the primitive forces of the land and the climate. Social intercourse and interaction exist on a small scale in South Dakota (and western) literature, mostly in the treatments of the formation of new settlements and towns on the frontier. Because people have never been packed together in large cities, their primary relationship has been with the land rather than with other people. When members of the Lewis and Clark expedition freeze their feet during a Dakota winter, Fisher has Lewis say almost casually, "I expect I'll be cutting off a lot of toes tomorrow." Not a particularly humane statement, it bows to the facts of the land.

Within the primitive environment, animalism in both of its aspects plays a major part in theme and characterization. In its first phase it is a characteristic attributed to men living away from the refinements and restraints of civilization. Applied to the white mountain men as well as to the Indians, and appearing in "contemporary" fiction (such as Frank Norris's *McTeague*) as well as historical novels, it is almost caricatured through exaggeration in *Tale of Valor*. Perhaps Fisher was simply trying to show the reactions of the explorers as they came in contact with customs which were strange to them; but he overworks the scenes in which the Indians literally attack carcasses like famished wolves, gulping down raw livers, kidneys, guts, and tubes of intestines while the blood pours from the corners of their mouths. There are many such descriptions, which are difficult to read while eating lunch. Behind them is the universal theme of hunger. More interesting, however, is the mystical feeling a man can have in the presence of a grizzly bear (or a white whale). Old Ephraim is the West's Moby Dick, to be hunted, feared, and respected. The Sioux traditionally held a high respect for all animals, especially the buffalo, which provided them with most of their food, shelter, arms, and tools and which was considered sacred, particularly when it was a rare white buffalo. In Fisher's novel, Lewis too has a mystical experience while out alone on the prairie, realizing that animals (in this case a grizzly) cannot be fully understood in scientific terms—the same thing Melville was getting at through the use of his interspersed "whale chapters" in *Moby Dick*. One must be close to nature, and away from books, to have this feeling.

Standard subject matter, aside from the Lewis and Clark expedition, includes Indians, cowboys, the cavalry (usually the Seventh Regiment), the fur trade, homesteading, railroad building, and the depression of the 1930s. These subjects are by no means confined to South Dakota; their ingredients may be found in the histories of other plains and mountain states. The Custer story, if fully fleshed out, includes a wide area, but, like the Sioux, Custer is associated with South Dakota even though his "major encounter" took place in Montana. As the subject of historical fiction, Lt. Col. George Custer is open to a variety of interpretations, which accounts for the number of novels written about him or based upon his career in the West. He has been seen as a man of destiny, as a tragic figure, as consumed by ambition, as an example of "pride goeth before the fall," as a fool, as a hero, and as a somewhat typical example of the white man's misunderstanding of the Indian. In order to keep his story alive, some writers have seen the events of the Custer campaign from the viewpoint of the Indians, some have established a "white renegade" among the Sioux in order to attempt a dual point of view, and some (like Ernest Haycox in *Bugles in the Afternoon*) have established a subplot which, in effect, becomes the main story, with the Battle of the Little Big Horn as a dramatic backdrop. Many "Custer novels" are simply frontier stories with Custer around somewhere as a figurehead or, more honestly, a gimmick.

Many possibilities are available to the writer who uses settlement of the West as his subject. Given a wide enough definition, "The American Dream" probably covers them all. South Dakota was hardly the sought-for Garden of Eden, but neither was California. There was no such thing, and what really lured people into the West was adventure, the pioneer spirit, a feeling of American expansion and manifest destiny, the hope for a fresh start, and, above all, free land. Many of these ingredients were the basis for South Dakota's only best-selling novels, one by Will O. Lillibridge, the dentist from Sioux Falls, and another by the brother-sister team of Kate and Virgil Boyles from Yankton.

Not a very strong man to begin with, the combination of practicing dentistry all day and writing novels at night led to Lillibridge's early death at the age of thirty-one. By that time he had already achieved considerable fame with, primarily, *Ben Blair: The Story of a Plainsman,* which was a national best seller in 1905 and was made into a motion picture. The story of a young man growing up on a Dakota ranch, and not unlike Wister's *Virginian* in some respects, the novel assumes the attainment of the dream on an economic level (Ben is assured of inheriting a ranch from his benefactor) and pursues it from another angle. Ben is an illegitimate child and, as such, is rejected by the woman he wishes to marry, the daughter of an English lord who ranches nearby. Having been spurned, Ben devotes his energies to seeking revenge against his father and to changing the mind of the girl of his dreams. When the father has been punished, Ben follows Florence to New York to persuade her to marry him. In the big city Ben is characterized as a "noble savage" who is inherently better (with an inner goodness derived from the land) than the socialites who confront him. Florence eventually sees this truth and returns to South Dakota with him. Lillibridge's other popular novel was *Where the Trail Divides* (1907); in some ways his most interesting piece was a novella, *Arcadia in Avernus,* included in a posthumously published collection of stories, *A Breath of Prairie* (1911).

Virgil Boyles was born in Illinois two years before his family settled a claim in South Dakota in 1874, and his sister Kate was born in Olivet a few years before the family moved to Yankton. Both were graduated from Yankton College, after which Virgil went into law and Kate became a teacher. Together they wrote novels about homesteaders, cattle rustlers, Indians, the Badlands, and the establishment of law on the frontier. Their view of the Indians in *The Spirit Trail* (1910) is sympathetic and idealistic. Hugh Hunt, a missionary, attends the signing of the Treaty of Laramie, is shocked by Custer's violation of the treaty in entering the Black Hills, and adopts many of the beliefs of the Indian. Katherine Mendenhall, daughter of an Indian agent, spends most of her time helping Hugh as he tries to help the Indians, but when she is captured by a West River tribe she wants nothing more than to escape from the West. Eventually she does so, with a man who in the novel represents the exile from eastern society. However, the Boyleses' most popular novel, *Langford of the Three Bars* (1907), was based on the exploits of outlaw Jack Sully and on his death at the hands of a much-needed frontier law. This novel probably had the largest sale of any work of fiction by a resident South Dakotan—over a hundred thousand copies. Whether lawlessness as theme proved to be the attractive element, or whether the two underlying love stories were the reasons for its success, *Langford* was Mc-Clurg's heaviest seller at the Chicago store for a long time.

Perhaps the largest body of South Dakota literature comes out of the homesteading period. The best-remembered fiction writers are Hamlin Garland, Ole Rölvaag, Laura Ingalls Wilder, Rose Wilder Lane, and J. Hyatt Downing. When the homesteads began to break up during the Dust Bowl of the 1930s, few local people had the time or the means to write, but Minnesota neighbor Frederick Manfred (writing as Feike Feikema) provided the state with its own *Grapes of Wrath* in a smaller but equally fine novel, *The Golden Bowl* (1944). As though South Dakota were returning the favor, its major contemporary novelist, Herbert Krause, set all three of his novels in Minnesota. (He was born there, not far from the Dakota border.) *Wind Without Rain* (1939) is an unexpectedly poetic farm novel, almost impressionistic in style, creating paradoxical beauty out of the harshness of the subject. In *The Thresher* (1946), Krause stayed more closely within the realism normally associated with the farm novel and produced a classic of the genre. His last novel, *The Oxcart Trail* (1954), turns to the fur trade, the *voyageur,* and an old trail between Saint Paul and Pembina (the latter a Canadian settlement in the northeast corner of North Dakota). In this historical setting, Krause probes the wilderness, its effects upon the characters, and the relationships between frontier whites and Indians.

Minnesota has indeed been an important factor in the cultural growth of South Dakota. Graduates of its university abound in the faculties of South Dakota schools. The Northwest Area Foundation (formerly the Louis and Maude Hill Family Foundation, formed from railroad money) made possible the founding of Dakota Press at the University of South Dakota, helped to support the state's only professional literary magazine—the *South Dakota Review*—and established a writer's residency at the university. These contributions have been of the utmost importance in a state which is still reluctant to support such non-practical activities as the development of writers. So Minnesota, once accused of an attempted political take-over of Dakota Territory, has done much to help South Dakota in its "struggle for culture."

While reciprocation has been small in quantity, it has been varied, it has occasionally been unique, and it has been of high quality. Dakota Press, operating on a small scale, has concentrated on regional materials which have interest outside the region as well, such as the first collection of contemporary American Indian poetry, fiction, and art, a collection which was tapped by almost every subsequent anthology of Indian writing published in New York. The *Review* frequently devotes special issues to the literature of the American West, bringing an extremely important group of writers to the attention of the nation as well as foreign countries.

Artists of various kinds have also made an impact beyond the state. Syd Fossum, of Aberdeen, became associated with the farm and labor movement in Minnesota, painted with a social conscience, and taught art at the University in Minneapolis. Raymond Parker, on the other hand, went from a small town in eastern South Dakota to New York where he has been known as an abstract painter, a member of the New York School, and where he has also taught. Some of the shapes in his paintings, as well as the colors, are subtle reminders of the landscape of his home state, although there is nothing obviously regional about them. James Fraser, reared on a farm near Mitchell, South Dakota, designed the famous Buffalo Nickel. Gutzon Borglum's faces on Mount Rushmore must be considered as sculptures which have had an impact upon the entire nation.

The two painters most highly regarded by their native state, Harvey Dunn and Oscar Howe, have used local materials almost exclusively, though in quite different ways. Dunn spent most of his life in New Jersey, but his work consists largely of boldly stroked prairie and farm paintings in a style midway between photographic realism and French impressionism. Titles such as "The Harvest Orator" and "The Prairie Is My Garden" have endeared him to most Dakotans and hang in the South Dakota Memorial Art Center in Brookings, an attractive gallery built originally to house Dunn's work. Although he maintained a studio in Tenafly, New Jersey, and taught for almost twenty years in New York City, he made frequent trips back to his home state.

Oscar Howe, full-blooded Sioux Indian, has remained in South Dakota all his life except for schooling in the Southwest and service in the U.S. Army during World War II. One of the leading Indian artists in the country—with R.C. Gorman, who is Navajo, and Fritz Scholder, who was once Howe's pupil at the Indian School in Pierre—Oscar Howe's paintings are in great demand by collectors. Traditionally, Sioux art was devoted largely to the painting of winter counts (chronological records) on animal skins and to the beadwork decoration of deerskin clothing. Howe's work springs from skin painting but has been refined and modernized through influences as far afield as Picasso. His paintings are done in tempera, are symbolically colorful, and are geometric to the extent that they are made up largely of straight lines (truth) and circles (unity of the Sioux Nation and of the universe).

Although Howe has not lived on the reservation for many years, his concern for the traditional values of Sioux beliefs, religion, ceremonies, and symbols shows in every painting. Even his techniques are derived from the old methods. Like the skin painters, he establishes points on the paper—which he calls esthetic points—to set off the basic division of space before he begins to put down the lines, or the structure, of the painting. He then proceeds into a design of the kind he has called "bi-vision," a blending of the abstract and the objective. Figures, whether human or animal, are recognizable as such, but they become an integral part of the design, so that neither shape nor color can be called "realistic" in the normal sense.

The phrase "struggle for culture" takes on an ambivalent meaning for Oscar Howe. His people, the Sioux, had a culture—an old one. It was not necessary for him to acquire a culture. The struggle came in making his own use of that culture, and in getting critics and viewers from another culture to accept his painted statements of his heritage. Howe has experienced racial prejudice, slum poverty, hunger, poor health, near blindness, the depression of the 1930s, and war, together with an almost total disregard of his work during the earlier part of his life. At one time he paid bills with paintings. He pleaded for recognition in the nation's art galleries. After many years he got it, and more. As artist-in-residence at the university of South Dakota he is part of the white community and highly respected, but he has not abandoned the beliefs of his people. In his paintings those beliefs are made available to a white culture which has finally recognized their value and the contributions they can make to a Christian and urban society.

Because of language problems (the Dakota language is not a written one and does not translate easily), the writing of poetry and fiction by the Sioux is slow in developing. However, the Sioux have an articulate spokesman in Vine Deloria, Jr., whose books combine a thorough knowledge of the non-Indian religions and laws with an insight into the ways in which the Sioux heritage can enrich the entire state and nation. Since the publication of *Custer Died for Your Sins* in 1969, the white population can never be as complacent as it once was toward Indian affairs.

Serious poetry was not one of the major achievements of non-Indian writers either, until very recently. It is likely that every frontier state has had its cowboy versifier. In South Dakota it was Badger Clark, whose *Sun and Saddle Leather* (1915) and other books led to his appointment as the first poet laureate of the state. Born in 1883, Clark attended Dakota Wesleyan University in Mitchell for one year; it has been said that he was then asked to leave because of his poor academic record. After two years of adventuring in Cuba he contracted malaria and returned to Deadwood. A year later he had tuberculosis, the same disease which had killed his brother, so he went to Arizona and lived on a ranch near Tombstone. It was here that he learned about cowboys and began to write verses. Perhaps his best-known poem is "A Cowboy's Prayer," which was widely reprinted. In 1910 he was back in Hot Springs, at the southern end of the Black Hills, and in 1925 he retired to his cabin at Legion Lake to spend a solitary life wandering through the Hills, reading and writing. He is one of the "heroes" of the South Dakota Poetry Society which was organized by a Danish immigrant, J. C. Lindberg, who taught at Northern State Teachers College. In 1926, with the help and suggestions of one of his students, Rudolf G. Ruste, Lindberg began publication of *Pasque Petals,* a magazine of verse, which is now in its fiftieth year.

Today there is a small but steady succession of young poets, some natives of the state, others escaping from the crowded cities to the east, who make use of regional themes, the landscape, and Indian motifs, but who write in contemporary forms and are published in magazines around the country. Some of these young poets stay; others go on to further studies of their craft at the University of Iowa Writers Workshop and similar programs in other states since the master of fine arts degree is not available to them in South Dakota. It seems that the vicissitudes of the state are of constant benefit to other states.

It is difficult to speak of "cultural centers" in a sparsely populated agricultural state. In local efforts, the two largest cities—Sioux Falls and Rapid City—have had the best chance at galleries, orchestras, and writing groups. The Black Hills Playhouse, begun in 1946 near Custer, has consistently mixed serious drama with musicals and melodrama to entertain summer crowds. The players are drawn both from South Dakota and from schools in other states. Primarily, however, it is the two universities which have in different ways been the cultural centers of the state. They, too, as institutions, have had a struggle in convincing the legislature and the regents of the human, spiritual, emotional, and even practical values of the arts. What has made the largest impact on the state as a whole has been the efforts of the National Endowment for the Arts in the past decade to bring poetry, music, theater, dance, and other arts into the public schools and into the small towns and rural areas. It is quite likely that this program will be much more beneficial to a state like South Dakota than to those more populous states which have on their own made the arts available through outstanding symphony orchestras, art galleries, and professional theaters. Some South Dakotans see a splurge of creativity growing among the younger people of the state and hope that some of it will mature and remain within the state. If it does, a genuine cultural climate could emerge and establish itself during the next decade or two. The interchanges of the past will undoubtedly continue: artists from elsewhere will seek refuge on the Great Plains and will bring a necessary contribution with them, and artists developed in the state will go elsewhere in their search for fulfillment and recognition. At the very least, under these conditions, the newfound culture will not stagnate as it does in some of the big metropolitan areas of the nation.

9

The Straddle of Time

$\mathcal{T}$HE frontier in American history has been defined as a line which separates civilization or society from the wilderness. For a while, the Missouri River was that line in South Dakota. The hypothesis was that as the line moved westward it was followed by law and order, by the niceties of a social system, by cultural activities and interests, by the arts, and, in short, by some kind of enlightenment. Since Frederick Jackson Turner said that the frontier closed—ceased to exist—in 1890, the assumption would be now that there is no wilderness in the United States, that there are no frontier conditions in any part of the nation, and that we are an enlightened people moving through various kinds of refinement toward a complete and successful civilization.

Assumptions are comfortable but they are sometimes too simple to reflect the entire context in which they are made. Wilderness areas are now preserved—although frequently under pressure from vested interests—and the meaning of the word "wilderness" has changed. Whereas it once conveyed a sense of danger, it now evokes the feeling of escape from a world which pits men and women against their own kind, daily, in the arena of "civilized" activities. And, although the frontier seems to have been dissipated by a continuous string of settled towns and counties and states from one ocean to the other, there are places where it is still real, either in memory or in fact.

159

Many communities in South Dakota have at least one person who was born before statehood, which means before the closing of the frontier. These people are a living link to the past and a reminder that the past still exists in the present. Their memories bridge a rather narrow gap, historically, between the struggling territory and the modern state. These people literally straddle the entire history of South Dakota. For one such person, Charlotte Cushman Clark, there was a frontier line going through Deadwood in the 1870s and 1880s. Descended from an official of the Plymouth Colony, Mrs. Clark arrived in Deadwood (from Denver) in 1878. She was three years old. In 1975 she was still there, celebrating her 100th birthday. Remembering the old days, she is a little upset by the attention always given to Wild Bill Hickok, Calamity Jane, Poker Alice, and "people of that sort." They represented the wild side of the frontier, whereas just across the line, in another part of town, were churches, respectable businessmen, lawyers, and many educated people. Mrs. Clark seems to remember the lawyers more clearly than anyone else, as though law were the real difference between civilization and barbarism.

Mrs. Clark is a reminder that South Dakota is a young state and that it, along with the rest of the nation, has undergone an almost traumatic change in the lifetime of one person. Her childhood trip by stagecoach from Denver to Deadwood took four days and three nights; at age ninety-eight she flew back to Denver (for a visit) in one hour.

Not everything has changed that much. It is true that South Dakota is a modern agricultural state. It ranks first in the nation in rye exports, second in flaxseed, third in durum wheat, fourth in other spring wheat and oats, fifth in alfalfa seed, seventh in alfalfa hay and barley, and tenth in other hay exports. These facts are impressive enough to suggest that perhaps (in one sense, at least) there really was a Garden of Eden west of the Mississippi River. Or they indicate technological advances in agribusiness. Nevertheless, the frontier may have lingered in this garden. Mrs. Clark remembers an incident involving Calamity Jane and the boy Horace who was to become Mrs. Clark's husband:

Well, she went into Horace's father's store and she had a gun, and I
don't know if she wanted to sell it or to just borrow money on it,
but anyway my husband was just a little boy and he was in there
and he reached up and wanted to handle the gun and his uncle who
was waiting on Calamity said, "Oh, no, don't touch the gun."
Calamity said, "Oh, let the boy handle it, it won't hurt him." [1]

The gun is a vital part of the frontier myth. It is also part of
another American myth, that which says a boy becomes a man
when he is given his first gun. Many Dakotans give guns to
their children as part of a maturation ritual quite different from
the vision quest of the Sioux. (South Dakota also grants driver's
licenses to mere children, a practice stemming from pre-school-
bus days when farm children needed to travel a considerable
distance to and from school.) Whatever the motivation may be,
there are an estimated 400,000 guns in a state whose population
is roughly 660,000. Two guns for every three people. This phenomenon has been explained as part of the state's heritage, as
an indication that the frontier is still a very real factor in the
lives of South Dakotans. It is not uncommon, especially in West
River, to see two or three rifles hanging in the back window of a
rancher's pickup truck. One-fifth of the state's population is
issued hunting licenses annually. During one of the periodic financial crises in the state (these are usually caused by crop failures), when it was difficult to attract teachers to the colleges and
universities, many of those who accepted employment in the
state did so because of the hunting opportunities. For years,
when two nonhunters met on the street, in any town, each was
surprised to discover that there was more than one who did not
like to hunt.

One writer, in attempting to differentiate between the East
and the West, links the development of long-range firearms to
the elusiveness of those animals which adapted themselves so
well to the western environment—the antelope, the jackrabbit,
and the prairie dog. Another writer insists that the American

---

1. John Barstow, "Charlotte Cushman Clark—The Last Pioneer," *Black Hills
Nuggets,* commemorative ed. (Rapid City: The Rapid City Society for Genealogical
Research, Inc., 1975), p. 66. Used with permission.

bison, or buffalo, once existed in greater numbers than any other species of four-legged animal living upon the earth. Considering that the buffalo came near extinction shortly before the closing of the frontier, and that during the antelope hunting season in the Black Hills area it is almost impossible to find (for one example) an auto mechanic on duty, it is not hard to believe that Americans have continually been at war with nature rather than living peacefully with it, that destruction rather than adaptation has been the mode of settlement, and that conquest still is—as it has been—a sign of strength, success, and psychological fulfillment. Richard Slotkin, examining these and other matters in his 1973 book, *Regeneration Through Violence,* evokes the image of hero Davy Crockett standing beside a mountain of bearhides and smiling in satisfaction, refers to the rifle shots of hero Daniel Boone as "prayer and poetry" within the context of the American frontier character and spirit, and deplores the substance of his own thesis, that Americans seem to have needed violence in order to achieve a regeneration of their own collective spirit. The title of the last chapter—"A Pyramid of Skulls"—leaves us wondering about the immensity of our sins committed during the search for, or the building of, a New World Garden of Eden.

The indictment is not localized, of course. And since South Dakota has an extremely low rate of violent acts in relation to other states (contrary to the image generated by journalists in reporting—or speculating—on certain incidents such as the one in 1973 at Wounded Knee), it would seem that gun ownership is at least partly a ritualistic remnant of the frontier, or a gesture in the cause of individual rights, or an indication of cultural lag determined by environmental factors, or, perhaps, the metaphor from some old American myth whose continued existence is possible in a region where outdoor life is still common.

Depending upon one's point of view, there may be romance or there may be danger in the straddle of time. The frontier lingers in South Dakota, allowing the dramatic struggles of the past to remain in the memory as elements in a success story of a new country while at the same time preventing the instigation and development of new and perhaps better ideals. Three coun-

ties populated largely by Indians are still without their own government, unorganized, attached to neighboring counties as they
were early in the history of the state. A federal appeals court
recently took one step away from this condition by ruling that
the three unorganized counties may take part in the election of
officials of the neighboring counties that govern them. By impli-
cation, the next step may be to allow people from the unorganized counties to run for office in the governing counties next to
them. A further complication on the reservations is that they are
in some ways more closely attached to the federal government
than to the state.

It might seem on the surface that the lack of state support to
the liberal arts within the institutions of higher learning also
reflects a frontier way of thinking, but such may not be the case.
The immigrants who came to South Dakota brought with them a
strong belief in educational opportunities and were particularly
concerned that their children (and their children's children, and
so on) should be able to rise above the level of learning of their
parents. The university, the first school of advanced learning to
be established, was given both a traditional and a practical cur-
riculum—science, literature, art, law, medicine, teacher training, and agriculture—although the inclusion of agriculture was
probably a device for obtaining financial aid under the Morrill
Land-Grant Act. Because none of the prospective students who
arrived for classes in October 1882 were prepared for college-
level work, the school existed for a while as a preparatory
school. Its principal was a former Jew, Ephraim Epstein, who
preached in Baptist churches in Yankton and Vermillion, who
also had a degree in medicine, but who was above all a scholar.
During the next forty years, six more territory and state institutions were established by law, at first emphasizing such things
as mining, agriculture, and the training of teachers. The curricu-
lums broadened gradually. The schools grew as the state grew.
When the population began to decline after 1930, and then to
fluctuate but never again to reach the 1930 figure, it slowly became apparent that the state would have difficulty in supporting
seven colleges and universities. In recent years, attempts to
close one or more of the smaller schools have met with local op-

position (as one might expect) and political maneuvering has kept the schools open.

Although for many years the schools were run on a somewhat personal basis, with dedicated faculties turning out exceptional students, recent developments (based partly on the assumption that education is a business) have led to political-type administrations which are increasingly divorced from the academic life of the schools and from humanistic interests. Administrators, whose function was once to serve the faculties, have become an elitist group, opening gaps between themselves and the real heart of the institutions—the faculties and students. The vision of the pioneers has given way to the corporate structures of modern life. At the same time, specific jobs and the training for them have taken precedence over the kind of liberal education which was, and still is, the best preparation for a good life as well as for good jobs.

Such problems are, however, more typical than unique. Although South Dakota is still close in time to the frontier, and although vestiges of that time are still apparent in some areas (even if only as a cultural lag), it has changed as the nation has changed, even to the proliferation of government (as though in imitation of the swelling federal government), and this in a state which once proposed a kind of sovereignty within the federal system and wanted as little governmental interference as possible.

As a place, however, as a big piece of land on which people are born and then either stay, or leave for a while and then return, or leave permanently, there seems to be a unique quality, combining both the remnants of the frontier and the changes undergone in the twentieth century, which fascinates as well as repels, which invokes love and awe as well as fear and irritation, and which points up again the many-faceted personality of the region, both land and people. This quality may be relatively undetectable to those who are close to it for a lifetime, but it is noticeable (though not easy to define) to those who look back at it from another vantage point, or those who come back to it after an extended absence, just as it has been striking to those who passed through, pausing only briefly.

Two contemporary accounts may help to clarify these issues. The first comes from Kathleen Norris, a young poet whose roots were in South Dakota but who lived elsewhere until her recent return to the family home.

Kathleen Norris [2]

"In the spring of 1974, David and I moved from the island of Manhattan, population about two million, to the town of Lemmon, South Dakota, population about two thousand. Often the move has seemed an enormous turnabout, like moving to another country. But it also feels like destiny, something I was always meant to do.

"I have lived in many places, from Virginia to Vermont to Hawaii. When I was a kid, my grandparents' house in Lemmon was a 'constant,' the place where we spent our summers. Consequently the old house and the town itself have carried for me the full weight of eternity and childhood memory. I practically learned to read in the town's library, and learned to swim in its pool. I was living in New York when my grandparents died, but it seemed the time for me to come here and claim my inheritance. I knew it was not to be found on any piece of paper, but in the old house, in the South Dakota grasslands.

"I love New York City. In my five years there I made a nest for myself: friends (many of them other writers), favorite places, neighborhood markets, and old movie houses. I had a demanding job that had become an important part of me. I grew in the city and wrote a book of poems there. Of course the city was often raw and terrifying, but I remember with joy the luxury of solitary walks along Broadway; or standing on the steps of the big public library, watching a wealth of people passing by, strangers in all shapes, sizes and colors. When I think of New York now I recall a vast medieval fair of traders and craftsmen, painters and sailors.

"I love South Dakota too, although I don't yet know it well.

2. Kathleen Norris, "Through the Looking Glass," *Sunday Clothes* 4 (Autumn 1975): 20–21. Used with permission.

Gertrude Stein wrote that 'In the United States there is more space where nobody is than where anybody is. This is what makes America what it is.' I feel close to that statement here, in northwestern South Dakota. It is still the frontier and in part because of that it bears a troubled relationship to the rest of the country. I am still a New Yorker, becoming a Dakotan, moving East and West.

"South Dakota is known to be a geologist's paradise, but I have found that it is also a paradise for anyone who enjoys the sound of speech. Many of the farmers speak in a way that is as eloquent as it is grammatically unorthodox. Their language must have its own set of rules, because one never hears a mistake in choice of word and seldom an error in phrasing. This is remarkable to the ear, since one has become accustomed to hearing people fumbling for words, speaking without style.

"There are many local speech peculiarities, among them one which never fails to startle me: 'I and he went hunting.' The speaker most often chooses the correct pronoun, but simply reverses the usual order. More interesting to me is the way farmers, young and old, use magnificent words such as 'farrow,' which were common English five hundred years ago, but which faded from use as society became industrial. I even heard one older man refer to a 'wain' for wagon. The word dates back to the Celts.

"I am used to hearing today's slackened English, full of misapplied words and the ugly-sounding phrases of sociology. It is a language that has lost much of its local shading, reflecting not a particular place but a national preoccupation with ideology and bureaucracy, with television and slick magazines. This language has certainly reached Lemmon. One hears it here, but it is good also to hear so much speech that remains unaffected by it.

"I am a devourer of newspapers and often read all three of the dailies available here, from Aberdeen, Bismarck, and Rapid City. They lack the awesome completeness of the *New York Times,* but are generally better than papers in some larger cities (Honolulu, and Syracuse, New York for example).

"The local weekly gives a responsible accounting of the affairs of the town and the local school board and frequently contains a wonderful column written by children in the rural schools, who report on such things as seeing a Snowy Owl, or finding gophers hibernating in a haystack. But plowing through the paper's prose each week is like driving on a road full of potholes. In every issue there are grammatical constructions that defy the imagination, even incomplete sentences. I am not overly anxious about correct English, especially in demotic speech; but I despair when people who write newspapers don't know something as fundamental as that all sentences have verbs.

"There is an interesting ambivalence about culture here. On the one hand there is the populism that defines an expert as 'someone who is 50 miles from home,' and on the other, the exaggerated respect for 'the arts' and formal education that is, I suppose, found in frontier areas everywhere. We have learned to expect just about anything. There are people who ask about our writing and then talk about their 'hobby,' which is stamp collecting. There are others who seem to idealize what we do. And I'm afraid we end up confusing everyone. We read a great deal and are preoccupied with language and literature; but by not always valuing education (certainly not equating it with knowledge) and by seeming indifferent to 'culture for culture's sake' we are often at odds with the role prescribed for us.

"Probably the most noticeable social change in the move to Lemmon has been the loss of the city dweller's anonymity and the gain of a sense of community. Lemmon is close-knit in a way that even the friendliest New York neighborhood cannot be. Ritual is more important here: the tribe is still of manageable size. Here one is born, one grows, marries, and dies, and the whole community participates, overseeing each event.

"Sometimes I resent not being able to be a stranger when I walk out my door, but on the other hand I find that living here has made me a more responsible citizen. Democracy is tangible in South Dakota and one feels more obligated to it than one can in New York. We have a state senator who answers by phone all the letters he receives from constituents. I can't even write that down without a feeling of awe.

"The smallness and isolation that make Lemmon a genuine community also make it extremely insular. I am used to living on the big, shifting ground of a city, among people who live in ways very different from my own—among blacks, Jews, Haitians, and Puerto Ricans. Here all life is centered in agriculture, and people more or less conform to one social code. The phrase 'that's different' is used to convey a range of feelings, from disgust and disdain to simple uncomfortableness.

"One thing I find extremely curious is the extent to which Indians in South Dakota are contained in a vacuum. They are truly invisible men and women: sometimes I feel that I could find out more about them in New York than I can here. After almost a year, I have finally made some Indian friends and hope to learn from them more about the realities of Indian life and the political issues surrounding it. I feel that I can breathe just a little easier now: not that I have solved anything, but simply broken through the surface. Before I felt helpless, part of a lie.

"Insularity has its odd effects. It is one of the ironies of history that New York, first colonized by the Dutch in the mid-1600s, should be so completely a twentieth-century city, while Lemmon, which had virtually no existence before 1907–1908, should still be clinging to its nineteenth-century underpinnings. The social clubs for both men and women are an example. For the most part they have a nineteenth-century structure (one must dress and act in a certain way to 'belong') mixed with a timeless American high school notion of 'fun.' For someone from so wildly egalitarian a place as New York City these clubs are bewildering, an anomaly. I'm afraid we blew it the first time we walked into the cowboy bar.

"David and I have inherited some of my grandparents' friends and have found some new ones. We were asked to be the advisors for a church youth group. But we are aware that we do not fit easily into the community's structure. Our habits often put us on a reverse schedule with the rest of the town: dinner at eleven or twelve at night, work until five in the morning. And we find ourselves at variance with local custom in many ways.

"The area in which the step through the looking glass, back in time, has been most apparent is feminism. We each have our own name and career, inasmuch as writing can be considered a

career. We have taken turns supporting each other. We tend not
to trivialize each other but see ourselves as partners, equals who
happen to enjoy reading, shooting guns, embroidery, playing
pool, and cooking. A good many of the people we went to
school with, friends on both coasts, wouldn't consider changing
their names in marriage, or don't want children, or consider a
group like NOW (National Organization for Women) to be
somewhat conservative. This is our normal frame of reference
and it is the reverse of what we find in Lemmon.

"This reversal of ground gives me a kind of double vision.
Having lived so long in the East, in a city, I am extremely
aware of many pressures being brought to bear on South Dakota
by other parts of the country. We are living on a thin line here,
by a grace that seems extremely fragile, a grace that is dependent on our underpopulation, or, in the popular phrase, 'under-
development.' The common trust that allows a Lemmon mer-
chant to provide counter checks from area banks, or a family to
leave its house unlocked, is a luxury that would quickly disappear in an energy boom. I am frightened when I read of towns
in Alaska and Wyoming where the population has quadrupled in
recent years. The crime rate inevitably skyrockets and much
community life is destroyed.

"What frightens me even more is that our nation's urban majority don't understand a place like South Dakota. They don't
connect what they consider to be the country's 'boondocks'
with the food they need for survival. They think our land is flat
and ugly: they have absolutely no idea of the beauty of a prairie,
with its buttes and varieties of grasses. Many people in a city
don't even know what land is and can't very well be expected to
care when it is destroyed to feed their subways and elevators.
The situation is an extremely dangerous one. Often I think we
are all Indians here, in as much danger of losing our land as the
Sioux of one hundred years ago. And if it happens, I fear we
will meet with the same massive national indifference.

"There are many blessings here: a friend's ranch on the
Grand River which must be one of the most beautiful places on
earth; the sky at night in the open spaces; the silvery cot-
tonwoods. Children come to see me, and I visit old women in
houses that have soaked up years and years of silence. Living

here has changed me in unexpected ways. I have learned things that were unthinkable before: how to knit, how to shoot a gun. I bake bread in my grandmother's big, comfortable kitchen with its old-fashioned flour bin and bread board.

"David and I have had to make room for ourselves in this house. We had to clear out my grandparents' belongings before we had room for our own. We spent months, it seems, opening cupboards and drawers—discarding artificial flowers, keeping old books on the history of Kansas. We are still borrowing from the dead, using their photographs, cooking utensils, and habits. But we manage to co-exist, if somewhat crazily. The Sir Joshua Reynolds portrait that has hung in the living room for as long as I can remember now stares across the room at a Matisse print. The city and the country co-exist here as well. An album of Cole Porter songs and a Waylon Jennings record sit side by side, both well-loved, frequently listened to.

"I find that I am still sorting things out between the past and present, defining the duties of inheritance. It has gone beyond discarding vestigial corsets and white gloves; now it is in my blood. At times I doubt my decision to come here. I miss old friends, other times. But there are days when I connect with my new life in ways that give everything meaning. I think of last summer, when I went to the fields at harvest time and learned what dust is, or when I sold wheat for the first time. I felt myself being pulled along by this new world; and soon I found myself working on a poem very different from any I had written before: 'Inheritance.' "

The second account comes from Tom Brokaw, who like Kathleen Norris was born in South Dakota, but who elected to leave the state and become a national news commentator for a television network, returning only for short visits.

Tom Brokaw [3]

"Wherever I go, and talk turns to home states, someone invariably says, 'I've never met anyone from South Dakota be-

---

3. Letter to the author.

fore,' and then asks a series of condescending questions suggesting that part of the prairie remains frozen in the nineteenth century, a primitive frontier where the buffalo and Indians still prevail and the weather is a never-ending cycle of dust storms and blizzards. 'Well,' I used to explain, 'certainly it isn't a place of bright lights, crowded streets, chic dinner parties where the rich and famous gather to be witty and wise, but South Dakotans stopped living in sod houses and gathering buffalo chips some time ago.' My explanations, no matter how clever, failed to generate little more than small smiles of little tolerance or fixed stares of boredom. So I have relaxed about my South Dakota birthright and the burden of explanation it carries with it. Instead, I've started thinking about what the state means to me and not what I might be able to make it seem to others.

"There always will be a little prairie dust mixed with Missouri River water running through my veins. Chances are I'll never return to the state to stay, but I treasure my occasional visits. All of my senses are assaulted as I step back onto the prairie and feel the steady wind sweep by, stirring an almost giddy pulse of freedom. I stare at the great blue and white umbrella of sky that stretches from horizon to horizon, conditioned as I am to a much narrower vision, fouled by yellow air and interrupted by grimy buildings.

"When I return I am reminded that South Dakota winds whistle through my mind even when I am not physically present to feel their effect. Wherever I am in the world, I am sixteen years old again when a burst of wind moves a patch of grass as if it were a school of minnows in a Missouri River backwater, first dark green and then silver as it catches the sun and suddenly turns away. Similarly, a cold wind howling in any darkness brings to mind snow drifting against a modest duplex my father rented on a bluff high above where the Fort Randall Dam bisects the Missouri River.

"Curiously, I left South Dakota as a boy fearing none of the elements and returned as a man to have small charges of fear triggered by common occurrences. Driving alone at dusk along a pencil mark of pavement drawn through dark green fields of

corn and soybeans, I have been transfixed by the sight of a summer thunderstorm building on a far horizon, throwing ever-
larger black clouds into a steadily darkening sky. En route from
Mitchell to Huron late one cloudy autumn night I stopped along
the road and stepped into an unrelieved darkness. Slowly, I
turned around, straining to see something else in the night,
another car, a house, a town, anything. There was nothing.
Suddenly, I was frightened by the absence of neon signs, honk-
ing horns, and headlights. Just as quickly, fear faded. Laughing, I thought, 'What the hell, Brokaw, here you are, ready to
trade a harmless South Dakota night for the perils of a city after
dark.'

"South Dakota blizzards have taken on new forms as well.
As a child I looked on a ferocious blizzard as a source of excitement. Trudging home from school through five-foot drifts, head
bowed against fifty-mile-an-hour winds, was a joyful challenge.
It was routine. Now I would probably record: 'Today I defied
the savage forces of nature and won. I walked a half-mile
through a South Dakota blizzard.' Whenever the weather turns
nasty in the East my friends grumble and turn to me to say, 'Of
course, Brokaw is used to this; he's from South Dakota.' I try to
assume a Gary Cooper smile of reassurance, all the while con-
cealing my own discomfort. As I say, a South Dakota birthright
does carry some extra burdens.

"While it is the land and the elements that shape it that come
first to mind, it is the people of South Dakota who have left the
deepest impression. It is more than their sturdy German phy-
siques or round Czech faces or pale blue Scandinavian eyes or
coal black Indian hair that I remember. It is how they live their
lives, how they value results more than mere ideas.

"It was a long time before I could define work as anything
other than long hours at manual labor. As one who makes his
living writing, reading, and talking, I still occasionally pause to
wonder when I'll be required to do some real work, the kind of
back-bending, muscle-wrenching, sweat-of-the-brow work my
father, Red Brokaw, has done nearly every day since he was
eight years old. Sure, I realize that much of the hard work of the
prairie has been simplified by mechanization. My father no

longer wrestles a team of horses and a clumsy wagon to haul dirt. He directs a crew of men outfitted with trucks and tractors, power mowers, and powerful cranes in the maintenance of parks and grounds around Gavins Point Dam. Still, he works hard, damn hard. It's in his bloodline. Hard work is a legacy of the generations who settled the prairie, broke the soil, built the sod houses, fought the droughts and grasshoppers and penny-a-pound prices for their products. It is a legacy that even those of us who leave carry with us.

"All of this work has produced what may be the single largest collection of powerful hands in the world. Hands I'll never forget belong to strangers I'll never know. A cowboy working a rodeo in the Black Hills outside of Rapid City rode slowly by, carrying an extra saddle as if it were a baseball glove, a huge freckled hand seeming to stretch from pommel to cantle. A burly farmer, plainly uncomfortable in a stiff white shirt and a blue suit that was cheap when he bought it ten years ago, sitting along the wall of the Lesterville dance hall, unconsciously rubbed the scar tissue of a thumb lost to a cornpicker.

"Other hands were more familiar. My sharp-tongued, Scotch-Irish maternal grandmother had long, graceful hands with the tensile strength of tempered steel. My brothers and I would stand quietly in awe as she'd split an apple by simply twisting it apart in her hands. A family friend, Oscar Johnson, a spartan, Swedish, bachelor immigrant, would visit in the winter when he was too old to carry on his house-moving business and various other nickel enterprises. He'd sit in our tiny living room dressed in a nearly new flannel shirt and blue overalls combination that was his uniform, page through back copies of *Life* and the *Saturday Evening Post* while my mother would wonder aloud how she could keep him busy. Before long, Oscar would have his own idea. He would decide to shovel the walk as soon as the snow stopped drifting. The moment the wind died he would be outside, knee-deep in snow, clearing the walk with powerful, easy strokes of a scoop shovel. I would stand off to the side, awaiting the ritual of Oscar's hands. It would go like this: shovel, shovel, shovel, clap, clap, clap. Oscar's hands had been frostbitten so many times cold turned them numb almost instantly, so he would revive them with a slow-motion applause.

"It will remain with me forever, the sight of that old man, bundled up in a long sheepskin coat and black wool cap, deliberately clapping his great mittened hands so he could get back to work. It never occurred to him that at his age his tortured hands should be spared snow shoveling.

"My father may some day bleed to death through the hands. They are never still, his hands, and they are never healed. After a day of working on his car or refinishing furniture or moving heavy machinery he will often enter the house ignorant of what appears to be an open wound on one of his hands. When it is called to his attention, the standard answer is, 'Oh, I must have skinned myself on that goddam pulley,' or whatever. Cold running water, preferably at the kitchen sink, is the antidote.

"South Dakota hands signal something else about the people who live there. Pick up a small town weekly newspaper in the state and there it is, a picture of a local farmer or businessman, a couple or even a group, all of them with their hands clasped awkwardly in front of their serious dresses or suits. Long before trendy psychologists on television talk shows were describing similar poses as a form of body language, I had figured out that in South Dakota, at least, this pose was a symbol of social uneasiness, a kind of mute expression of embarrassment. Much of life in South Dakota is a solitary experience and public appearances often don't come easily. As a result, hands that are functional and busy most of the day in South Dakota become clumsy and out of place when a camera is raised and they must be still.

"This social Stoicism gives way to an honest friendliness and plain, straightforward hospitality as soon as strangers show interest in South Dakota. I remember how swiftly word would spread through the small town of my youth whenever a car with out-of-state license plates would stay overnight. My friends, and friends of my parents, would look over the passengers and throw out some observation, generally on the weather, a sure-fire, twenty-four-hour-a-day topic of conversation in South Dakota. If the out-of-staters took that conversational bait, they'd be on the receiving end of a short but well-rehearsed description on the virtues of South Dakota, its people, and the quality of life on the prairie. The strangers might be asked if they had ever heard of Joe Foss, the marine who won a congressional Medal of Honor. 'Yes? Well, he's a South Dakota boy. You bet. And Mamie Van Doren, she's from Rowena. Casey Tibbs, the world champion cowboy, is from Fort Pierre and he married a Miss South Dakota. Hell, we got clean air, pheasant hunting, the Black Hills and cool summer nights.'

"I guess it's the physical and cultural remoteness of South Dakota that compels everyone to memorize almost every South Dakotan who has left the state and achieved some recognition. As a child I would pore over magazines and newspapers, looking for some sign that the rest of the world knew we existed. I was even proud when an obscure insurance agent from, say, Watertown would have his name listed in a *Life* advertisement along with a thousand other agents of a national company.

"Strangers who turn out to be former South Dakotans are treated as if they're uncles thought lost at sea. Confidences are immediately shared. Familiarity takes over. 'So you're from Yankton. Know George B. German? The hell you say. Mother and I went to California to visit the kids last winter. Never could get used to all those freeways, but we saw Johnny Carson and Bob Barker on "Truth or Consequences." Barker is a South Dakotan. Born out on the reservation somewhere, but he's not an Indian. Damn, I don't know what we're going to do with the Indians. You're from around here. You know what they're like.'

"Yes, I think I do, but the difference between what I think of Indians and what many other South Dakotans think of Indians seems to widen with each year. To be sure, the Indians of my youth were a race apart. Yet the divisions were not so deep as they are now. Or maybe nothing has changed except to my perception, changing as it has from a boy's to a man's.

"As a boy there was no one quite so special as Sylvan Highrock, a Yankton Sioux who lived in a rough cabin with his parents and assorted brothers and sisters along the Missouri River. At home, Sylvan spoke only Sioux dialects, something

he kept from the rest of us. What he shared with us was a remarkable range of athletic abilities, a natural grace, and the
most efficient force of mongrels any rabbit hunter ever has had
the pleasure of working. In a state where a man is measured in
part by his marksmanship, Sylvan should have been a feudal
prince. A cottontail moving quickly, but erratically, through
heavy brush was safe as long as he stayed in my sights. If Sylvan raised his barrel, it was good-bye rabbit. He'd shoot carp
out of the murky waters of the Missouri River from forty yards
away. Through it all, his heroics on the basketball floor or football field, his success on the hunt, he would remain even-tem-
pered and good-humored, the first to pull off his cap when entering a house, the first to say thank you. He was embarrassed
by drunk Indians just as the rest of us were embarrassed by
drunk white men making fools of themselves in the local bowling alley or highway cafe.

"When I last saw Sylvan he was reduced to working on a
garbage truck. He was practically stone deaf from an industrial
accident for which he received no compensation. His teeth and
complexion had seriously deteriorated. He lived in a tiny frame
house on the Indian side of a dusty West River town. He hoped
to get together enough money to buy a pickup for the deer
season. He was bitter about whites, something I had never heard
him express during our untold hours together as boys.

"That worries me. I am equally worried by outbursts of racial
hatred on the part of my white South Dakota friends. It can
become a cancer on the community, for that's what South Dakota is, a community more than it is a state. A community that
can take great pride in the achievements of Olympic champion
Billy Mills and artist Oscar Howe, Indians, as well as the
achievements of baseball star Dick Green and bandleader
Lawrence Welk.

"Two years ago my mother, Jean Conley Brokaw, presented
each of her sons with a remarkable personal reminiscence of her
childhood days in South Dakota. It was startling to read just
how primitive conditions were in the twenties and thirties. It
was a struggle for survival against fierce natural elements made
even more demanding by the economic conditions of the times.

A people who could overcome those years and still flourish has resources enough to overcome another, more ancient, evil: prejudice.

"My bicentennial hope is that the answer to that challenge is the South Dakota standard, 'You bet.'"

Epilogue

ORE than fifty years ago the grandfather of poet Hayden Carruth asked how South Dakota should know itself and how it should develop individuality. In many ways, the state is like its prairie or Great Plains neighbors. All were settled from east to west, so that the larger cities and the state universities are in the eastern half, while the population dwindles, the land elevation rises, and rainfall diminishes in the western half. Going down the line from north to south, North Dakota, South Dakota, Nebraska, Kansas, Oklahoma, and Texas are all transitional states, linking one section of the nation to another. Even Iowa and Minnesota touch on this transitional space. Montana, Wyoming, and Colorado are somewhat different from the other plains states because they harbor the mighty Rocky Mountains. To travel through these plains states is to know the similarities, sense the differences, and, like Carruth, have difficulty in defining those differences. In relation to South Dakota, one can say with too much ease that Minnesota is more cosmopolitan, Iowa has more farmers (as opposed to ranchers), North Dakota is colder and flatter, Nebraska has more "sameness," Texas is bigger and richer and its people therefore less humble, Oklahoma has more Indians and some wealth through oil, and so on. All of which still leaves us with Mr. Carruth's question, posed in 1923: "What is the Soul of South Dakota?"

He could not answer his own question. On the surface, at least, it appeared to him that Dakotans were an agricultural people who cared more about rain than about science and the arts, who put a great deal of money (per capita, not total) into educational institutions but did not know what education was, who continually had to remind outsiders that Sioux City was not in South Dakota and that Deadwood was not in Wyoming, and who, if Christ came to the state, would make sure that He received a quarter-section of land but would not listen to His ideas. In an effort to reconcile this somewhat humorous view of the people with his laudatory view of the prairie—the closest thing America has to nirvana—Carruth arrived at the possibility that the prairie, in spite of its unequaled beauty, might have more negative qualities than positive, and that the state simply followed its geographical location in exhibiting the same negative qualities.

The Carruth attitude is almost typical of the running commentaries, however slight, on South Dakota during the twentieth century. Reactions to this place in the center of the continent are contradictory, and when the conflicting views cannot be reconciled they are quickly turned into a rather grim humor. Some writers have simply denied that there is actually such a place. We can dispense with this notion. There are few locations in the United States where a sense of place, a feeling of really being somewhere, is as strong as it is in Dakota. John Graves, the Texas writer, said recently that places are becoming harder and harder to find; his brief explanation of the sense of place in Texas did not include Dallas or Houston or oil but confined itself to the people's rootedness in the land and an unexplainable agricultural mysticism. Lacking Dallas and Houston and oil (the oil production in South Dakota has been negligible), Dakotans are perhaps extraordinary in their attachment to the land. They are indeed rooted in a place. To which the bright young lads and the ornery old men of the cities, especially to the east, reply that, yes, rootedness is precisely the problem in South Dakota and other agricultural states. The people can't move; they are anchored (rooted) in place. Their vision is limited. They are caught in a dying world.

It is only the brittle and superficial mind that thinks attachment to a place is detrimental to growth. In the very image of rootedness there is the quality of natural growth, as with a tree whose nourishment is derived from the soil and from water and whose branches grow up and out, toward the sun, into the sky, until one day the tree is tall, full-bloomed, and strong. Applying the metaphor to people does not necessarily imply that rooted people vegetate. Some do, of course, but equally in every part of the nation, including the "lively" cities. Attachment to a place is different from being chained to a place. At the very least, there is an element of choice involved in the distinction. To choose a place—even though one leaves it with various degrees of frequency to travel the world—is to stake a claim on the permanence and continuity of life. The choice does not preclude knowledge of the rest of the world.

Particularly in our own time in history, with all of the electronic wonders that bring information almost instantly from any part of the globe, and with the ease of air travel, no people in geographically isolated areas are literally cut off from events, artistic achievements, or cultural changes in the so-called centers of sophistication. The "hick farmer" disappeared long ago.

In manners and intellectual techniques, there may of course be a difference between the young person growing up in a town so small that it is almost invisible and his counterpart in the city, even a city the size of Sioux Falls, or a smaller city like Vermillion which is, however, dominated by the university. The difference, though, is on the surface. Young Dakotans are inherently intelligent, healthy, and capable of learning whatever is necessary to get along in any segment of business, society, the professions, or the arts.

Negative qualities are more fun, and jokes abound within the state—the weather, the legislature, the educational system, rural life, the South Dakota colony in Arizona, and so on. What is significant in Carruth's conclusion (and that of others) that the prairie might be more negative than positive, even though the prairie is possibly the most beautiful landscape anywhere, is the obvious and troubled complexity of what is supposed to be an elementary and simple place and character. A simple question like that of the soul of a region does not, unfortunately, have a simple answer, even in South Dakota.

Believing in an individual soul does not help solve the question of the collective soul. For one thing, how far afield do we go to establish the group-entity which might have this soul? State boundaries are often arbitrary and superficial, and it would be a mistake to claim that there is a "South Dakota Soul" or spirit which stops at Milbank, or Jefferson, or Wewela, or Pine Ridge, or Spearfish, or Lemmon, or Winship and instantly turns into something else in Minnesota, Iowa, Nebraska, Wyoming, Montana, or North Dakota. Furthermore, in a state as varied as South Dakota, is the soul to be found in East River or in West River? Or in the middle of the Missouri River?

Too often a culture is judged entirely on the basis of the achievements of a few people—the leaders, heroes, political figures, or outstanding artists or scientists or the nationally-known in whatever field. South Dakota has had such people, some of whom have been mentioned earlier. Just among the Sioux Indians, who can deny the importance—and in some ways the contributions—of Spotted Tail, Crazy Horse, Sitting Bull, Gall, Black Elk and his son Ben, Vine Deloria and his son Vine, Jr., or Oscar Howe? Even if, for example, the exploits of Crazy Horse do not meet with favor among the non-Indian population, it would be unfair to say that his spirit has not become part of the soul of the region. We have already noted the relationship to the state of Karl Mundt, George McGovern, Hubert Humphrey, Ole Rölvaag, and Harvey Dunn, influential in different ways. Other notable people have come from South Dakota, bringing various talents to the state or to the nation.

Ernest O. Lawrence received the Nobel Prize in physics for his contributions in the discovery and development of atomic energy. Wallace Carothers is known as the developer of nylon fiber. Joe Foss was the first fighter pilot of World War II to equal Eddie Rickenbacker's record for the number of planes shot down in World War I; he went on to become governor of South Dakota, first commissioner of the American Football League, and host of a sportsman's show on television. Casey

Tibbs epitomized the rodeo bronc rider, winning the world championship so often that when anyone thought of rodeos he automatically thought of Tibbs. Mamie Van Doren, actress, Myron Floren, musician with the Lawrence Welk orchestra, Joe Robbie, well-known in professional football, and Cameron Hawley, best-selling novelist, all South Dakotans, are but a few of the variously distinguished people who might be called notables.

Although I do not wish to slight the achievements of these people, I point to Jack Schaefer's statement in a speech before the Western Literature Association that it is only a myth—and a bad one—which says we must judge ourselves as a race, or a culture, or even a species, on the basis of the achievements of a few people who have reached a high level of accomplishment. Better that we rate ourselves (or perhaps even identify ourselves) on our collective actions.

Which brings us back to the word "collective" as applied to the soul or to the spirit. If people of differing beliefs, nationality backgrounds, and activities gather in a place, it is possible that the place becomes the key to the people. So does the particular time. Consider that we in Dakota may well have a distinctive character which is in keeping with the quality of the place. The earth, and our working of it, or on it, keeps us basically primitive in spirit. This would mean that our values (at least many of them) are fundamental, and are less artificial or faddish than some of those values which are associated with sophistication. The distances between noticeable landmarks can give us a sense of isolation, or privacy, which is different from the "loneliness in the crowd" of the large metropolitan areas elsewhere. The isolation in turn makes us independent, occasionally to the point of orneriness, but it also makes us aware of the importance of companionship, of willingness to help neighbors, and so we are (collectively) a friendly people.

There is a problem, though, which South Dakota shares with only two or three other states. Through geographical and historical accidence, we are caught between the old and the new, between the earth and the sky, between the mysteries and traditions of the past and the mysteries and possibilities of the future.

The region is geologically old but politically and socially very young—only an infant, in fact. Twenty years ago, when the first man-made satellites were circling the globe, many Dakota towns were celebrating their seventy-fifth birthdays; men grew pioneer beards, women put on their grandmothers' dresses, and at least one ox-cart caravan re-enacted a journey from a primitive time only seventy-five or eighty years in the past. In other words, we are living so close to our past that its primitivism almost collides with the space age. South Dakota is not yet a hundred years old, and yet man has several times walked on the moon.

Because we plains people live in a large and open country, with both earth and sky spread out before us, we are closer in a physical sense to the earth and the sky than anyone else. In a spiritual sense we may even be unique. Never before in history has man stood with one foot in his primitive origins and the other poised on the moon. Psychologically, this is perhaps the most important moment in the entire existence of man. Whole new concepts have opened out before us, some of them staggering the imagination, and we haven't had time yet to become accustomed to our simple and immediate past. At the very least, it is disquieting to examine—especially through the arts—our past, in an effort to discover who we are and to make our short tradition usable, while simultaneously facing space travel, the dangers of atomic warfare, and problems of hunger and employment in a world which, beyond our own little world, is overpopulated. One way of training the imagination to comprehend past and future in an intellectual and emotional fusion is to study those regional writers who have attempted to understand who and what we are in terms of our origins and our landscape and at the same time to read reliable science fiction. This kind of study is becoming popular in the schools, so that in a generation or two our two worlds may come together in a particularly important insight. What this will do to our collective psyche is not easy to predict, since South Dakotans will still be tied to the land in a very practical agricultural way, and anything smacking of mysticism may be limited to a small minority.

Consider the place. As John K. Sherman of the *Minneapolis*

Tribune once said, geographical flatness is not spiritually flat. A horizon line—as witnessed in some painters—can have a mystical appeal. The horizontal line of the prairie contrasts sharply with the vertical lines of skyscrapers and other buildings in a large city, where these verticals often imprison the urban dweller. If the vertical (and the city) is the line of ambition and aspiration, then the horizontal (and the prairie) is the line of meditation and peace. For the city-oriented person to go out onto the open prairie is to experience—at least sometimes—an aversion to what looks like a desert, but the problem for this person is that there is nothing to lean against, nothing for him to prop himself against, and nowhere for him to hide.

Writers speak of the "smell of distance," of the "pull of the horizon," and of the great quietness broken only by the wind. The wind can be both irritating and soothing. It can pick at a person, as though to pluck him, piece by piece. It can carry his voice away, so that he is without not only his props but also his call for help, and he must fall back upon his own resources to control himself and adapt himself to his environment. The distance can be frightening if never seen before, but once a man is accustomed to it he feels hemmed in by buildings and by hills. And, perhaps most important, on the prairie one can see the skeleton and arteries and veins and skin of the land, open, exposed, not covered by concrete. The earth, unlike concrete, accepts tracks, paths, the mark of a foot; a man can leave a trail as evidence of his life on this earth.

There are differences that depend upon a point of view. For those who prefer cold statistics, a book of records will show that at a place in northwest North Dakota, in 1936, the temperature ranged from 60 degrees below zero to 121 degrees above zero, a difference of 181 degrees. This is a world record, "disputed" by the Russians, who claim the record of 192 degrees in Siberia, but whose measurements have not been accepted as official elsewhere, nor were the high and low temperatures recorded in the same year, only in the same place. Browning, Montana, in 1916, set the world record for the greatest temperature change in one day, from 44 degrees above zero to 56 degrees below zero, a twenty-four hour change of 100 degrees. Almost everyone on the plains has experienced changes of 40 or

50 degrees in a matter of hours. Does this do something to the soul as well as to the body? The most freakish rise in temperature ever recorded in the world occurred at Spearfish, South Dakota, January 22, 1943, from 4 degrees below zero to 45 degrees above zero—a change of 49 degrees—in two minutes.

These are weather extremes, only one of them occurring in South Dakota but the others close enough to be pulled into our collective consciousness. At various points we have seen other kinds of extremes: an elevation of land that changes from about 800 feet in the northeastern part of the state to over 7,000 feet in the Black Hills; moist air at one end, and dry air at the other; areas of bleak monotony contrasted with sublime beauty and with eerie beauty; spring thaw in January with the chinooks, and snow in June (though this is rare); harshness and softness, of both land and climate; restlessness and contentment in the people; the coming-in of people who are dissatisfied with the crowds and traffic jams of the city, and the going-out of young South Dakotans who feel that there is nothing for them to do on the farms or in the small towns.

Extremes. Perhaps the key word for Dakota. The travel department calls it infinite variety. What happens with extremes is that they come together, and the result is a kind of tension. The point of tension, paradoxically, is both the weakest point and the strongest point in the pull from both ends of the scale. Where the pull occurs, we can break under the pressure, or we can come to grips with the extremes and find the strength which comes from a fusion of opposites. Over many generations, South Dakotans have found that strength. This may be the very quality which will, one day, serve an urbanized nation, reminding it of landed values, of a morality which is often considered old-fashioned, and of the pioneer spirit which stood the country in good stead for many years before it began to fade as the frontier faded.

As a frontier state, South Dakota is isolated from urbanized and industrialized areas. Curiously, it is isolated in another way, which may cause an unconscious restlessness in its people, an urge they do not fully recognize. We, as a species, are said to have come from the sea. There may still be in us, built in biologically, a desire to return to the sea. It may be more than port facilities and trade with foreign countries that foster the building of cities along the coasts and draw large populations to within striking distance of the oceans. The most remote place in the world is said to be an unmapped point in the desert in China, more than 1,500 miles from the open sea in any direction. From a point in South Dakota it is more than 1,200 miles to the nearest sea. Motels have on their walls more ocean than prairie pictures. In North Dakota, before World War I, there was a newspaper called the *Inter-Ocean Journal*. Most of our ancestors came from across the sea; many were seafaring people. Ole Rölvaag, in *Giants in the Earth*, describes the prairie as a sea of grass.

An interesting question comes to mind. Do we have a subconscious desire to get away from the isolated center of the continent, a desire which is at least equally as strong as the sense of place on the prairie? Or are we content to stay here because the prairie comes the closest of all land formations to resembling the sea? To complicate matters further, South Dakota was once an inland sea, millions of years ago. The largest prehistoric marine turtle skeleton ever discovered was found in Custer County in 1895. Lewis and Clark saw what appeared to be a strange giant fish skeleton along the Missouri River. The Badlands are a rich reservoir of petrified bones of dinosaurs and other ancient reptiles and fish. We live above the bed, or floor, of an ancient inland sea, and have become a link in the continuity of life, embracing the sea in our imaginations and the land in reality.

I do not know whether many South Dakotans think of these things. Hayden Carruth wrote of the state's "prairieness" as though it were a holy word, a quality to be revered and cherished; but, he wrote before the depression, before World War II, before the sculpting of Mount Rushmore. South Dakota is still affected by the depression. The state government insists upon maintaining a bank balance, some kind of insurance against the possibility of another depression. It is economically careful, conservative. And it is quite likely that most of the people think not of an inland sea but of the Morrell Company in Sioux Falls, or Gurney's Nursery in Yankton, or Wall Drug (with its road-sign advertising all over the nation), or pheasants, or hunting, or the huge earthen dams on the Missouri River, or, somewhat more exotic, EROS, the Earth Resource Observation Systems in Minnehaha County, which record information from orbiting satellites. These are practical things, to accompany crop prices and the cattle market. Dakotans are a practical people. Education is no good unless it leads to jobs.

Whether it is understood or not, we live within two dichotomies. First, the state is both new and old: EROS reads the orbiting satellites in space while nineteenth-century Swedish bishops point their fingers across the sea and warn us not to stray from the fold. Second, the people are practical but have in their environment the potential for a mystical view of the world around them: they are most interested in economic survival, but as that problem lessens they may discover (as some already have) the spiritual values latent in Indian traditions, in the inland sea, and in essential prairieness.

Meanwhile, we are full of contradictions, which may seem strange to non-South Dakotans who consider us a simple rural people. While the state has gone by several names, the most common one is the "Coyote State." Consider the coyote. Thomas Say, the naturalist who accompanied Maj. Stephen H. Long's expedition to the Rocky Mountains in 1820, called this animal *Canis latrans,* which means "barking dog." Early Anglo-Americans called the coyote a "prairie wolf." Other names given it were "brush wolf," "barking wolf," "American jackal," "heul wolf," "steppen wolf," and "cased wolf." The last of these names came from the method of skinning the coyote without making a slit down the belly but simply peeling the skin off. The word "coyote" comes from Mexican-Spanish, from an Aztecan word, "coyotl." The Aztecs were in awe of the coyote and its abilities and might have chanted this kind of song:

> The expanse of earth is wide.
> My brother the coyote spoke,
> "Behold the wideness of the earth,
> The coyotes know the earth is wide."

The coyote may be found in Aztecan legends and superstitions, coyote symbols figured in Aztecan religious rituals, and, more recently, the coyote totem has been cherished among the Zuñi and other American Indians.

In myth and in several Indian beliefs, the coyote is considered a two-sided being. Some see him primarily as a sly and deceitful trickster who works to thwart the plans of the benevolent but not all-powerful creator god. In this role he often imitates in a rather ridiculous way the works of the creator or culture hero. He is a mocker. But he often appears as the hero himself, as the powerful magician who not only destroys but also brings about order in the chaotic world. Put the two roles together and the coyote becomes the artist of the wild creatures in myth, destroying, making, and then mocking what he has made. In this characterization he could well be the modern white man's cultural hero.

The Sioux Indians have several names for the coyote, perhaps the most common being the Teton *Sunk-mani-tu*—dog in the wilderness. However much they may honor the coyote, especially as a natural wonder, they do not revere this creature as much as they do the buffalo, the eagle, the bear, and the wolf. And although the coyote is South Dakota's official animal, it is now the only one on which the state pays a bounty—five dollars for an adult and two dollars for a pup. (Some districts add to these payments, especially in sheep country, so that it is possible to collect as much as fifty-five dollars for a pelt.) In 1975 the Game, Fish, and Parks Department verified almost 3,000 livestock losses from coyotes. In the past thirty years, more than 140,000 coyotes have been bountied. Yet, there is disagreement over the bounty system. The animal control specialists feel that it is a waste of money because the coyote is so adaptable that if he is threatened he will simply produce more offspring. But West River sheepmen insist that there are no good coyotes, only the kind that eat sheep, and that everything possible should be done to eliminate them.

Honor it and kill it. The complexities of the attitude are indicative of the complexities of a state which includes very practical people who want nothing to stand in the way of their livelihood and, on the other hand, people who sense, and perhaps see, long-term values which might be destroyed by practical measures. It would be the minority, of course, who place the coyote alongside Moby Dick and Old Ephraim and who recognize that the historical and biological facts do not always explain a "creature" fully, that there might be not only an ecological importance but a significant symbolical and religious belief worth preserving in the coyote. The attitude of the Sioux toward animals, birds, and all nonhuman life has become increasingly important to many non-Indians in recent years, but, as the Sioux have already discovered, it is difficult to reconcile traditional values with the modern dictates of economy and political expediency. Such a reconciliation would be a kind of salvation, not only for South Dakota but for the entire nation.

Who is to do it? Jefferson dreamed of a democracy in which freethinking land owners, independent of political and economic pressures, would guide the nation. Urbanization discredits much of that theory, if not all of it. Yet, it is not impossible that a young state like South Dakota, a frontier state even today, with its fulfillment still in the future, may be the proving ground for the ideas and resolutions of the next century. Whether such ideas will come from politicians, economists, ecologists, or demographers is hard to say. Consider at least the role of the writer, of the artist. Herbert Read, the British scholar of the arts, has said that what produces great art is a concentration of infinite time in a finite place. Given the geological age of South Dakota, as well as its strong sense of place, we can at least wonder whether it might one day hold the destiny of the nation in its hands.

Such notions are for prophets. Before South Dakota can entertain thoughts of leadership it has much to do for itself. It is not so much a matter of changing the image of the state (that will happen in due time) as it is of understanding it through examination. The Scandinavians and other Europeans who make up much of the population are not a glib people. They do not easily reveal themselves, either through speech or writing, and for this reason are often called cold or unfriendly. What they really are is private, so it is difficult to determine why they vote the way they do, and to what extent they may feel the soul or spirit of the land and of themselves as a group. The Sioux are also private but they are certainly an important part of the collective soul which grows through its relationship to what I have called (among other things) the "mysticism of the land." The immediate problem seems to be the same one which James Michener identified in his novel, *Hawaii,* as a kind of dullness and a waste of the human intellect caused by lack of understanding of the place and its people. What Michener suggested for Hawaii seems to be the solution for South Dakota as well: people must speculate about the state, and write about it. Only then will they understand themselves and their place fully. Only then will they be prepared to contribute more meaningfully to that whole of which they are a part.

The process may be a long one, because a state which is agricultural and conservative is slow in recognizing the need for writers and in encouraging their development. However, for this time, and for this place, what matters is that the process has begun.

Suggestions for Further Reading

The history of South Dakota is recorded in a wide array of literature. The most useful key to it for the general reader is the reading list in Herbert A. Schell's *History of South Dakota* (Lincoln: University of Nebraska Press, 1975); it is organized topically and chronologically and offers annotation on major works. Schell's book is also the most comprehensive, recent history of the state, though the Works Progress Administration's *Guide to South Dakota* (New York: Oxford University Press, 1952) still contains a lode of valuable information. The greatest concentration of periodical literature on South Dakota can be found in the South Dakota Historical Collections and in *South Dakota History,* the magazine of the State Historical Society.

For the reader interested in the general history of the plains region and the forces which have molded its development, the best place to begin is with Walter Prescott Webb's classic study, *The Great Plains* (New York: Houghton Mifflin Co., 1936). Carl F. Kraenzel, *The Great Plains in Transition* (Norman: University of Oklahoma Press, 1955) views the problems of the area from the Dakotas to Texas from a sociological perspective, while Mary Wilma Hargreaves, *Dry Farming in the Northern Great Plains, 1900–1925* (Cambridge: Harvard University Press, 1957) provides a look at the land-use issues in Great Plains agriculture. The South Dakota Geological Survey's *Geography of South Dakota,* by Stephen S. Visher (Bulletin no. 8, 1918), contains factual material on the state's landforms and natural setting.

The native Americans who were the first South Dakotans have been the subject of a number of good books. A useful introduction to the Plains Indians' social organization can be found in Robert H. Lowie, *Indians of the Plains* (New York: McGraw-Hill Book Co., 1954). For good histories of specific tribes important in the area which would become South Dakota, the reader should consult George E. Hyde, *Red Cloud's Folk: A History of the Oglala Sioux Indians* (Norman: University of Oklahoma Press, 1937), and *Spotted Tail's Folk: A History of*

191

the Brule Sioux Indians (Norman: University of Oklahoma Press, 1961). Insight into the messiah craze among the Teton Sioux emerges from Robert M. Utley, *The Last Days of the Sioux Nation* (New Haven: Yale University Press, 1963), and tribal voices speak for themselves in a recent collection of tape-recorded interviews, *To Be An Indian: An Oral History* (New York: Holt, Rinehart and Winston, 1971), edited by Joseph H. Cash and Herbert T. Hoover.

Lying in what many believed to be a path to the Pacific, South Dakota saw the passage of numerous explorers and trappers long before the first sod was broken. The elder Vérendrye is the subject of a good biography by Nellis M. Crouse, *La Verendrye: Fur Trader and Explorer* (Ithaca: Cornell University Press, 1956) while the more famous wanderings of Meriwether Lewis and William Clark are best documented in the explorers' journals themselves. Of the several editions to choose from, probably John Bakeless, *Lewis and Clark: Partners and Discoverers* (New York: William Morrow and Co., 1947) and Reuben Gold Thwaites, *Original Journals of the Lewis & Clark Expedition, 1804–1806,* with an introduction by Bernard De Voto (New York: Arno Press, 1969), are most useful for modern readers. On trappers in the South Dakota region, John F. Sunder, *The Fur Trade on the Upper Missouri* (Norman: University of Oklahoma Press, 1965) provides valuable information.

The period from the beginnings of white settlement until statehood has been well-chronicled. Studies of the territorial period include the older, two-volume work by George W. Kingsbury, *History of Dakota Territory* (Chicago: S. J. Clarke Publishing Co., 1915) and the more recent, interpretive study of political behavior, Howard R. Lamar, *Dakota Territory, 1861–1889: A Study of Frontier Politics* (New Haven: Yale University Press, 1956). Behind the politics, the quality of everyday life on the plains frontier comes into focus in Everett Dick, *The Sod House Frontier, 1854–1890* (New York: D. Appleton-Century Co., 1937); Seth K. Humphrey, *Following the Prairie Frontier* (Minneapolis: University of Minnesota Press, 1931); and William J. Hyde, *Dig or Die, Brother Hyde* (New York: Harper & Bros., 1954).

Cows and cowboys get good coverage in studies of the cattle business by Edward Everett Dale, *The Range Cattle Industry: Ranching on the Great Plains from 1865 to 1925* (Norman: University of Oklahoma

Press, 1930; reprint, 1969) and *Cow Country* (Norman: University of Oklahoma Press, 1945; rev. ed., no. 27, Western Frontier Library, 1968). Bob Lee and Dick Williams provide a more specific look at South Dakota's ranching experience in *Last Grass Frontier: The South Dakota Stock Grower Heritage* (Sturgis, S.D.: Black Hills Publications, Inc., 1964). For a personal sense of what that life was like, the reader could do no better than turn to *Ike Blasingame, Dakota Cowboy: My Life in the Old Days* (New York: G. P. Putnam's Sons, 1958), and Walker D. Wyman, *Nothing But Prairie and Sky* (Norman: University of Oklahoma Press, 1954). More exotic but still central to South Dakota history in the nineteenth century, the Black Hills mining frontier is the subject of Watson Parker's excellent *Gold in the Black Hills* (Norman: University of Oklahoma Press, 1966), while the story of the region's most famous mine is told in Joseph H. Cash, *Working the Homestake* (Ames: Iowa State University Press, 1973). On one of the Black Hills' more famous sojourners, the reader should see Donald Jackson, *Custer's Gold—The United States Cavalry Expedition of 1874* (New Haven: Yale University Press, 1966).

The shape of South Dakota political life since statehood emerges in broader works on the midwest plains region, such as Russell B. Nye, *Midwestern Progressive Politics: A Historical Study of Its Origins and Development, 1870–1950* (East Lansing: Michigan State University Press, 1951), and Theodore Saloutos and John D. Hicks, *Agricultural Discontent in the Middle West, 1900–1939* (Madison: University of Wisconsin Press, 1951). For a good biography, the reader should see Gilbert C. Fite, *Peter Norbeck: Prairie Statesman* (Columbia: University of Missouri Studies, 22, no. 2, 1948). More recent developments are covered in Alan L. Clem, *Prairie State Politics: Popular Democracy in South Dakota* (Washington, D.C.: Public Affairs Press, 1967). The fight of women for political participation, meanwhile, is examined carefully in Dorinda Riessen Reed, *The Woman Suffrage Movement in South Dakota* (Vermillion, S.D.: Governmental Research Bureau, Report No. 14, University of South Dakota, 1958).

No list would be complete without noting at least some of the fiction which, if not all written by South Dakotans, has been largely inspired by South Dakota themes and characters. Among historical novels, there are few better than Vardis Fisher's *Tale of Valor* (Garden City, New York: Doubleday, 1958), a romantic rendering of the Lewis and Clark expedition. Among works dealing with the early settlement of the plains, Will O. Lillibridge's *Ben Blair: The Story of a Plainsman* (New York: A. L. Burt Co., 1907) and *Where the Trail Divides* (New York: A. L. Burt Co., 1907) still provide good reading. Probably the most substantial body of fiction came out of the homesteading era, when writers like Hamlin Garland, Ole Rölvaag, and Laura Ingalls Wilder achieved lasting fame and popularity with stories set on the Great Plains. The grim passages in Garland's *Main Traveled Roads* (New York: Harper & Row, 1891) went far to shape the negative image which burdened the region for so long, an accomplishment shared by Rölvaag's *Giants in the Earth* and its tale of pioneers overwhelmed by the land. Wilder's happier endings have even won latterday acclaim through television serialization. A shift in the image of grim Dakota came in the wake of the Great Depression with the sardonic humor of Frederick Manfred's *Golden Bowl* (St. Paul: Webb Publishing Co., 1944). Later, in the work of Holger Cahill, *The Shadow of My Hand* (New York: Harcourt, Brace, 1956) the dry and rugged Dakota region takes on an almost mystical quality, while Lois Phillips Hudson's novel of the depression, *The Bones of Plenty* (Boston: Little, Brown & Co., 1962) added a new dimension to the imaginative literature about a place known as much through its images as anything else. Finally, for those who prefer a wide sampling between two covers, there is John Milton's recent anthology, *The Literature of South Dakota* (Vermillion, S.D.: Dakota Press, 1976).

Index